Green Writing
Romanticism and Ecology

Green Writing
Romanticism and Ecology

James C. McKusick

St. Martin's Press
New York

Contents

Permissions

Foreword

Walking up a mountainside, alone, in a cold Montana winter, I noticed the tracks of a bear in the freshly fallen snow. Examining them carefully, I realized that the long, deeply indented claw-marks must be those of a grizzly. Somewhere ahead of me, I supposed, it was walking uphill, through a forest of tall pines bearing their dark cones in silence. I followed in its footsteps, wondering whether I would see it and how we might appear to each other, meeting suddenly in the snow-laden woods. The bear kept climbing along a dim path known only to itself, and to the occasional deer, and now to me, as we continued upward through the snow. The tracks were fresh, and just then I remembered how a friend of mine had told me of a grizzly he once encountered, in those same mountains, in a clearing where neither man nor beast had expected to find the other. The bear peered at him, grunting with surprise, then reared back on its hind legs and roared out its identity with fierce determination. My friend, moved by an utterly instinctive reaction, stood his ground and roared back in a strange, inhuman voice that he did not know he possessed. Thus we rise, as if by hidden knowledge, to occasions we never anticipate.

On this occasion, however, I did not see the bear. He vanished into a thick tangle of branches, noiselessly, with that unconsidered elegance of motion given only to those who inhabit the wild. Perhaps not seeing the bear that day left a greater impression upon me than seeing him would have done. Twenty years later, I still follow his tracks in the snow and I still wonder when he may appear, unexpectedly, and what those dim traces may portend.

Tracks in the snow, broken thorns, torn pieces of bark, the intense odor of decaying logs, and the sound of crackling brush—all of these are signs by which we and other creatures come to recognize the prey that we seek, the mate whom we desire, the rival whose fierce antagonism lurks beyond the next hill. We of human kind are not alone in our manifold ability to sense the presence of other creatures, and we share with many other species the instinctive means of reading those signs of passage. Bears especially, I am told, see rather poorly and therefore perceive their surroundings most acutely through the sense of smell. If bears had a system of philosophy, their concept of mind would very likely be predicated on the sense of smell: "I sniff, therefore I am."

Twenty years later, I remember most keenly the visceral sensation of the bear's presence, as if he were walking beside me, and I understand better how in many indigenous cultures the discovery of an animal companion marks the transition from childhood into full-fledged adulthood. So I still walk in the footsteps of that bear, whose powerful paw-prints are the only visible sign of his passage in that remembered forest. The snow still falls gently on the forest floor and lingers on the branches. He walks on ahead of me, as do all creatures that know their way by trails as yet undiscovered by our kind.

Acknowledgments

I am grateful to Marilyn Gaull, who showed great confidence in this book project and who offered friendly guidance as it was being written and revised. Jonathan Bate provided inspiration and generous encouragement. Karl Kroeber assisted with timely advice and constructive criticism. Robert Essick showed me new ways of seeing the poetry of William Blake, and Morton Paley helped me to fathom Blake's ideas of apocalypse. Eric Robinson offered a wealth of information on John Clare and the history of technology. Ronald Limbaugh shared fruitful ideas on how best to approach the work of John Muir. Eugene Parker guided me to a deeper understanding of environmental science. Bridget Keegan has been a close collaborator with me on many projects, and this book shows the congenial influence of her keen observation and her thoughtful engagement with all intellectual issues.

The Huntington Library provided financial support for my research in their magnificent rare book and manuscript collections, particularly the Mary Austin Collection. The Holt-Atherton Library at the University of the Pacific provided unfettered access to the John Muir Collection. I am grateful to the British Library for extensive access to its rare books and manuscripts. The Bancroft Library of the University of California, Berkeley, provided convenient access to its collection. The Gerald Peters Gallery in Santa Fe, New Mexico, kindly allowed me to peruse every nook and cranny of the Mary Austin House.

This book manuscript was completed with generous fellowship support from the National Endowment for the Humanities, the Mellon Foundation, and the University of Maryland, Baltimore County. Portions of this manuscript have previously been published in *Studies in Romanticism, The Wordsworth Circle, The Keats-Shelley Journal,* and *University of Toronto Quarterly.* I am grateful to the editors of these journals for permission to republish.

Warm personal thanks are due to Kirk McKusick and Eric Allman, whose home in Berkeley provided a base for explorations all over the West. My father, Blaine McKusick, has encouraged my love of nature since I was young enough to get lost in tall grass. And my deepest debt of gratitude is due to my wife, Paige McKusick, whose considerate responses, even to my wildest notions, have been invaluable.

Introduction

As I write these words, I peer out the window of my study across open fields and gnarled trees crusted with ice. Beyond those trees I see cars and trucks dashing along a busy interstate highway past dirty piles of melting snow that still remain from last week's snowstorm. This is the city of Baltimore, where I live. Like many of my readers, I have spent most of my life in urban and suburban settings. Growing up during the 1950s in the mid-Atlantic region, I became quite accustomed to the sounds and smells of smokestack industry, the penumbra of smog pervading the city on summer afternoons, the rainbow sheen of oil glistening on puddles in the street. Even small excursions into the natural world, whether it was gathering chestnuts along my sidewalk when still a young child, or walking immersed in tall grass along the banks of the Brandywine River, or just contemplating the noisy activities of squirrels and bluejays in a local park, aptly named the "Happy Valley," fired my five-year-old imagination. The astonishing sense of discovery that I felt when, as a teenager, I first ventured upon the vast open spaces of the American West, still resonates deeply in my memory.

Wilderness means something different to those who come upon it from a modern city. The English Romantic poets lived at the dawn of the industrial era, and for Blake, and Coleridge, and Keats, the green world of field and forest was a remote, mysterious, and magical place that existed in sharp disjunction from the smoke, crowded streets, and noisy machinery of London, where they lived for most of their lives. To be sure, such a contrast between country and city life has existed in some form since the dawn of civilization, but this dichotomy has taken on new dimensions of meaning in the aftermath of the Industrial Revolution. New modes of transportation have brought the two realms into much closer proximity; on rapid stagecoaches or by steam-powered ships and railways, the later nineteenth-century writers could travel from one realm into the other far more quickly, and with much less effort, than was previously imaginable. Today we travel swiftly by airplane through the vast spaces of the American West, crossing deserts that were still terrible, uncharted terrain for the pioneer wagons of the mid-nineteenth century, pressing westward across the wild frontier to California and the Oregon Territory.

An Opportunity to Forget the Old World

In his classic essay "Walking," Thoreau invokes and develops the contrast between city and country, which he maps out as a journey from East to West:

> Eastward I go only by force; but westward I go free. . . . Let me live where I will, on this side is the city, on that the wilderness, and I am ever leaving the city more and more, and withdrawing into the wilderness. I should not lay so much stress on this fact, if I did not believe that something like this is the prevailing tendency of my countrymen. I must walk toward Oregon, and not toward Europe.[1]

The "prevailing tendency" to conceive of the West as a place of freedom and wildness is indeed one of the most powerful archetypes in all of American literature, and Thoreau accurately identifies it as one of the underlying polarities of his own imaginary geography. In his celebration of the American West, however, Thoreau overtly rejects all the qualities associated with the East: urbanization, commerce, and the decadence of the Old World. Indeed, he goes so far as to acknowledge the necessity of *forgetting* one's place of origin in order to carve out a space for wildness and freedom:

> We go eastward to realize history and study the works of art and literature, retracing the steps of the race; we go westward as into the future, with a spirit of enterprise and adventure. The Atlantic is a Lethean stream, in our passage over which we have had an opportunity to forget the Old World and its institutions. (668)

Such an "opportunity to forget" the urban civilization of the Old World is entirely typical of American writers in the Transcendentalist tradition, and such a gesture reveals something of the essential underlying motivation for the Westering impulse in American culture throughout our history. The West has always been a blank slate upon which the destiny of the nation may be written. D. H. Lawrence, in his seminal *Studies in Classic American Literature* (1923), argues that the essential symbolic act of the American is the murder of Father Europe, and another is re-baptism in the Wilderness. Wilderness is thus mentally constituted by an act of forgetting.

What is forgotten, or erased, by such a constitutive act? At the dawn of the twenty-first century, we have grown justly suspicious of the archetypes of Wilderness as an empty space, virgin land, or pathless void. Something was there already, and our cultural predisposition is not to see it. Of course, secretly we know what was there, and therefore I need not belabor the fact that entire ecosystems, with their unique flora and fauna, indigenous peoples, autonomous cultures, free-flowing waterways, and unfenced horizons, were mapped, plowed, hunted, eradicated, exterminated, ditched, dammed, bulldozed, channelized, and utterly destroyed in the westward course of American empire. These things we know, although our curious cognitive apparatus enables us not to think about them. "Wilderness" is therefore a deeply suspect concept. Thoreau helps us to see that it entails an act of forgetting.

What else is forgotten in the act of Westering? Thoreau calls the Atlantic Ocean a "Lethean stream," and it is precisely the Old World origins of American culture that are forgotten, or intentionally repressed, in the making of a New World. We may see this moment of repression quite overtly in Thoreau's treatment of English literature in the essay "Walking," a personal *tour de force* that was his signature piece throughout his travels on the New England lecture circuit, and intentionally held back from publication until 1862. "Walking" is Thoreau's declaration of independence from the English literary tradition. He writes:

> English literature, from the days of the minstrels to the Lake Poets—Chaucer and Spenser and Milton, and even Shakespeare, included—breathes no quite fresh, and in this sense, wild strain. It is an essentially tame and civilized literature, reflecting Greece and Rome. Her wilderness is a greenwood, her wild man a Robin Hood. There is plenty of genial love of Nature, but not so much of Nature herself. Her chronicles inform us when her wild animals, but not the wild man in her, became extinct. (676)

Such a dismissive appraisal of English literature is entirely typical of the Transcendentalist writers; Emerson evinces a similar attitude in "The American Scholar" and "Self-Reliance." The overt rejection of British culture is of course a deeply held American attitude that was expressed in political terms by Thomas Paine in *Common Sense* (1776) and is inscribed in the foundational document of American government, the Declaration of Independence, which itemizes and denounces the corrupt practices of the wicked King George.

There is more to this act of rejection, however, than rowdy American chest-beating or revolutionary geopolitics. Thoreau rejects English literature, and specifically the work of the Lake Poets, because they are too "tame and civilized." Just as the wolf, the boar, and the aurochs have vanished from the primeval British forests, so too the "wild man" has become extinct in all of Britain. According to this view, the study of English poetry is akin to the study of Latin and Greek, dead languages that Thoreau studied at Harvard and found to be of little relevance to his life in the woods. Thoreau imagines a new, utterly wild American literature that is free of any decadent Old World influences. Emerson likewise advocates a new, self-reliant kind of American literature in "The Poet," an essay that arguably unleashed the "barbaric yawp" of Walt Whitman upon the world, to Emerson's initial acclaim and later consternation.

Yet in Thoreau's essay on "Walking," the category of "wild" literature remains an empty one. He regretfully concedes, "I do not know of any poetry to quote which adequately expresses this yearning for the Wild." To be sure, he imagines a future mythology to be generated out of the land itself, much as the ancient Greek mythology "is the crop which the Old World bore before its soil was exhausted, before the fancy and imagination were affected with blight" (677). In some future epoch, Thoreau hopes that "the poets of the world will be inspired by American mythology" (677). In the meantime, however, the utter vacuity of the concept of "wild" literature should alert us to the act of intentional forgetting that it perhaps unwittingly manifests. The "wild" is constituted here as the erasure of all previous literature, especially that which is *written* (in contrast to the *orality* of ancient mythology). And the most immediate target of Thoreau's ironic dismissal is the writing of the Lake Poets, known today as the founders of English Romanticism: Wordsworth and Coleridge.

There is certainly an ironic tone implicit in Thoreau's sweeping dismissal of all English writers, because elsewhere in the same essay he cites their works approvingly, in support of his own ideas. Chaucer, for instance, is cited on the topic of pilgrimages (669), Milton's *Lycidas* is quoted in favor of westward journeys (669), and the following anecdote is recounted of the leading Lake Poet: "When a traveller asked Wordsworth's servant to show him her master's study, she answered, 'Here is his library, but his study is out of doors'" (663). This latter example is especially telling because it reveals that the *topos* of rejecting book-learning in favor of meditative walking out-of-doors is in fact immediately derived from Wordsworth. Indeed, it should be apparent to any reader of Wordsworth's poetry that the main theme of the "Walking" essay is largely indebted to such poems as "Expostulation and Reply" and "The Tables Turned." Both of these poems develop a contrast between boring, irrelevant book-learning and the vital stimulus of meditative wandering in the natural world. The symbolic significance of westward travel is most explicitly developed in Wordsworth's poem, "Stepping Westward," which describes a walking tour by William Wordsworth and his sister Dorothy into "one of the loneliest parts" of the Lake District.[2] Anticipating Thoreau's characteristic emphasis on wildness, this poem evokes travel to the West as "a *wildish* destiny":

> *"What, you are stepping westward?"—"Yea."*
> —'Twould be a *wildish* destiny,
> If we, who thus together roam
> In a strange Land, and far from home,
> Were in this place the guests of Chance:
> Yet who would stop, or fear to advance,
> Though home or shelter he had none,
> With such a sky to lead him on?[3]

In the two following stanzas, this poem develops the symbolic resonances of a journey "through the world that lay / Before me in my endless way" (25-26). Such contemplative wandering into the boundless realm of the unknown is indeed one of the most characteristic and distinctive themes of Wordsworth's poetry.

What could possibly have motivated Thoreau to deny the influence of the Lake Poets while overtly citing Wordsworth in the same essay? Is he being ironic or merely perverse? One is tempted at first to rely upon a neo-Freudian psychological explanation, invoking what Harold Bloom terms the Anxiety of Influence.[4] According to this theory, every writer must clear out space for his own creative activity by symbolically killing off his precursors. Yet such a grim Oedipal struggle for dominance seems utterly out of keeping with the sauntering, jocular tone of the "Walking" essay. By claiming to reject British influence, yet frequently citing British authors (along with classical Greek and Roman texts), Thoreau perhaps evinces nothing more than an uncouth American irreverence for the monuments of European greatness, much as Mark Twain does in *The Innocents Abroad*

(1869). Like Ben Franklin and James Audubon before him, Thoreau is appearing in coonskin cap and fringed leather garb to enact the Noble Savage before his shocked and delighted Anglo-European audience. It is merely a pose, a theatrical mask.

Or is it? Can we imagine a more plausible motivation behind Thoreau's simultaneous rejection of and reliance upon his English Romantic precursors? If the political, psychological, and theatrical explanations of such perverse posturing are regarded as inadequate, then what mode of explanation could possibly suffice? Perhaps for a writer like Thoreau, so deeply attuned to the significance of the places he chose to inhabit, a more adequate explanation may emerge from a thoughtful investigation of mental geography. For Thoreau, as for many other Americans, East and West are mapped onto many other opposing categories: city and country, tame and wild, servile and free, civilization and wilderness. Such binary oppositions are intrinsically unstable and prone to collapse into each other because they are grounded in acts of ontological bad faith: one category in each pair is constituted as the negation or absence of the other, and therefore has no substantial existence on its own account. Thoreau's playful irony emerges from his intuitive awareness of the acts of bad faith (and historical injustice) that underlie the great American mythology: Northern freedom entails Southern slavery, and the making of the American Wilderness entails the wanton destruction of its former inhabitants. In wildness is the decimation of the world.

Forgetting Romantic Origins: Some Further Examples

It might be argued that Thoreau's "Walking" is merely an isolated instance of such complexly motivated forgetting, and that for the overwhelming majority of American nature writers, the influence of the English Romantic poets is so pervasive and so freely and openly acknowledged as to be merely a commonplace. It is quite "obvious" to all observers that the American nature writers, particularly those in the Transcendentalist tradition, are overtly indebted to the Romantic tradition as it emanates from the English Lake District to the shores of Walden Pond and thence to the Big Wilderness of the American West. And if something is obvious, then why bother to talk about it?

Yet there is always something gained by investigating the things that everyone knows, since the most valuable information may be hidden in plain sight, like Poe's Purloined Letter. And Thoreau is certainly not the only American nature writer to hide his indebtedness to the English Romantic poets through a strategy of foregrounding his knowledge of their writings while denying the Romantic origins of his most fundamental insights. To take a contemporary example, in a fascinating and provocative 1995 essay entitled "The Trouble with Wilderness," William Cronon sets out to re-examine the historical roots of the idea of wilderness.[5] As one of the pre-eminent modern historians of environmental ideas, Cronon is well aware of the significance of the English Romantic poets in the formation of contemporary awareness of the natural world, and he spends several pages describing the emergence of the Romantic Sublime in the writings of Edmund Burke, Immanuel Kant, and William Gilpin, and its deployment in such key passages of Romantic poetry as the Simplon Pass episode in Wordsworth's *Prelude* (1850). Cronon convincingly argues that the concept of the Romantic Sublime was pervasive in the establishment of the first National Parks:

> God was on the mountaintop, in the chasm, in the waterfall, in the thundercloud, in the rainbow, in the sunset. One has only to think of the sites that Americans chose for their first national parks—Yellowstone, Yosemite, Grand Canyon, Rainier, Zion—to realize that virtually all of them fit one or more of these categories. Less sublime landscapes simply did not appear worthy of such protection. (73)

Cronon goes on to describe the other essential elements in the cultural construction of the American Wilderness: the primitivism of Jean-Jacques Rousseau and the rugged individualism of the American frontier. Composed of these largely mythical elements, the American Wilderness is, in Cronon's view, essentially a fantasized or fictional place from which any dissonant elements (such as Indians, large predators, and any lingering evidence of forestry or agriculture) have been forcibly removed:

> The removal of Indians to create an "uninhabited wilderness"—uninhabited as never before in the human history of the place—reminds us just how invented, how constructed, the American wilderness really is. To return to my opening argument: there is nothing natural about the concept of wilderness. It is entirely a creation of the culture that holds it dear, a product of the very history it seeks to deny. (79)

Cronon's argument here is forceful and compelling, especially his claim that the American Wilderness arises from a "thoroughgoing erasure of the history from which it sprang" (79). There is indeed a motivated forgetting that underlies the construction of "Wilderness" out of places that have been inhabited by Native Americans for thousands of years. Cronon's call for a return to historical awareness, and a corresponding sense of responsibility for the displaced inhabitants of the landscape, is one that any ethical person would surely endorse.

Yet Cronon himself falls prey to the same lack of historical awareness that he so accurately diagnoses in other American nature writers. Toward the end of his essay, he calls for a rejection of the "romantic legacy" (88) that conceives wilderness as vast, remote, and sublime. As an antidote to this kind of Big Wilderness, Cronon proposes that we develop a sense of wonder for cultivated landscapes and everyday experiences:

> Wilderness gets us into trouble only if we imagine that this experience of wonder and otherness is limited to the remote corners of the planet, or that it somehow depends on pristine landscapes we ourselves do not inhabit. Nothing could be more misleading. The tree in the garden is in reality no less other, no less worthy of our wonder and our respect, than the tree in an ancient forest that has never known an ax or a saw. (88)

Cronon's argument here is powerful and persuasive, but he is mistaken in his view that this argument comprises an antidote to the "romantic legacy." Indeed, "the tree in the garden" is a familiar *topos* of English Romantic poetry, and the notion that beauty can be found in everyday objects, not just in vast and sublime ones, is nowhere better expressed than in Coleridge's poem, "This Lime-Tree Bower My Prison."[6] Composed in June 1797, almost exactly two centuries before Cronon's essay, "This Lime-Tree Bower My Prison" expresses the poet's sense of frustration and longing as his friends set off to climb a local mountain. Temporarily lamed by a household accident ("dear Sara accidentally emptied a skillet of boiling milk on my foot"), the poet remains trapped at home while his friends are off enjoying the sublime scenery of the Quantock hills:

> Now, my friends emerge
> Beneath the wide wide Heaven—and view again
> The many-steepled tract magnificent
> Of hilly fields and meadows, and the sea,
> With some fair bark, perhaps, whose sails light up
> The slip of smooth clear blue betwixt two Isles
> Of purple shadow! (20–26)

Although this landscape is not uninhabited wilderness, it is nevertheless a clear instance of the Romantic Sublime, replete with intimations of divine presence and power:

> So my friend
> Struck with deep joy may stand, as I have stood,
> Silent with swimming sense; yea, gazing round
> On the wide landscape, gaze till all doth seem
> Less gross than bodily; and of such hues
> As veil the Almighty Spirit, when yet he makes
> Spirits perceive his presence. (37-43)

Thus far Coleridge's poem is little more than a standard late-eighteenth-century evocation of sublime landscape, evocatively presented, to be sure, but of limited originality. The poem becomes a lot more interesting when Coleridge suddenly shifts the perspective back to his garden bower, the scene of composition, where he has been wallowing in self-pity while his friends are out having exciting adventures:

> Nor in this bower,
> This little lime-tree bower, have I not mark'd
> Much that has sooth'd me. Pale beneath the blaze
> Hung the transparent foliage; and I watch'd
> Some broad and sunny leaf, and lov'd to see
> The shadow of the leaf and stem above
> Dappling its sunshine! (45-51)

In a bold swerve away from the Romantic Sublime, Coleridge evokes a renewed sense of wonder in the restricted surrounding of a lime-tree bower in his neighbor's garden. He discovers beauty in commonplace objects, not scenery on a grand scale, and finds pleasure in the gentle "dappling" of sunshine made by leaves waving in a soft summer breeze.

Coleridge goes on to argue that "Nature" is to be found everywhere:

> Henceforth I shall know
> That Nature ne'er deserts the wise and pure;
> No plot so narrow, be but Nature there,
> No waste so vacant, but may well employ
> Each faculty of sense, and keep the heart
> Awake to Love and Beauty! (59-64)

For Coleridge, then, the perception of "Nature" need not be confined to settings of Big Wilderness; even the most humble garden plot, when seen through eyes awake to "Love and Beauty," can respond to our innate sense of wonder in the presence of things we have not created ourselves. This poem seeks to rekindle the sense of "otherness" that William Cronon invokes as the single most important task for contemporary environmentalism.

Although he disregards it here, Cronon must surely be aware of this "homely" element in English Romanticism, since the evocation of beauty in commonplace objects is one of the most familiar hallmarks of the new poetic style pioneered by Wordsworth and Coleridge. Throughout the *Lyrical Ballads* (1798), and especially in those poems where Wordsworth describes the humble routines of everyday life in the vernacular language "really used by men," the sudden shock of mild surprise in the presence of unexpected natural beauty pervades his poetic language, imagery, and ethos. Geoffrey Hartman has written a splendid book on *The Unremarkable Wordsworth,* examining precisely these moments when strange glimmers of "otherness" poke through the veneer of ordinary experience.[7] No sensitive reader of English Romantic poetry could possibly fail to notice the "spots of time" (as Wordsworth termed these events) when the uncanny presences of the natural world suddenly obtrude themselves into consciousness. Coleridge's Conversation Poems record an analogous sense of wonder in the presence of the commonplace, nowhere more eloquently expressed than in "The Nightingale," where, on a dark pathway in the midst of the forest, he finds "a pleasure in the dimness of the stars" (11). Such haunting evocations of the most subtle of natural phenomena, quite distinct from the *Sturm und Drang* [Storm and Stress] of the Romantic Sublime, are entirely characteristic of the poetry of Wordsworth and Coleridge.

Why, then, does William Cronon claim to be making a bold departure from the "romantic legacy" in his argument that "we need to embrace the full continuum of a natural landscape that is also cultural, in which the city, the suburb, the pastoral, and the wild each has its proper place" (107)? Such an argument is itself a vital part of the Romantic legacy, and perhaps Cronon's critique of the "romantic legacy" is merely a tactical move—he needs to destroy a straw-man version of Romanticism in order to carve out space for a this-worldly, purportedly post-Romantic way of living in the devastated post-industrial landscape. Yet one wonders if there is not a deeper kind of motivated forgetting at work, just as Cronon himself astutely observes "the flight from history that is very nearly the core of wilderness" (96). Cronon is not the first, and will surely not be the last, to derogate and demonize the "romantic legacy" as a way of laying the foundations for a supposedly more sophisticated, more "modern" way of understanding the concept of Nature and the complex interrelation between people and the places where they live, work, and play.

Whatever its motivation, such a one-sided caricature of the "romantic legacy" entails a distinct loss of our intellectual and cultural heritage. The Romantic tradition offers a far more rich and varied set of responses to the natural world than is dreamed of in the conventional history of ideas. If the American environmental movement seems to be perpetually in a state of crisis, lurching from one dam disaster to the next, perhaps one reason is an intellectual impoverishment that arises from the worldview of the "true believer." Contemporary American nature writers do not need to know their own intellectual history, because everything they need to know is written in the Good Books of Emerson, Thoreau, and Muir. Amid this pantheon of Green Saints, what need to investigate the Romantic origins of American environmentalism?

"Our birth is but a sleep and a forgetting."[8] Thus Wordsworth describes the emergence of our souls from a Platonic realm of pre-existence into the concrete material world. Forgetting is the price that all humans must pay for not being strong enough to withstand the terror of complete knowledge. Yet the price of ignorance, in a world beset by the mindless pillage of vast machines, is too great to be sustained. It is only by understanding our history that we may come to know ourselves, and by such knowledge we may learn to abide what the future holds in store.

On the Methodology of Ecocriticism

This book describes the emergence of ecological understanding among the English Romantic poets, arguing that this new holistic paradigm offered a conceptual and ideological basis for American environmentalism. Coleridge, Wordsworth, Blake, John Clare, and Mary Shelley all contributed to the fundamental ideas and core values of the modern environmental movement; their vital influence was openly acknowledged by Emerson, Thoreau, John Muir, and Mary Austin. In tracing the transatlantic tradition of Green Writing, this book will employ an interdisciplinary method that encompasses the history of science and environmental history, as well as more traditional approaches to literary analysis. It seeks to elucidate the role of the Romantic poets in creating a new, holistic way of perceiving the natural world, and to explore the ramifications of this view in the later history of science and culture. At the dawn of the third millennium, we are only too aware that the life and death of humankind is inherently linked to the life and death of our planetary ecosystem. A re-examination of the environmental concerns of the English Romantic period can provide a fresh perspective from which to view the historical development of American environmentalism, and it may well suggest possibilities of remedial intervention and progressive social action that are presently outside the mainstream of political and literary discourse.

As a method of literary analysis, ecocriticism emerged in the late twentieth century as a means of investigating the relation between literary texts and their environmental contexts. The term "ecocriticism" was first devised in 1978 by William Rueckert in his pioneering essay, "Literature and Ecology: An Experiment in Ecocriticism."[9] The development of a coherent methodology of ecocriticism has occurred at a time of growing public awareness of environmental issues. Rachel Carson sparked the formation of the modern environmental movement with the publication of her book *Silent Spring* (1962), which described the lethal effects of chemical pollutants in the air we breathe, and the water we drink, in chilling and scientifically accurate detail. Carson's previous nonfiction book, *The Edge of the Sea* (1955), brought a deep ecological understanding to its lyrical depiction of shoreline habitat, and this best-selling book likewise did a great deal to create an environmental sensibility among its readers. Aldo Leopold's influential essay, "Thinking Like a Mountain" (1949), is another important instance of environmental advocacy that actually brought about a significant change in public awareness. Leopold's elegy for a dying wolf not only created a strong sense of outrage in its readers, but also kindled a desire to see his preservationist "land ethic" realized before America's last wild creatures were hunted into extinction. During the twentieth century, as never before, environmental writing had a direct effect on public awareness and public policy. The passage of landmark environmental legislation, such as the Endangered Species Act (1966), the Clean Air Act (1970), and the Clean Water Act (1972), owes much to the persistent and eloquent advocacy of writers like Carson and Leopold. In recent decades the American environmental movement has evolved into a mainstream political force to be reckoned with.

There is always a danger that by becoming mainstream, a movement that began as a radical critique of modern consumer culture may become tamed and assimilated to the point that it is entirely co-opted by the very forces that it set out to oppose. The modern phenomenon of "green" advertising and "environmentally friendly" merchandising carries such dangers for the environmental movement. To be sure, no political move-ment can lay claim to pristine moral purity in the pursuit of its goals, and we would be mistaken to mythologize the origins of contemporary envi-ronmentalism as a sort of hagiography, a collection of Green Saints' Lives. Such mystification of origins is a danger that lurks in the denial or forget-ting of history, and the only effective antidote lies in the accurate recovery of the history of ideas.

Since the time of Emerson and Thoreau, a fictional version of Ameri-can nature writing as self-begot, self-originating, has prevailed in popular awareness and even in more scholarly studies. Within the academy, the departmental and disciplinary boundaries between English Literature and American Studies have effectively discouraged thoughtful scrutiny of the linkages and affiliations between British and American nature writers. It is perhaps known in a general way that the Transcendentalists were "influ-enced" by the English Romantic poets, but the scope and results of this "influence" have not been fully investigated or generally understood. The Emersonian myth of American self-reliance is alive and well within the academy, and it has prevented the modern environmental movement from truly knowing its origins.

Perhaps the term "influence" is part of the problem. The old-fashioned history-of-ideas approach to literary criticism focused mainly on the linear, cause-and-effect relationship between the "source" of an idea and its "recurrence" in later texts. Although this traditional method allowed room for an idea to develop into multiple variant forms, it did not really provide much scope for the creative autonomy of the individual writer, nor did it envisage the genial flow of conversation and mutual exchange of ideas that commonly occurs within a community of writers, especially those engaged with a common sense of purpose in the promulgation of a literary move-ment. These shortcomings effectively doomed the history-of-ideas approach to a gradual demise in the middle part of the twentieth century, to be supplanted by the approach known as the New Criticism.

The New Criticism placed useful emphasis on the autonomy of the lit-erary artifact, and it allowed ample scope for the individual creativity of the author, especially as it was manifested in the spontaneous and often baroque efflorescence of word-play, vivid imagery, and complex metaphors. Yet such an emphasis on uniqueness and individuality carried with it the dan-ger of losing touch with the personal, intellectual, and social contexts out of which a text was written; the living, breathing writer was prone to dis-appear entirely into the literary artifact. Indeed, the artifact or "poem" itself was thought to provide its own "context," and the notion of organic form (which the New Critics derived ultimately from Coleridge by way of the Practical Criticism of I. A. Richards) was invoked to provide a means of describing the *ontology* or unique mode of existence of a literary work. Yet the New Critics' concept of organic form was reductive in a way that was hard for anyone to perceive during the 1940s and 1950s, the triumphal moment of American consumerism. For the first time in their history, middle-class Americans were able to accumulate the gleaming appliances that signified their entry into postwar affluence: washers and dryers, radios and televisions, Jeeps and Thunderbirds. Amid such rampant commodity fetishism, it is not hard to see how the literary text, conceived as a totally unified "organic form," and regarded as analogous to a living organism (whether hothouse flower or sturdy spreading oak), came to be shorn of its roots. The "poem" was understood by the New Critics as a self-contained object, in virtually total disjunction from its social, historical, and geographical context. No one wanted to think about how or why it came to be there. In the era of Disneyland, literature itself became a theme park, filled with discrete simulacra of lived experience.

The advent of Structuralism in American universities during the 1960s and 1970s marked the end of such ostrich-like obliviousness to the broader contextual elements that shape the meaning of any text. The "text" replaced the "poem" as the object of critical scrutiny, and Roland Barthes went so far as to declare the Death of the Author—partly as a form of deliberately outrageous intellectual carnival, but also out a serious desire to understand how the overarching structure of *langue* (language) pervades and thoroughly conditions the possibility of any individual *parole* (utterance).[10] Such a linguistic approach provided a useful corrective to the New Critics' excessive emphasis on the uniqueness of the literary text, since it showed how all texts must emerge from the given possibilities of their native language and culture. Yet Structuralism was limited by its dualistic and essentially Cartesian emphasis on binary opposites that exist in a kind of pure mental space; the impersonal *langue* posited by Ferdinand de Saussure was ultimately as abstract and bloodless as Plato's disembodied realm of the Ideas. The exuberant ferment of post-Structuralism during the 1970s eventually succeeded in dismantling the systematic tyranny of *langue,* but the bewildered readers of Derrida's *Grammatology* (1967; English translation, 1976) were left to wander aimlessly amid the rubble of all previous philosophical systems. After the advent of Deconstruction, it was unclear whether any text could have determinate meaning. The reader was lost in a dark night in which all cats were gray.

The New Historicism came riding to the rescue in the 1980s, bearing a renewed emphasis on the social and political subtexts of literary works, and lending new attention to the way that the concrete economic process of publication often freights a text with hidden meanings. This renewed emphasis on the concrete material existence of the literary work in its own historical moment revitalized the study of literature and lent new relevance to the academic discipline of literary theory by engaging it in the critique of race, class, and gender. Curiously excluded from most New Historicist analyses, however, was any attention to the most material circumstance of all: the environmental context that surrounds the production of any literary work, providing "raw materials" that range from sensory inputs for the writer's cognitive production of imagery to the physical paper, ink, cloth, and leather that make up the finished book. These materials come from *somewhere* out there—a place beyond the purely social realm that we may designate "Nature" without stipulating a definition of the latter term.

It is unfortunate that the New Historicism came to see itself as antagonistic to the emergence of ecocriticism during the 1990s, because the two methods share a common interest in what Clifford Geertz has termed "thick description": the elucidation of the *total material context* of literary production. Much of the squabbling between New Historicists and Ecocritics has been carried on in deplorably simplistic and even *ad hominem* terms. To the extent that there is a serious issue at stake, it centers around the question of whether Nature "really exists" or is merely a construct of social and political history. Alan Liu has gone so far as to claim that "there is no nature except as it is constituted by acts of political definition made possible by particular forms of government."[11] A typical counter-claim by Karl Kroeber is that English Romantic poetry was "the first literature to anticipate contemporary biological conceptions," and he goes on to stake out the ground for a radically materialist ecological criticism founded on the Malthusian concept of grim competition for scarce resources.[12] Both of these claims are dangerously reductive, in my view, since they tend to paint their proponents into narrow corners labeled "Nature" and "Culture," both of which are conceived in the absurdly comprehensive form, "Everything is X." The advocates of "Nature" are left in the posture of Samuel Johnson, who responded to the subjective idealist philosophy of George Berkeley by kicking a stone and saying "thus I refute him, Sir."

I cannot rescue the New Historicism from its own reductive acts of self-caricature, but I do advocate a form of ecocriticism that evades the trap of crude materialism. There is more to "Nature" than cold, hard objects, and there is more to "Literature" than pure, isolated images of the natural world. As a first step on the path beyond such a materialist reduction, I would recommend a careful reading of *The Spell of the Sensuous* by David Abram, a work that develops many valuable insights about the interrelation of mind, language, and nature.[13] Abram provides a provocative, engaging account that seems quite relevant to the study of Romanticism, even though he doesn't explicitly devote much attention to that literary movement. Abram is especially insightful in his discussion of language as a medium for the conception and exchange of sensory information. He describes how language, and especially pre-literate language (as spoken, for example, by Wordsworth's orally inventive Lakeland shepherds), is correlative with the moment of experience, part and parcel of our active engagement with the natural world, not simply an objective description. Yet for Abram, "alphabeticism" stands as the downfall at the origin of the Hebraic (monotheistic, providential, and linear) understanding of history, and of the Greek rationalist approach to natural science.[14] According to this view, any written text necessarily participates in the pernicious process by which nature is surveyed, consumed, and ultimately betrayed by culture. In short, we are back to the familiar dichotomy of wild, spontaneous Nature versus cold, rational Culture.

Why is this dichotomy a false one? I have imagined a couple of possibilities (both of which I find persuasive): First, the concept of Nature is capacious enough to contain both nature-as-ground and nature-as-construct. Karl Kroeber points out that consciousness arises from natural processes, and David Abram develops this point, especially with regard to language. Even conceding this assertion, however, it remains excruciatingly difficult to discover or describe the process by which consciousness emerges from the raw sensory data of experience, since human beings always do that kind of meta-analysis through an invisible cultural/political filter.

Second, the disjunction between Nature and Culture rests upon an unexamined premise that the social production of human behavior is entirely distinct from the means by which the "lower animals" learn to hunt, hide, play, and fight. Yet the science of ethology provides numerous examples of animal species whose learned behaviors exhibit several of the most distinctive traits of human culture. The songs of whales, for instance, are invented by particular individuals, are frequently imitated and sung by other whales, become enormously popular, and eventually pass into oblivion, much like hit songs on American Top Forty radio.

In my view, the dichotomy between nature-as-ground and nature-as-construct is false when it is posed as an either/or alternative, much as the nature-versus-nurture argument is silly and meaningless if it is posed in absolute terms. To be sure, our perception and conception of "nature" is always filtered, categorized, and constructed by our perceptual/cognitive apparatus. Kant had some good insights about the way that our understanding is constrained by *a priori* categories, as did Marx and his followers from a more historical and social determinist angle, and Sapir and Whorf from the standpoint of linguistic relativity (the latter topic is usefully addressed by David Abram). But even the most ethereal of philosophers must inhabit physical bodies that are always liable to interrupt the contemplation of abstract ideas with unruly urges to eat, sleep, and procreate.

Or to put it another way, the reproduction of knowledge and culture depends on, and indeed presupposes, a material infrastructure that is not entirely or even primarily cognitive or cultural. Living as we do in a continually worsening state of environmental crisis verging upon catastrophe, we have come to understand more clearly than Kant or Marx that our continued existence is radically contingent upon the ecological cycles of energy and matter that sustain and nourish us. In this material sense, nature is a ground of existence. Consider also, from a biological perspective, that life evolves through the exchange and reproduction of information, encoded mainly in DNA, and for humans (and certain other animal species capable of symbolic exchange) also embedded in language and culture. So there is no clear boundary between the material substrate and the cognitive content of information, from an evolutionary point of view.

This is why I think the idealist tendency of various major Romantic poets and prose writers is not incompatible with, and indeed foreshadows, the prevailing contemporary understanding of how ecosystems work. M. H. Abrams calls Coleridge a "cosmic ecologist," suggesting that his hunt for an all-encompassing, energetic and dynamic Idea is cognate with modern ecological thought.[15] And, I would add, in the internet era we are well situated to see how cultural evolution occurs through the exchange of information and ideas. So we need not imagine a cruel, ravenous Darwinian nature "red in tooth and claw" as somehow utterly disjunct from our own pristine and hygienic ivory-tower world of human language, culture, and consciousness. It's not just that we are animals—naked apes—but also that many animals (especially the predator and prey species) are already fully involved in semiotic exchange.[16]

Alan Liu's notorious claim that "there is no nature" actually provides a healthy antidote to the notion that organic unity somehow inheres in the object of perception, whether it is a living creature or a work of literature. And yet, to the Ecocritic, the concepts of the organism and the ecosystem must be regarded as more than merely heuristic; they necessarily correspond to something *really out there,* since otherwise humans would not exist as members of an intelligent, tool-using species. It seems to me that any form of social or cultural determinism must ultimately deny whatever reality can be attributed to the concept of "ecosystem," and to the Ecocritic such forms of intellectual analysis are therefore merely tendentious, not helpful or expedient to our inquiry. Cultural historians cannot explain the origin of culture. Nor will they have much to say in the event that environmental degradation threatens an end to human existence, and thus an end to history as we know it.

For all of the reasons just cited, ecocriticism offers the most effective and relevant means of literary analysis in an era of increasing human impact upon the terrestrial environment. Perhaps the most significant and useful tool that modern science offers to the literary critic is the concept of the ecosystem, which, as a consequence of recent environmental research, is now regarded as a much more chaotic and unstable structure than the classic scientific understanding of the "balance of nature" might have suggested. Such chaotic and unstable interrelationships are well known to those who study the development of literary movements, and thus it may prove useful for our present purposes to posit the existence of Romantic poetry as a literary ecosystem, a vibrant community in which competition and synergy, exchange of ideas and flow of information, predators and prey, hosts and parasites, all coexist in the turbulent vortex of a shared intellectual environment. Perhaps such a suggestion is more than just an analogy, since for *Homo sapiens* during the last several millennia, cultural evolution has been far more important than biological evolution, and the pace of changes in our conceptual repertoire has far outstripped the pace of changes in our DNA. In this very concrete sense, the old-fashioned study of the "history of ideas" may be usefully re-conceived for our time as a study of the dynamics of intellectual ecosystems.

Whatever its merits as a description of what actually occurs in the unruly ferment of a new intellectual movement, such an ecocritical approach offers some distinctive possibilities for a new approach to the study of literary history. It suggests that the linear analysis of "sources and influences" should be enlarged and perhaps even supplanted by a study of the dialogical exchange of ideas among a community of writers. Such a community should be regarded as a dynamic entity, sometimes verging upon utter chaos, and always in the process of becoming something other than itself. The borders of such a community are drawn quite arbitrarily, and often upon purely aesthetic criteria, since the entire living planet may legitimately be regarded as a single ecosystem; but for the present purpose of analysis the notion of a "language community" makes sense as a provisional or heuristic device. Throughout the nineteenth century, the community of English-speaking writers extended to both sides of the Atlantic, and the borders of the modern industrial nation-state often proved quite permeable to the exchange of persons and texts traveling in both directions.[17] This book will therefore concern itself with the transatlantic community of Green Writers who flourished in England and America during the Long Romantic Period, which we may generously extend from the dawn of the Industrial Revolution to the turn of the twentieth century.

On the Origin of Ecological Consciousness

The claim that English and American writers of the Long Romantic Period made significant innovations in the development of environmental ideas will likely be scoffed at by historians of earlier periods, who may claim with some justification that everything in the Romantic lore of nature had been strongly foreshadowed in previous epochs. Such a claim is not without merit. Some degree of environmental awareness is surely inherent in every civilized people since the dawn of urban life in the ancient Middle East, and it would be rash indeed to claim that the English Romantics were the unique point of origin for all of our modern ideas about ecology. Indeed, the English Romantics were well aware of their participation in a literary tradition of immemorial standing, whose most proximate version was the concept of Pastoral, mediated by writers from ancient classical times to the sentimental writers of the later eighteenth century.[18]

Yet this study does make a historically determinate claim, arguing that the Romantic writers formulated an innovative and in many respects original way of understanding the world. Such an understanding may authentically be termed "ecological," since for the first time in the Western intellectual tradition it evinces the essential elements of a modern ecological worldview. The originality of the ecological understanding of the Romantic poets may best be demonstrated by situating them within the larger historical context of the Western tradition of environmental writing. Although such a distinguished critic as Karl Kroeber has described the Romantics as merely "proto-ecological" thinkers,[19] the present study advances a stronger claim that the English Romantics were the first full-fledged ecological writers in the Western literary tradition. Such a claim will require at least some cursory scrutiny of their precursors in that tradition.

Environmental writing has very deep historical roots, harking back to the archetypal image of the Garden, as canonically represented in the Garden of Eden, and often described in the classical mode of pastoral poetry as the *locus amoenus* or "pleasant place," a garden of earthly delights.[20] Such archetypal images may indeed embody a cultural memory of agricultural fertility and abundance, before deforestation and intensive irrigation had converted the paradisal landscapes of the ancient Mediterranean world into barren deserts.[21] The pastoral eclogues of Theocritus and Virgil are likewise grounded in a concrete understanding of the negative consequences of the social and technological complexity of life in an urban setting. Both Theocritus and Virgil regarded the formation of the imperial city-state as a recent and pernicious phenomenon; Virgil in particular writes his pastorals out of aversion to the tyranny of Augustus. The pastoral mode was to provide one of the most enduring and influential modes of expression for environmental awareness, representing the life of simple shepherds as a desirable alternative to the stress and frivolous consumption of city dwellers. Throughout the bleak history of Western colonial expansion and technological development, the pastoral mode has provided a vicarious escape to the green world of field and forest, and (with varying levels of seriousness and sincerity) has advocated a return to a local, sustainable, low-tech agricultural lifestyle. Raymond Williams, in *The Country and the City,* has exposed the material basis of the pastoral ideal as it developed from these classical precursors into the full-blown pastoral poetry of Sidney, Spenser, Marlowe, Herrick, and Marvell. Williams argues that the pastoral mode, in its presentation of an idealized golden age, tends to efface the harsh working conditions of agricultural laborers; but despite this element of distortion—typically the result of a dominant class ideology—there often remains a firm foundation of vividly realized images drawn from country life.[22] During the eighteenth century, the pastoral ideal was re-externalized in the construction of "English gardens" that imitated the idyllic disorder of natural landscapes, rather than formal geometric patterns. The English landscape, it was believed, by thoughtful care and nurturing, could return once again to the primeval innocence of the Garden of Eden.

This archetypal image of the Garden is related (at a deep psychic and historical level) to the feminine principle of fertility and abundance, represented in Paleolithic fertility figures and in the ancient cult of Gaia, the pre-patriarchal Earth-goddess.[23] Analogues of the Great Goddess occur in many ancient cultures, such as Isis in Egypt, Ishtar in Canaan, the Sumerian goddess Nanshe, and the Celtic goddess Cerridwen. Greek mythology tended to personify diverse attributes of this goddess, regarding Demeter,

Hera, Athena, and Aphrodite as discrete embodiments of this generative yet destructive female power, which also manifested its uncanny presence in the Bacchic orgies and the Eleusinian Mysteries. The Christian tradition, despite its alleged patriarchal and logocentric tendencies, has always found a place for the corresponding embodiments of female power in the figures of Eve, who assured Adam of an earthly destiny, and Mary, who nurtured Christ in an earthly body. The Christian doctrine of the human steward-ship of nature, often dismissed as environmentally exploitive, nevertheless proved congenial to St. Francis of Assisi, whose intensely joyful "Canticle to Brother Sun" (circa 1225) should be recognized as an early aspiration toward total harmony with the generative forces of nature. These forces are embodied for St. Francis in the figure of "Mother Earth, who nourishes and watches us while bringing forth abundance of fruits with colored flowers and herbs."[24] The final strophe of this canticle, addressed to "Sister Death," invokes the complementary destructive aspect of nature. St. Francis's acceptance of poverty, his work among marginal social groups (including lepers, robbers, beggars, and Saracens), his advocacy of peace, and his fond-ness for animals, make him an attractive role model for modern environ-mentalists, suggesting (among other things) that ecological awareness must go hand in hand with individual responsibility and social activism.[25]

Growing up alongside the literary and religious traditions of nature writing, but at first largely distinct from them, was the scientific tradition of natural history prose. From Aristotle's various treatises on animals, this tradition developed through Pliny's comprehensive *Historia Naturalis* (circa 77 A.D.), which inspired numerous medieval herbals and bestiaries. The Renaissance brought a renewed emphasis upon empirical observation; Francis Bacon called upon scientists to investigate nature rather than books, and his appeal eventually bore fruit in the weighty *Transactions of the Royal Society* (founded 1665), with its motto, *nullius in verba* ("nothing in words"). Meanwhile, John Ray's treatise, *The Wisdom of God Manifested in the Works of the Creation* (1691), promoted the scientific study of nature from a non-anthropocentric viewpoint, foreshadowing modern ecological thought by emphasizing each creature's participation in a cosmic plan, a clockwork universe cunningly constructed by a watchmaker God. William Derham's *Physico-Theology, or, A Demonstration of the Being and Attributes of God from His Works of Creation* (1713) was a further development of Ray's views, advanc-ing the study of natural history through its perception of total design in nature, and focusing especially on the adaptation of organisms to their habitats.[26] But the holistic view of natural phenomena advanced by the physico-theologists was not sustained in the eighteenth century, an era of rational analysis that fostered an essentially taxonomic approach to natural history. The effort to describe and catalogue all known species was launched by Carolus Linnaeus in his famous *Systema Naturae* (1735), which proposed a Latin nomenclature of genus and species for all flora and fauna; henceforth the common vernacular names would be discarded by most scientists in favor of these bloodless but precise Latin terms.[27]

The rebirth of empirical science in the Renaissance also marked the (re)discovery of the New World and its teeming wilderness, vividly described by European explorers from Christopher Columbus onward. In the English language this exploratory genre of natural history writing takes shape with Thomas Hariot's *A Brief and True Report of the Newfound Land of Virginia* (1588), which extravagantly praises the fertility of the New World and catalogues several of its species. Hariot's account, along with many others, was published in Richard Hakluyt's *Voyages* (1589-1600), a vast compendium of Elizabethan travel writing that contains extensive descriptions of exotic flora and fauna in their remote habitats. During the eighteenth century, the breathless tone of New World exploration was sustained by William Bartram's *Travels through North and South Carolina* (1791), which describes risky close encounters with Indians and alligators, while a gentler, more domestic landscape prevails in Crèvecoeur's *Letters from an American Farmer* (1782). Meanwhile Captain Cook's scientific expeditions girdled the globe, gathering specimens of unknown flora and fauna from uncharted Pacific islands and the trackless wilderness of Australia. Joseph Banks, the leader of the scientific party on Cook's first voyage and later the president of the Royal Society, became a major figure in the popular dissemination of natural history knowledge, encouraging the scientific expeditions of younger naturalists and establishing Kew Gardens as an open-air laboratory for the propagation of the exotic flora discovered on their voyages.[28] All of these British naturalists applied the prevailing Linnaean nomenclature, describing their taxonomic discoveries in precise but rather colorless prose studded with the Latin names for genus and species.

Closer to home, pastoral poetry was becoming imbued with the empirical spirit of scientific description, augmenting the classical and Renaissance pastoral mode with a more circumstantial depiction of rural landscapes. Ambrose Philips incorporated some realistic details of English country life in his *Pastorals* (1709), earning him the derisive nickname "Namby Pamby" and the vehement scorn of Alexander Pope, who cultivated a more austere classical correctness in his own *Pastorals* (also published in 1709). Most notable in this new vein, however, is James Thomson's *Sea-*

sons (1726-30), which marks a fresh departure in the presentation of natural phenomena in English verse. Unlike most of his precursors in the pastoral tradition, Thomson does not confine himself to the abstract evocation of rural landscapes, but projects an air of facticity through the taxonomic description of actual species, while admitting pests, parasites, predators, hazardous marshes, gloomy mountains, and frightful storms into the world of his poetry. Thomson's miscellaneous farrago of pastoral convention, scientific description, and sublime scenery proved to be one of the most popular and enduring poetic modes of the eighteenth century, closely imitated by the later poets of Sensibility such as William Collins, Thomas Gray, and William Cowper, and ardently admired by the first-generation Romantic poets. Thomson's *Seasons* was the first book of poetry that John Clare ever purchased (at age 13), and it exerted a strong formative influence on his poetic style and his way of representing the English landscape.

The tradition of Sensibility, as it developed from Thomson through the poets of the later eighteenth century, falls short of an authentically ecological understanding of the natural world; it reflects an essentially touristic and hierarchical awareness centered on the most spectacular or "sublime" aspects of nature, and it dramatizes the poetic persona in its sensitive, tasteful response to these outlandish phenomena. The poet is just passing through, on his way to ever more astonishing and delightful scenes; he is not a native inhabitant, and he knows little about the local environment or the everyday activities of the local residents. Even Cowper, the most "rooted" of these poets, shares Thomson's tendency to privilege dramatic response over circumstantial description. In Cowper, however, we find the most articulate expression of a concern for the rights of animals, a crucial aspect of ecological awareness that had only gradually gained prominence during the eighteenth century, challenging the Cartesian view of animals as unfeeling automata and the prevailing conception of nature as an inexhaustible stockpile of raw materials to be exploited for man's use. In *The Task* (1784), Cowper argues that all created beings possess intrinsic value, not just utility for human purposes: "they are all—the meanest things that are— / As free to live, and to enjoy that life, / As God was free to form them at the first."[29] Cowper expressed his commitment to animal rights in his tenderness for small, helpless creatures, even worms and snails; among his contemporaries, Samuel Johnson, Lawrence Sterne, Christopher Smart, and William Blake expressed a similar solicitude for animals, along with a growing sense of "th'oeconomy of nature's realm" as possessing value in its own right, distinct from human purposes.[30] This increased respect for the autonomy of the natural world, and the corresponding view of human beings as responsible for the integrity of that world, was a vital legacy of the poetry of Sensibility.

George Crabbe injected a further note of realism into his depiction of village life, acknowledging the difficult working conditions of agricultural laborers in *The Village* (1783). Crabbe expresses deep sympathy for the rural poor, and his evocation of social and environmental devastation due to exploitive farming practices is unprecedented in the pastoral tradition, which had tended to depict a timeless, idealized mode of existence. Crabbe rehistoricizes the landscape by representing it as the product of class conflict and technological innovation, and in this respect he foreshadows the poetry of John Clare, where the impoverishment of the land and people is regarded as the tragic outcome of a concrete historical process. Clare greatly admired Crabbe, and often imitated him (especially in his early poetry), but he nevertheless considered Crabbe to be an outsider, an itinerant "parson poet" lacking the firsthand experience of a native inhabitant or a member of the working class, and thus liable to a patronizing tone that undercuts the validity of his social and environmental critique:

> I have seen 1 vol of Crabb (last winter) called 'Tales' . . . I lik'd here and there a touch but there is a d———d many affectations among them which seems to be the favourite play of the parson poet— . . . whats he know of the distresses of the poor musing over a snug fire in his parsonage box—if I had an enemy I coud wish to torture I woud not wish him hung nor yet at the devil my worst wish shoud be a weeks confinement in some vicarage to hear an old parson & his wife lecture on the wants & wickedness of the poor.[31]

Despite his genuine sympathy for the poor, Crabbe maintains a detached, moralistic perspective that prevents him (in Clare's opinion) from fathoming the real situation of the land and people or discovering a workable solution to their problems. Just as all politics is local, so too all ecology is local; and a true ecological writer must be "rooted" in the landscape, instinctively attuned to the changes of the Earth and its inhabitants.

William Wordsworth has often been regarded as a climactic figure in the development of ecological consciousness. He was a native inhabitant of the Lake District, and his poetry, beginning with *Descriptive Sketches* and *An Evening Walk* (both published in 1793), expresses a deep intuitive knowledge of his native region while adapting the poetic conventions of Sensibility to a more intense imaginative response to natural phenomena. These early poems depict the picturesque landscape of the Lake District and the sublime mountain scenery of the Alps in the approved Thomsonian manner, but they clearly grow out of a detailed knowledge of the local environment. Wordsworth's contributions to *Lyrical Ballads* (1798) are less concerned with sublime scenery than they are with everyday occurrences among people who live in harmony with their natural surroundings. In particular, his poem "Michael" (1800) imparts historical realism to the pastoral mode by describing actual English shepherds attempting to live a simple, independent life in a remote corner of the Lake District. Despite their best efforts, however, these shepherds are ultimately trapped in the tentacles of the mercantile urban culture. In his concern for the economic fate of the local people, and in his valiant efforts to mitigate the environmental impact of the proposed Kendal and Windermere Railway, Wordsworth inaugurates a new era of environmental activism.[32]

In his most characteristic works, however, Wordsworth tends to subordinate the description of nature to the inward exploration of poetic self-consciousness. Even more than Thomson, Wordsworth seeks to dramatize the subjective response of the beholder, so that in "Tintern Abbey" (1798) and *The Prelude* (1850) the essential narrative development consists of the growth of the poet's mind as it evolves from an immediate sensation of pleasure in natural objects toward a more mediated response that exults in the power of imagination to modify and recombine the objects of perception. This quintessentially Romantic celebration of self-consciousness—what Keats called the "wordsworthian or egotistical sublime"—exists in uneasy tension with a more circumstantial depiction of nature, and it often threatens to obliterate the concrete details that provide its empirical foundation.[33] Dorothy Wordsworth, in her *Grasmere Journals,* describes how she once took a walk with her brother and discovered a group of daffodils, along with a few "stragglers," by the lakeshore. In William's poetic revision of this account, these "stragglers" are omitted, along with their habitat of "mossy stones" and even his erstwhile companion; only the abstract "host of golden daffodils" remains as an emblem of the imagination's power to recreate experience.[34] For Wordsworth, this imaginative power is fundamentally at odds with the detailed perception of flora and fauna, or the discovery of their complex interrelations; and for this reason his poetry is best regarded as an evocation of lived experience, rather than a scientific description of the natural world.

Gilbert White, another great admirer of Thomson, found it possible to combine the mode of Sensibility with the scientific precision of natural history, enabling him to compose *The Natural History and Antiquities of Selborne* (1789), a landmark in the development of ecological consciousness.

This delightfully rambling and anecdotal collection of informal letters seeks to encapsulate a complete "parochial history" of the district of Selborne, providing not merely a dry taxonomic description of its flora and fauna, but a detailed account of each species's habitat, distribution, behavior, and seasonal variation or migration. White's penchant for anecdotal presentation, and his frequent use of vernacular or dialect words to supplement the "official" nomenclature of Latin words for genus and species, pioneers a new, more colorful and engaging kind of nature writing.

Some of the most essential insights of modern ecological thought were first developed in the writings of Gilbert White. Throughout *The Natural History of Selborne,* he evokes the "economy of nature" on a local scale, describing in meticulous detail the interaction of plant and animal species throughout the parish. Even insects and reptiles, in his view, are essential to the cycling of resources through the food chain:

> The most insignificant insects and reptiles are of much more consequence, and have much more influence in the economy of Nature, than the incurious are aware of; and are mighty in their effect, from their minuteness, which renders them less an object of attention; and from their numbers and fecundity. Earth-worms, though in appearance a small and despicable link in the chain of Nature, yet, if lost, would make a lamentable chasm.[35]

Such evident fondness for even the most "despicable" creatures is typical of White's attitude toward nature, and marks an important step toward the idea of a biological community in which all organisms play an essential role. Especially in his later years, White often questioned the value of human intervention in the natural world, mourning the loss of favorite trees to the woodcutter's axe and resisting the conversion of "waste" areas to farmland.

White's sincere affection and concern for all living creatures is, however, qualified by his philosophical allegiance to the traditional Christian doctrine that the Earth was created for human purposes. White tends to evaluate various species in terms of what they can contribute to human existence; the swallows, for instance,

> are a most inoffensive, harmless, entertaining, social, and useful tribe of birds: they touch no fruit in our gardens; delight, all except one species, in attaching themselves to our houses; amuse us with their migrations, songs, and marvelous agility; and clear our outlets from the annoyances of gnats and other troublesome insects. . . . Whoever contemplates the myriads of insects that sport in the sunbeams of a summer evening in this country, will soon

be convinced to what a degree our atmosphere would be choaked with them was it not for the friendly interposition of the swallow tribe. (134)

Although White would hardly condone the ruthless pillaging and exploitation of the land that characterized much economic activity during the Industrial Revolution, he nevertheless sees the rural landscape primarily as a source of scientific knowledge and aesthetic pleasure, and he is not averse to killing scientific specimens, hacking trails through the woods, or carving scenic "prospects" out of wild natural landscapes. Such intrusive activities are certainly benign by eighteenth-century standards, but they do indicate the historical distance that separates White's worldview from that of modern environmentalists, who would make a much clearer distinction between wilderness, existing for its own sake, and land that is managed for human purposes. Gilbert White's love for the natural world remains anthropocentric at a deep ethical and emotional level.

Nevertheless, White's scrupulous attention to the living organism in its local habitat marks a significant step beyond the single-minded specimen collecting and cataloguing that typifies eighteenth-century natural history.[36] Moreover, despite his conservative political views, White took a sympathetic interest in the poor people of his parish, seeking on one occasion to defend their common rights against the threat of enclosure.[37] White's intense curiosity about the habitat and behavior of birds and animals, his lively anecdotal mode of presentation, and his use of informal vernacular language, would later prove essential to John Clare as he struggled to express his own poetic vision of the natural world. Clare possessed two different editions of White's *Natural History,* and it is largely from this work that Clare evolved the means of expression and the technique of description that enabled him to become one of the first true ecological writers in the English-speaking world.[38] Clare's unique accomplishments as a self-taught poet and naturalist will be more fully examined in chapter 3.

The Emergence of Romantic Ecology

This book describes the emergence of ecological awareness among the English Romantic poets and its subsequent development among the American nature writers in the Romantic tradition. It examines the work of five English Romantic writers who inaugurated a radically new conception of humankind's relationship to the natural world: Samuel Taylor Coleridge, William Wordsworth, John Clare, William Blake, and Mary Shelley. It seeks to assess the vital significance of these poets for later American environmental writers who developed and articulated a more detailed understanding of ecological processes and advocated the preservation of wilderness areas. The most essential insights of ecological thought—namely, the adaptation of species to their habitats, the interrelatedness of all life forms, and the potentially catastrophic effects of human intervention in natural systems—are first expressed by the English Romantic poets, and more explicitly developed by American nature writers of the later nineteenth century. There is a direct link between the basic ecological concepts of the English Romantic poets and the bold speculations of the American Transcendentalists.

Perhaps the single most important figure in the development of a full-fledged ecological consciousness in Britain and America was Samuel Taylor Coleridge. Coleridge was the first of the English Romantics to articulate a holistic conception of poetic form and to relate this conception to the scientific concept of the organism. In his later prose works, particularly *Aids to Reflection* (1825), Coleridge provided a coherent philosophical basis for regarding the natural world as pervaded by holistic and cyclical processes, a view that later sparked the development of American Transcendentalism. To be sure, Coleridge's transcendental view of the natural world has been sternly criticized by those who posit a materialistic, neo-Malthusian basis for scientific ecology; Karl Kroeber, for instance, in his groundbreaking study, *Ecological Literary Criticism,* dismisses the latent idealism of Coleridge and Percy Bysshe Shelley. Kroeber has especially harsh words for Coleridge's allegedly narcissistic transcendentalism and Shelley's "retreat into a form of Platonic idealism."[39] Yet it was precisely the transcendentalism of these two poets that appealed to a later generation of American nature writers, including Emerson, Thoreau, and Muir, and that continues to inspire such contemporary ecological visionaries as Gary Snyder and Barry Lopez. It is therefore with Coleridge that this book will begin its analysis of the emergence of ecological consciousness in the English Romantic period.

The crucial importance of the natural world to Wordsworth and Coleridge, both as a locus of imaginative energy and as a potent source of intellectual ideas, has long been recognized by Romanticists, although many scholars are reluctant to describe them as "nature poets," especially if this phrase is taken to imply merely the scenic description of wild natural areas. Wordsworth and Coleridge are more than just itinerant observers of scenic beauty; they are dwellers in the landscape of the Lake District, and the poetry that they composed in this region often adopts the persona of a speaker whose voice is inflected by the local and personal history of the place he inhabits. Such a perspective may legitimately be termed an eco-logical view of the natural world, since their poetry consistently expresses a deep and abiding interest in the Earth as a dwelling-place for all living things. The word *ecology* (first recorded in the English language in 1873) is derived from the Greek word οἴκος (*oikos*), meaning *house* or *dwelling-place,* and the poetry of Wordsworth and Coleridge clearly foreshadows the mod-ern science of ecology in its holistic conception of the Earth as a house-hold, a dwelling-place for an interdependent biological community.[40]

John Clare expresses an even more compelling ecological vision. As an impoverished agricultural laborer in the village of Helpston, 80 miles north of London, Clare obtained only the rudiments of a formal education, but from an early age he was an enthusiastic observer of the local flora and fauna. Clare deplored the changes that economic "progress" brought to his village—the wholesale destruction of forests and wetlands, the disappear-ance of streams, and the enclosure of common fields. Clare regarded the natural world as a realm possessing intrinsic value, distinct from human purposes, and he strongly advocated the preservation of wild and "waste" areas. Clare's meticulous description of birds and animals in their natural habitat is conveyed in a new kind of literary language, which he calls a "green" language, grounded in his own regional dialect with its colorful deviations from the lexicon, grammar, and spelling of standard English. These themes are explored in chapter 3, "The Ecological Vision of John Clare," with particular attention to his seminal conception of a "green" lan-guage.

The idyllic Romantic conception of the natural world as a place of vital sustenance and peaceful coexistence is complemented by its nightmare vision of a world threatened by imminent environmental catastrophe. Although the apocalyptic theme has long been regarded as integral to the Romantic World Picture, the environmental implications of this theme have been overlooked or undervalued by several generations of literary critics. This book will articulate a revisionary understanding of the apoca-lyptic narratives of the major Romantic writers, examining how Blake's poetry, from the *Songs of Experience* to *Jerusalem,* engages in a sustained and bitter critique of the material conditions of production—the "dark Satanic mills" that constituted the coal-fired industrial base of Britain's mercantile empire. Blake's quest for a utopian alternative to such destructive tech-nologies is accompanied by a prophetic vision of the death of all life forms and the Earth itself in a final apocalyptic conflagration. Such global anni-hilation, often regarded as a mere poetic fiction, bears a more urgent bur-den of possibility in the present era of global warming and impending environmental catastrophe. Blake's visionary protest against the Industrial Revolution offers informative parallels to our own ecological concerns.

The novels of Mary Shelley, particularly *The Last Man* (1826), provide further evidence that the destruction of the Earth's capacity to sustain human life was a vital concern of the English Romantic writers. In *The Last Man,* Shelley paints an apocalyptic picture of a world in which mankind has perished as the result of a mysterious plague unleashed by the harsh conditions of warfare in an arrogant masculine quest for world domination. The narrator of this novel, Lionel Verney, emerges as the last survivor amid the ruined grandeurs of Rome in the year 2100, further adumbrating the apocalyptic theme of first and last things. Mary Shelley evinces a strong awareness of gender issues that might well be termed "ecofeminist," since her vision of a ruined Earth is mediated by a critique of patriarchal meddling with the underlying organic powers of generation and nurturance, a view also apparent in *Frankenstein* (1818), in which the inadvertent creation of a violent, uncontrollable "new species" foreshadows the nightmare potentiality of genetic engineering in our own time.

The main purpose of such an ecological approach to the English Romantic writers will be to elucidate, and perhaps to defamiliarize, the ways in which crucial aspects of their literary language emerge from their perceptual and affective engagement with local and global environmental issues. An ecological reading of these writers will enable certain aspects of their conception of poetic form and their actual poetic practice to be understood more adequately than previous critical perspectives have allowed. In particular, the synergistic relationship between an individual organism and its habitat, which was first coming to be understood in its full complexity by late-eighteenth-century science, offers a fresh and suggestive model for analyzing the role of organicism in Romantic poetry and aesthetics. These topics are introduced in chapter 1, "Coleridge and the Economy of Nature," which examines "The Rime of the Ancient Mariner" as a parable of ecological transgression. Subsequent chapters sustain and enlarge this discussion of perennial literary issues from an environmental perspective.

The American writers of the Transcendentalist movement were deeply affected by the work of Wordsworth and Coleridge. Many of Coleridge's American disciples remembered his philosophical engagement with the concept of organic form and cherished his inspiring remarks on the essential knowledge revealed in the perception of everyday objects. Among these admirers of Coleridge was Ralph Waldo Emerson, who visited Coleridge at Highgate in 1832, and who developed an essentially

Coleridgean theory of perception in the fourth chapter of *Nature* (1836), especially in his assertion of a symbolic correspondence between words and natural objects. Henry David Thoreau is less explicit in his acknowledgment of Coleridge's influence, even (on the 1854 titlepage of *Walden*) expressing disdain for the decadent sort of writer who would write an "Ode to Dejection," but his description of Walden Pond as an organic community nevertheless owes a great deal to a Romantic conception of nature. Thoreau invokes the familiar Romantic image of the Aeolian harp on several occasions in *Walden,* using it to express a vital sense of participation in larger organic processes.

The first American writer to articulate a scientific ecology was George Perkins Marsh, whose treatise, *Man and Nature* (1864), takes stock of the devastation visited upon the American continent by modern technology and suggests practical means by which the Earth's organic processes might be restored. His cousin, James Marsh, was the American editor of Coleridge's *Aids to Reflection* (1829) and *The Friend* (1831). James Marsh's eloquent prefaces to these works were widely influential in Transcendentalist circles, perhaps because they stressed the holistic dimension of Coleridge's philosophy. Through a thoughtful reading of these prefaces, George Perkins Marsh may have come to realize the ecological implications of Coleridge's concept of organic form, which bears a clear affinity with Marsh's own view of the natural world as an interdependent biological community.

Among the pantheon of American environmental writers, no single figure looms larger than John Muir, an early explorer of the Sierra Nevada in California who became widely known for his books that extolled the pristine beauty of these mountains and passionately advocated their preservation as wilderness for future generations. Muir has sometimes been described as a belated Transcendentalist, and his connections with Emerson and Thoreau have been thoroughly examined, but his profound awareness and lifetime study of English Romanticism has not been given adequate attention by historians of the environmental movement. More than simply a popularizer of Romantic ideas, John Muir was engaged for most of his adult life in a careful close reading and critical response to the work of the Romantic poets. Through careful study of John Muir's personal library, I have traced his response to the English Romantic poets, particularly his annotations in the works of Coleridge and Percy Bysshe Shelley.

The last chapter of this book examines the work of Mary Austin, an environmental writer whose classic evocation of the California desert, *The Land of Little Rain* (1903), is unsurpassed in its treatment of the harsh beauty of that region. Austin tempers Muir's celebration of wilderness by introducing a more austere depiction of desert creatures that live in a permanent condition of scarcity, and her sensitive characterization of the Paiute and Shoshone Indians enables her to establish her own voice from a place outside the traditional pastoral representations of a benign and sheltering Earth. Like Muir, Austin criticizes human intervention in the natural environment, and she provides an ecofeminist perspective upon the radical changes in the land that were being wrought by early exploiters of the California landscape. As a twentieth-century inheritor of the Transcendentalist view of nature, Austin is fully attuned to the Romantic tradition of nature writing; but her struggle for existence in a harsh desert climate, complicated by a troubled relationship with her domineering husband, resulted in an ecofeminist revision of the Romantic aesthetic that still serves as an influential model for contemporary environmental writers.

My analysis of this group of Green Writers is deeply indebted to the work of many other scholars in the rapidly growing field of environmental literary studies, and throughout the following chapters I have made every effort to document my indebtedness to several distinguished scholars for many of the ideas developed here. This book is nevertheless distinguished from previous works in its field by two main features: (1) its historical focus on the English Romantic period, and (2) its analysis of the transatlantic connections between British and American thought. Standard histories of ecological thought, such as *Nature's Economy* by Donald Worster (1977), *The Background of Ecology* by Robert McIntosh (1985), and *The Norton History of the Environmental Sciences* by Peter Bowler (1992), tend to overlook or undervalue the contributions of the English Romantic poets, stressing instead the achievements of Linnaeus, Gilbert White, Charles Darwin, and their disciples in the field of natural history prose writing. The essential contributions of the Romantic poets and their American followers, especially their conception of the natural world as an interrelated organic system and their passionate advocacy for the preservation of wild creatures and scenic areas, have been disregarded by many intellectual historians. A more literary approach to the development of environmental ideas is taken in *The Idea of Wilderness: From Prehistory to the Age of Ecology* by Max Oelschlaeger (1991) and *The Environmental Imagination* by Lawrence Buell (1995). In particular, Buell's excellent study, which focuses on Thoreau and ranges widely throughout the history of American environmental thought, is in my view the single most incisive and significant work to date in the field of ecocriticism. The broad historical scope of these two latter studies is exemplary, but once again the English

Romantics get short shrift. Two recent books have devoted more sustained attention to the contributions of the Romantic poets: *Romantic Ecology: Wordsworth and the Environmental Tradition* by Jonathan Bate (1991) and *Ecological Literary Criticism* by Karl Kroeber (1994). Both of these works, however, are conceived as preliminary surveys of the terrain, rather than comprehensive analyses, and neither is concerned with the relation between British and American writers in the Romantic tradition.

The present study is intended to provide a more adequate understanding of the intellectual history that underlies the emergence of ecological thought during the Romantic period, and to describe the subsequent development of this ecological paradigm among several American nature writers in the Romantic tradition.

Chapter 1

Coleridge and the Economy of Nature

T his chapter seeks to assess the significance of ecological thought in Coleridge's intellectual development, and to examine the relevance of this way of thinking to our understanding of his poetry and prose. The main purpose of such an approach to Coleridge will be to elucidate, and perhaps to defamiliarize, the ways in which crucial aspects of his poetic language emerge from his perceptual and affective engagement with the local environment. An ecological reading of Coleridge will enable certain aspects of his conception of poetic form and his actual poetic practice to be understood more adequately than previous critical perspectives have allowed. In particular, the synergistic relationship between an individual organism and its habitat, which was first coming to be understood in its full complexity by late-eighteenth-century science, offers a fresh and suggestive model for analyzing the role of organicism in Coleridge's poetic thought.

The Economy of Nature

The youngest of ten children, Samuel Taylor Coleridge was born in 1772 in the rural village of Ottery St. Mary in Devonshire. His father died in 1781, leaving the nine-year-old Samuel with limited means of support. He was sent to London and enrolled as a charity boy at Christ's Hospital, a preparatory school of some intellectual repute, but a cold and inhospitable place for the young and impressionable orphan. Coleridge's extraordinary intellectual talents were soon noticed by his teachers, who promoted him to the elite class of "Grecians" destined for the university. Coleridge's mathematics teacher was William Wales, a professional astronomer on Captain James Cook's second voyage, who told his students fascinating tales of his exploits in the Antarctic Ocean, where he encountered icebergs, albatrosses, and strange luminous phenomena. In 1791–94, Coleridge attended Cambridge University, where he became an academic prodigy, but he left without taking a degree. Together with Robert Southey, Coleridge devised a utopian (and ultimately impractical) scheme called Pantisocracy, which aspired to create an ideal agrarian community on the banks of the Susquehanna River in Pennsylvania. Since only married couples were expected to embark on the Pantisocratic adventure, Coleridge soon found himself engaged to Sarah Fricker, the sister of Southey's fiancée. Married in 1795, the couple moved into a cottage at Nether Stowey, a rural village fifty miles southwest of Bristol.

Coleridge's residence at Nether Stowey was one of his happiest and most productive periods, as he embarked upon an intensive collaboration with William Wordsworth. In July 1797 Wordsworth and his sister Dorothy moved into Alfoxden House, just three miles away from Coleridge's cottage. Coleridge spent much of his time in their company, often walking out in stormy weather to discuss their literary projects. Among these was a collaborative volume of poems, *Lyrical Ballads,* published in September 1798. *Lyrical Ballads* marks a bold new departure in English verse, heralding the advent of Romanticism as a literary movement. Some of its most innovative features are the revival of ballad stanza, reliance upon the language of everyday life, and extensive use of natural imagery drawn from direct personal observation. In their composition of *Lyrical Ballads,* Wordsworth and Coleridge shared a common perception of the natural world as a dynamic ecosystem and a passionate commitment to the preservation of wild creatures and scenic areas.

In his Preface to *Lyrical Ballads,* published in the second edition of 1800, Wordsworth justifies his preference for the language of "low and rustic life . . . because in that condition the passions of men are incorporated with the beautiful and permanent forms of nature." Wordsworth's advocacy of simple vernacular diction is predicated on his view that human passion *incorporates* the forms of nature. His metaphor of incorporation, or embodiment, is essentially ecological since it suggests that all language, and therefore all human consciousness, is affected by the "forms of nature" that surround it. The natural world is a home (οἶκος), a birthplace and vital habitat for language, feeling, and thought. Although Coleridge did not fully accept Wordsworth's theory of poetic language, he certainly shared the view that linguistic form must emerge from a distinctly local set of conditions; this is the main premise of his poetic style in the Conversation

Poems, and it is explicitly developed in his early informal prose. In a note-book passage of 1799, written shortly after his return from Germany, Coleridge affirms his conviction that the naming practices of the Lake District are related to the inhabitants' sense of political independence and their proximity to wild natural phenomena: "In the North every Brook, every Crag, almost every Field has a name—a proof of greater Independence & a society more approaching in their Laws & Habits to Nature."[1] Like Wordsworth, Coleridge was fascinated by the naming of places, and he often compiled lists of local place-names during his wanderings in the Lake District.[2] Coleridge regarded this aspect of language as a key instance in which words are generated by complex interaction between the features of the landscape and the local residents. Language, most evidently in the case of place-names, is the result of an ongoing conversation between the land and the people who dwell upon it.

In the *Biographia Literaria* (1817), Coleridge's insight into the nature of language is stated in terms of organicism, an aesthetic doctrine that owes something in the detail of its formulation to the eighteenth-century scientific concept of the organism. More than Wordsworth, Coleridge was attuned to the scientific controversies of his era, and by reading such works as Erasmus Darwin's didactic poem, *The Botanic Garden* (1791), and his medical treatise, *Zoonomia; or, the Laws of Organic Life* (1794-96), Coleridge became steeped in the contemporary conception of the organism as an autonomous, cyclical, and self-regulating entity.[3] This organic metaphor is apparent in his poetry as early as 1795, when it provides a conceptual foundation for the speculative pantheism of "The Eolian Harp":

And what if all of animated nature
Be but organic Harps diversely fram'd,
That tremble into thought, as o'er them sweeps
Plastic and vast, one intellectual breeze,
At once the Soul of each, and God of all? (lines 44-48)

The term "organic" is used here with scientific precision; this passage asserts that all living creatures, no matter how "diversely fram'd," must possess an internal process of self-regulation. Coleridge's emphasis falls not on the autonomy of the organism, but on its vital response to an external stimulus, represented here as an "intellectual breeze" that sweeps over it. Although this passage is manifestly about the nature of sentient beings, it implicitly refers to the making of poetry and the ontology of the poetic artifact. If poems are organisms, then they should not merely be tightly woven structures, but they should also exist in harmony with their surrounding environment (metaphorically understood as a literary or discursive context). Such a conception of the poem as an organism residing in a local habitat is implicit in Coleridge's poetic practice in the *Lyrical Ballads,* and it represents the culmination of an eighteenth-century tradition of speculation about the nature of poetic form. Before exploring the aesthetic implications of this concept any further, however, it seems appropriate to investigate its scientific origins.

During the eighteenth century, a holistic conception of the natural world was gradually articulated as the result of a growing scientific understanding of the dynamic operation of closed systems, ranging from the individual organism to a more global scale. The biological sciences made particularly striking advances in their understanding of how animals distribute and regulate their energy resources. The anatomist William Harvey (1578-1657) demonstrated in 1628 that the heart works as a pump to circulate blood in a closed cycle.[4] This unexpected discovery led to further striking developments in the field of physiology during the eighteenth century, and it held enormous implications for the conception of living systems generally, since it demonstrated that all higher organisms, including humans, are permeated by a cyclical process that distributes nutrients throughout all parts of their bodies. The Dutch anatomist Anton Van Leeuwenhoek (1632-1723) continued the investigation of circulatory processes at the microscopic level; he was the first to describe red blood cells, and he extended the scientific knowledge of capillary function. Leeuwenhoek is perhaps best known for his discovery of "animalcules," microscopic organisms whose ubiquity in such common substances as rainwater suggested the presence of a teeming microcosm that lurked just beyond the normal boundaries of perception. Luminescent "animalcules" were observed in seawater during Captain Cook's first voyage, lending the ocean an eerie glow that later contributed to its luster in "The Rime of the Ancient Mariner."

On a larger scale, the Swedish botanist Linnaeus (1707-78) envisioned the entire terrestrial globe as an interlocking web of cyclical processes, using the hydrological cycle of evaporation, condensation, and precipitation as a paradigmatic instance.[5] In an influential essay entitled "The Oeconomy of Nature" (1751), Isaac Biberg (a disciple of Linnaeus) described how the hydrological cycle distributes water everywhere on Earth, sustaining all forms of life; he also described how predators and prey coexist in a hierarchical food chain that serves to maintain the population balance of various species. Biberg's essay provides a classic formulation of the prevailing eighteenth-century scientific conception of the world as a harmonious, self-regulating system: "By the Oeconomy of nature we understand the all-wise disposition of the Creator in relation to natural things, by which they are fitted to produce general ends, and reciprocal uses."[6] All natural things, according to this view, exist in reciprocal relation to other things, resulting in a complex order of cyclical processes that was termed the "economy of nature," and that bears some functional resemblance to our modern conception of a global ecosystem.

The chemist Joseph Priestley (1733-1804), in announcing his accidental discovery of photosynthesis in 1772, likewise employed a cyclical model, describing the respiration of plants as a "restorative" process that uses the energy of light to cleanse the "vitiated air" produced by animals and humans.[7] Exploring the global implications of this hypothesis, Sir John Pringle (the President of the Royal Society) stated in 1774 that the vegetation of "remote and unpeopled regions" is essential to cleanse the polluted air produced by cities. In Pringle's view, "good air" and "bad air" are circulated by wind currents in a process analogous to the hydrological cycle.[8] Erasmus Darwin, in Part 1 of *The Botanic Garden,* entitled "The Economy of Vegetation" (1791), further described the vital environmental role of green plants in producing oxygen and sugar by means of photosynthesis; he also proposed a theory of evolution that in some respects foreshadows that of his grandson, Charles Darwin, especially in the assertion that competition among individuals can lead to beneficial changes in the species.

From Linnaeus through Erasmus Darwin, an economic metaphor is employed to suggest that these cyclical processes in the natural world promote the efficient distribution and consumption of resources in much the same way that Adam Smith's *Wealth of Nations* (1776) had described the circulation of goods in a free-market economy. The "Economy of Nature," according to eighteenth-century science, operates very much like a capitalist economy, with the assurance that some "hidden hand" will optimize the results of individual action. Human intervention in the natural world is not generally seen as a controversial issue by these scientists, since human activities on a local scale, even if apparently destructive, are regarded as tending toward the improvement of the landscape and the development of its natural resources.

The new holistic sciences of the eighteenth century were thus quite limited in their understanding of the possible deleterious effects of human encroachment upon natural systems. There was also a significant gap, especially in the biological sciences, between macrocosm and microcosm.

Despite the rapidly growing understanding of the inner dynamics of organisms and the large-scale cyclical processes of the terrestrial environment, there was very little effort to integrate these theoretical perspectives by investigating how particular plants and animals relate to each other within a regional context. In the field of taxonomy, there was a vast increase in the number of species described and catalogued, but only limited attempts to describe the range and habitat of each species, or to observe its behavior and life cycle as a member of a biological community. This type of detailed local investigation, forming a link between the individual organism and its role in the global "Economy of Nature," was pioneered by Gilbert White, whose *Natural History and Antiquities of Selborne* (as previously discussed) was a landmark in the development of ecological thought.[9] White's scrupulous attention to the living organism in its local habitat marks a significant step beyond the narrow-minded specimen collecting and cataloguing that typifies much eighteenth-century natural history.[10]

Some of the most essential insights of ecological thought—the adaptation of species to their habitats, the interrelatedness of all life forms, and the potentially catastrophic effects of human intervention in natural systems—are first explicitly stated in the scientific writings of the eighteenth century. As Ian Wylie has demonstrated in *Young Coleridge and the Philosophers of Nature* (1989), Coleridge was well-versed in the scientific writings of this period and had fully internalized the broader implications of the new discoveries in chemistry and biology. In particular, Coleridge was fascinated by the new cyclical understanding of natural processes, and (as John Livingston Lowes first pointed out) he planned to use this scientific model as the basis for a series of hymns to the elements.[11]

For Coleridge, this scientific model also had social and political implications; his Pantisocracy scheme was evidently intended to create an "Economy of Nature" on the banks of the Susquehanna River. Coleridge's radical democratic politics received welcome support from his view of the natural world as an egalitarian biological community. The main political doctrine of Pantisocracy, "the equal government of all," went hand in hand with the economic doctrine of Aspheterism, "the generalisation of individual property"; and the economy of nature, as Coleridge conceived it, could provide a working model for both principles.[12] Rather than subscribing to the laissez-faire model of the economy of nature extrapolated from Adam Smith, Coleridge regarded the natural world as tending toward an equality of condition in which each individual organism can develop its unique potential. This egalitarian view of the economy of nature is implicit in his poem "To a Young Ass," in which Coleridge hails the beast as a "*Brother*" and evokes the Pantisocratic community as a "Dell / Of Peace and mild Equality" where beasts and humans can live together in harmony. The political and economic doctrines of Pantisocracy are thus allied with an idealistic (though perhaps naive) ecological doctrine that advocates the possibility of restoring the natural world to its original Edenic state of peaceful coexistence among all creatures. The radical Adamicism of this view is reminiscent of Blake's visionary politics, and although Coleridge would later repudiate his youthful radicalism, his turn to more conservative and essentially Burkean political views (in such late works as *On the Constitution of Church and State*) remains compatible with an organic conception of social organization, since he envisions an evolving and (ideally) self-regulating relationship between individual members of the "clerisy" and the established institutions of the church and state. Coleridge's commitment to an organic model of human society may be regarded as a constant element that underpins the shifting and often inconsistent expression of his political views during the course of his intellectual career.

A Most Romantic Vale

Coleridge's observations of the natural phenomena of the Lake District, as recorded in his *Notebooks*, tend to reflect a holistic awareness of the plant and animal communities native to that region. On his extended walking tour of the Lake District in August 1802, for instance, Coleridge lists several plant species that are found in association with each other: "Dial plate Flower, & wild Thyme roam up the Fells in company—with them the Fox's Tail—Fern, Rushes, &c" (*Notebooks*, 1:1216). Like Gilbert White, Coleridge expresses a distinct preference for the common vernacular names of species over the standard Linnaean terminology, largely because of the close association of vernacular names with local history and a personal sense of identity. In a notebook entry of 1803, Coleridge envisions "a noble Poem of all my Youth nay *of all my Life*," including "One section on plants & flowers, my passion for them, always deadened by their learned names" (*Notebooks*, 1:1610). He further resolves "Yet ever to note those [plant species] that have & may hereafter affect me," and his notebooks from this period evince a sustained effort to record specific information about the habitat and association of particular plant species. In December 1800, Sara Hutchinson transcribed several pages of English vernacular plant names into Coleridge's notebook from the index of William Withering's *Arrangement of British Plants* (1796). This list includes some interpolations by Sara, based on her personal knowledge of regional plant names; a brief citation will indicate something of the character of the list and of Sara's interpolations:

> Upland Burnet. Valerian. Velvet leaf. Venus comb. Venus Looking glass. Vernal Grass. Vervain. Vetch. Vetchling. Vine wild. Violet. Violet Calathian. Viper Grass. Virgins' Bower (=Traveller's Joy, Great Wild Climber, Honesty, Clematis).[13]

This colorful list of vernacular names indicates Coleridge's concern for the rootedness of English words in the soil of common experience, and the list of alternative names for "Virgins' Bower," added by Sara, suggests that her knowledge of regional plant names was confident and extensive. Coleridge presumably regarded this list as a source of raw linguistic material for subsequent literary adaptation.

Throughout his August 1802 walking tour, Coleridge typically regards human dwellings, pathways, and activities as indigenous to the landscape of the Lake District, as if they were self-generated features rather than embodiments of particular historical processes. Thus he describes the natural setting of Ulpha Kirk as "a most romantic vale, the mountains that embosom it, low & of a remarkably wild outline. . . . The Kirk standing on the low rough Hill up which the Road climbs, the fields level and high, beyond that; & then the different flights of mountains in the back ground" (*Notebooks,* 1:1225). Human agency is tacitly elided from this description, which assigns finite verbs to the things themselves: the kirk *stands,* the road *climbs.* Active verbal constructions are used in a subsequent passage: "from this House the <line of the> Beck *runs* almost straight up to its Fountain head / and a beautiful Road *serpentizes* over the Hill" (*Notebooks,* 1:1227; emphasis added). The lowly shepherds' cottages of Eskdale take on a special charm from their imbeddedness in the local topography: "never sure were lovelyer human Dwellings than these nested in Trees at the foot of the Fells, & in among the intervening Hills" (*Notebooks,* 1:1222). All of these human artifacts are seen as organic forms, in the sense that they are autonomous and self-sufficient; yet they also represent integral elements of the larger landscape.

Coleridge's mature theory of aesthetic organicism, although derived in part from German sources, may be seen as a logical development of these early views on the integrity and interrelatedness of the natural world. From an ecological perspective, just as the concept of the organism needs to be completed by a consideration of its habitat, so too the inner form of an aesthetic object (whether it is regarded as a well-wrought urn or a self-consuming artifact) is less significant than its relation to the linguistic and cultural environment that surrounds and nourishes it. Coleridge's journeys in the Lake District, as recorded in his notebooks, offer evidence that he was working through the concept of organic form toward a new and more concrete understanding of the various ways that human artifacts can work in harmony with their natural surroundings.

Coleridge's fascination with the natural and social ecology of the Lake District was combined with a renewed appreciation for the vital and evolving nature of language within a local environment. We have already described his interest in the origin of local place-names and in regional vernacular names for flora and fauna. As a professional man of letters, Coleridge was actively engaged in the word-making process of linguistic evolution, and his poetry and prose frequently bear witness to his intentional coinage of new words.[14] Especially in his early notebooks, Coleridge's coinages occur most frequently in the context of landscape description, and they reflect his understanding of linguistic form as the result of an ongoing conversation between the land and those who dwell upon it. By turns playful and profound, Coleridge's informal prose evinces a richness of lexical innovation that is unmatched by any other writer of the Romantic period. There is an abundant class of new words ending in the collective suffix "-age," suggesting that Coleridge was learning to see natural objects in complex aggregations. Thus we find the words *treeage, hillage,* and *cloudage* at various points in these notebooks, generally used of natural objects encountered on his wanderings in the Lake District. He coins the term *kittenracts* as a playful diminutive of *cataracts,* and the words *breezelet* and *wavelet* are diminutives of the same order. He creates the terms *waterslide* and *interslope* to describe specific aspects of waterfalls, and *twistures* to denote the convoluted appearance of trees growing out of cracks in the rocks. Features of the terrain are animated with vital energy, or marked as if by disease: he describes *offrunning* mountains, a *bulgy* precipice, a *scabby* tarn, *scorious* rocks, and a *scarified* hillside. The term *lacustrial* refers to the enduring presence of lakes in the local topography. The exquisite word *greenery,* first recorded in "Kubla Khan," recurs three times in Coleridge's notebook accounts of his German walking tour, each time to designate a symmetrical (and perhaps magical or sacred) clearing in the forest. The term *rockery* is coined, evidently by analogy with *greenery,* to designate a symmetrical collocation of rocks.[15]

The boldest of these word-coinages occurs in Coleridge's plan for a series of Hymns to the Elements, which was intended to culminate in "a sublime enumeration of all the charms or *Tremendities* of Nature."[16] The freshly minted term *tremendity*, along with the coinages previously cited, reflects Coleridge's striving to express his developing perception of the natural world as a systematic collectivity, rather than merely a set of discrete objects. This new way of looking at the world as an integral community is vitally expressed in new lexical forms that seek to denote the organic relationships among natural objects. These newly created lexical forms might well be collectively described as an *ecolect,* in the literal sense of a language that speaks for the οἶκος: the Earth considered as a *dwelling-place* for all living things.[17] Unlike certain other writers of the Romantic period whose poetic diction was virtually indiscernible from the cultural mainstream, Coleridge largely succeeded in creating a uniquely ecological idiom, an *ecolect* that reflects local environmental conditions and expresses his own distinctive way of perceiving and responding to the natural world.

The Shadow of the Ship

Coleridge's engagement with the integrity of the natural world, and his concern for its preservation, is apparent throughout his contributions to *Lyrical Ballads,* a volume that is constructed with thoughtful attention to the situation of poems in a larger discursive context. "The Rime of the Ancyent Marinere," a deliberately archaic narrative poem in ballad stanza, appears as the very first poem in the 1798 edition of *Lyrical Ballads.* Its placement at the head of the collection serves to emphasize its role as a stark and compelling statement of themes that will receive more varied expression later in the volume. Regarded in this way, "The Rime of the Ancyent Marinere" may be read as a parable of ecological transgression. The Mariner, an Everyman figure on a voyage of exploration in "the cold Country towards the South Pole," encounters a frigid realm that is apparently devoid of life: "Ne shapes of men ne beasts we ken— / The Ice was all between."[18] The word "ken" suggests that the Mariner's plight is fundamentally a crisis in Western ways of *knowing:* an epistemic gap (or deep Romantic chasm) that separates him from the hidden creatures of the Antarctic. The Mariner embarks on this voyage as a Cartesian dualist, a detached observer who is cut off from any feeling of empathy or participation in the vast world of life that surrounds him.

The Albatross appears out of the epistemic "fog" as an emissary from the Antarctic wilderness. In a spontaneous act of identification, the mariners hail it as "a Christian soul," as if it were a human being like themselves:

> At length did cross an Albatross,
>   Thorough the Fog it came;
> And an it were a Christian Soul,
>   We hail'd it in God's name. (lines 61-64)

The Albatross crosses from the wild ice to the world of men, and its act of "crossing" the boundary between nature and civilization indicates a possible resolution of the Mariner's epistemic solitude. The Albatross brings companionship to the lonely mariners, it guides them through the pathless ice, and returns "every day for food or play" (line 71). The 1798 version of the poem specifies that "The Marineres gave it biscuit-worms" (line 65), a homely detail that concretely renders the symbiotic exchange between man and beast: the mariners provide nourishment for the Albatross, while the bird provides them with more intangible benefits of companionship, guidance, and play. These biscuit-worms are more than mere vermin; they play an essential role in the web of life, and they suggest that what we regard as ugly or obnoxious may nonetheless be appealing when considered from another (inhuman) perspective.[19]

The Mariner kills the Albatross with his "cross bow" (line 79), a weapon that embodies the relentlessly destructive tendency of European technology at the same time that it invokes, with some irony, the traditional Christian imagery of sacrifice and atonement. If the Albatross is regarded as an innocent emissary from the unspoiled natural realm of the Antarctic, then the Mariner's deed represents an unmotivated act of aggression against all the creatures of that realm. But the Antarctic, through the agency of the Polar Spirit, wreaks a terrible vengeance upon the Mariner, who must witness the death of his shipmates and the decay of the entire living world around him, as if the destruction of a single creature had disrupted the whole economy of nature:

> The very deeps did rot: O Christ!
>   That ever this should be!
> Yea, slimy things did crawl with legs
>   Upon the slimy Sea. (lines 119-122)

These slimy creatures with legs, unknown to any textbook of natural history, represent with apocalyptic intensity the death of nature as a result of destructive human acts. On a concrete historical level, the voyage of the Mariner may be compared to Captain Cook's second voyage, which mapped the Antarctic region, described the incredible abundance of its fauna, and thereby ushered in an era of wholesale destruction of seals, whales, birds, and other marine life.[20]

As the Mariner's vessel "made her course to the tropical Latitude of the Great Pacific Ocean," a community of living things is gathered around her.[21] Any wooden sailing ship in tropical waters will gradually accumulate a host of fellow travelers, ranging from barnacles and seaweed to schools of fish that shelter within her shadow. The ship comes to resemble a floating reef, and the teeming flora and fauna offer both perils and opportunities to those aboard her. As Coleridge could have learned from several narrative accounts of maritime exploration in tropical latitudes, the fouling of a ship's bottom and the rapid rotting of her timbers can lead to her destruction, but the abundance and variety of marine life surrounding the ship was cause of wonder and amazement for many British explorers. John Livingston Lowes cites a typical passage from Captain Cook's third voyage:

> During a calm, on the morning of the 2d, some parts of the sea seemed covered with a kind of slime; and some small sea animals were swimming about. . . . When they began to swim about, which they did, with equal ease, upon their back, sides, or belly, they emitted the brightest colours of the most precious gems. . . . They proved to be . . . probably, an animal which has a share in producing some sorts of that lucid appearance, often observed near ships at sea, in the night. (Lowes, 42)

The slimy creatures found in the vicinity of Cook's ship display unexpected flashes of beauty to the scientific observer, just as the water-snakes in Coleridge's poem are revealed to be vital participants in the ship's local ecosystem. Their repulsive aspect is eventually shown to have been the result of the Mariner's flawed perception, not their intrinsic nature. The Mariner's act of blessing the water-snakes enables him to see them, with a striking intensity of vision, as creatures that inhabit "the shadow of the ship," an *ecotone* (or boundary region) that provides rich habitat for an abundance of marine life:

> Within the shadow of the ship
>   I watch'd their rich attire:
> Blue, glossy green, and velvet black
> They coil'd and swam; and every track
>   Was a flash of golden fire. (lines 269-273)

As Ian Wylie has pointed out, the luminescent trails of these sea-snakes strongly resemble the tracks of light described by Erasmus Darwin in "The

Economy of Vegetation," which are attributed by Darwin to the "incipient putrefaction" of "fish-slime."[22] Finding the hidden beauty in such slimy substances, the Mariner discovers that all life forms, even microscopic ones, play a vital role in the natural world.

By blessing the water-snakes, the Mariner is released from his state of alienation from nature, and the Albatross sinks "like lead into the sea" (line 283), crossing back from civilization into the untamed ocean. The Mariner has learned what the Albatross came to teach him: that he must cross the boundaries that divide him from the natural world, through unmotivated acts of compassion between "man and bird and beast" (line 646). In its concern for boundary regions, "The Rime of the Ancyent Marinere" foreshadows some of the most seminal thoughts of contemporary environmental writers. Romand Coles, in a recent essay entitled "Ecotones and Environmental Ethics: Adorno and Lopez," describes the ethical and imaginative significance of such boundary regions:

> Natural ecologists know that ecotones—with their intermingling borders— are especially fertile, "special meeting grounds" charged with "evolutionary potential." When we combine this knowledge with the etymology of *ecotone*, *oikos* (dwelling), and *tonus* (tension), we evoke an image of the fertility and pregnancy of dwelling at the edge of the tension between different people, beings, landscapes. . . . "What does it mean to grow rich?" [Barry] Lopez asks in the prologue to *Arctic Dreams*. It seems to me that he poses one answer to this question through a dazzling display of the biological and metaphorical wealth of Arctic ecotones. Yet the most profound ecotone in the book—and he knows this—is the one that occurs at the dialogical edge between the self and the otherness of the world, between Lopez and the light, the beings, the people of the Arctic.[23]

"The Rime of the Ancyent Marinere" likewise ponders the ethical significance of dwelling on boundaries between different realms. In the poem's initial episode, an Albatross crosses from the inhuman world of ice "as green as Emerauld" (line 52) into the human community of the mariners. At the poem's climax, the "shadow of the ship" (lines 264, 269) delineates a rich tropical ecotone inhabited by sea-snakes that the Mariner must "bless" in order to survive. At the end of the poem, the Mariner returns from sea to land, drifting across the "Harbour-bar" (line 473) and rowing ashore with the help of a Hermit who inhabits yet another ecotone, "that wood / Which slopes down to the Sea" (lines 547-548). All of these boundary regions serve as points of departure and arrival for the poem's profound meditation upon the green world of nature and the destructive tendencies of human civilization. The wedding-guest is transformed by the Mariner's tale into "a sadder and a wiser man," having learned that the deliberate destruction of any wild creature may bring unforeseen consequences. Written explicitly in defense of "all things both great and small" (line 648), this poem exemplifies the environmental advocacy that is integral to Coleridge's ecological vision.

Coleridge's use of language in "The Rime of the Ancyent Marinere" provides crucial evidence of his endeavor to construct a new ecolect. As Lowes points out in *The Road to Xanadu* (296–310), the 1798 version of the poem is more than just a fake antique ballad on the model of Percy's *Reliques* and Chatterton's "Rowley" poems. Lowes demonstrates that Coleridge combines three fairly distinct types of archaic usage: first, the traditional ballad lexicon (*pheere, eldritch, beforne, I ween, sterte, een, countrée, withouten, cauld*); second, the diction of Chaucer and Spenser (*ne, uprist, I wist, yspread, yeven, n'old, eftsones, lavrock, jargoning, minstralsy*); and third, seafaring terminology (*swound, weft, clifts, biscuit-worms, fire-flags*). All three types of archaic usage are severely curtailed in the 1800 edition of the poem, perhaps in response to a reviewer in the *British Critic* (October 1799) who denounced the poem's "antiquated words," citing *swound* (line 397) and *weft* (line 83) as flagrant examples of nonsensical diction. Coleridge omitted the vivid seafaring term *weft* in 1800, along with most of the other words listed here. The merits and demerits of Coleridge's 1800 modernization and his later addition of a marginal gloss in *Sibylline Leaves* (1817) have been widely debated; Lowes regards Coleridge's revision of "The Rime of the Ancyent Marinere" as a definite improvement, and more recent critics tend to accept this established opinion. Yet the accessibility and stylistic coherence of the 1817 version is accomplished at the expense of the multifaceted syncretic quality of the original version, which bespeaks the author's desire to reassemble the surviving fragments of archaic language into a richly textured and deeply expressive mode of poetic discourse.

In my own view, the 1798 version of "The Rime of the Ancyent Marinere" enhances the poem's ecological themes through its conservation of lexical diversity. Coleridge's use of archaic diction and spelling goes beyond the mere intention to appear quaint, or to follow a literary fashion. Rather than seeking to epitomize the English language at a single time and place, the poem draws eclectically upon many strands of diction from discrete historical periods and social strata. The purpose of this lexical variety is to construct an idiolect for the Mariner that embodies polyglossic and diachronic features; the adjacence of modern and archaic words enables the poem to characterize the Mariner as a wanderer through geographic space and historical time, and to situate his discourse at the (ecotonal?) conjunction of modernity and Romantic *Sehnsucht*. Moreover, the use of archaic diction provides a linguistic analogue to the poem's main environmental theme, since the extinction of an archaic word can have unforeseen repercussions upon the integrity of a language. If the English lexicon is regarded as a close-knit organic system, then the loss of a single word may result in consequences as dire as the Mariner suffers upon killing an albatross. Coleridge elsewhere describes "words as living growths, offlets, and organs of the human soul," and he urges writers to employ the entire "reversionary wealth in our mother-tongue."[24] From the perspective of this organic conception of language, it seems apparent that "The Rime of the Ancyent Marinere" aspires to enrich and revitalize contemporary poetic diction through the recovery and preservation of archaic words.

A particular example may help to elucidate this thesis. Coleridge's term "Lavrock" (line 348) derives from Middle English *laveroc,* a precursor of the Modern English *lark.* The Lavrock (like the Nightingale encountered later in the *Lyrical Ballads*) is a "most musical" bird, and Coleridge's impression of this bird evidently derives from his recollection of Chaucer's version of *The Romaunt of the Rose:*

> There mightin men se many flockes
> Of Turtels and of *Laverockes . . .*
> Thei song ther song, as faire and wel
> As angels doen espirituell . . .
> Layis of love full wel souning
> Thei songin in ther *jargoning.*[25]

Coleridge likewise uses the word "jargoning" to describe the Lavrock's song:

> Sometimes a dropping from the sky
> I heard the *Lavrock* sing;
> Sometimes all little birds that are
> How they seem'd to fill the sea and air
> With their sweet *jargoning.* (lines 347-351; emphasis added)

The Lavrock enters the poem at an ecotonal boundary of "sea and air," lending its mellifluous voice to the Mariner's growing sense of ethical redemption. The "sweet jargoning" of the Lavrock is metaphorically related in subsequent stanzas to the sound of human instruments, the song of angels, and the "singing" of a quiet brook. All created beings, and even inanimate objects, are accorded some form of linguistic expression. The voice of the Lavrock exemplifies a radical environmental usage, suggesting that the animate creation has its own language, and its own way of responding to the aeolian influences of the One Life. The word *Lavrock* contains a hidden lexemic trace of the word *rock,* possibly foreshadowing the Mariner's return to solid ground and the "kirk . . . that stands above the *rock*" (lines 503-504; emphasis added). When Coleridge substituted "sky-lark" for "Lavrock" in the 1800 edition, this subliminal trace of the word *rock* was lost, along with the word's Chaucerian echo and its distinctive contribution to the poem's lexical diversity. The 1800 edition of this poem, bowing to the critical demand for stylistic decorum, was severely impoverished by the loss of such words as *weft* and *Lavrock.* Indeed, the deletion of *Lavrock* obscures the main thematic point of the word "jargoning," which (according to the *American Heritage Dictionary*) is "probably of imitative origin," and thus refers to the inscrutable sounds one might hear in a language contact zone (or linguistic ecotone). The archaic word *Lavrock* represents the admixture of heteroglossic elements that constitutes a *jargon,* in the same way that the Lavrock's song traverses the boundary between human and inhuman language. Just as the Lavrock's song is perceived as a "sweet jargoning" by the Mariner, so too the word *Lavrock* contributes to the poem's distinctive "jargon," which might properly be termed an ecolect that emerges from the encounter between humankind and the natural world.

In their collaborative composition of *Lyrical Ballads,* Wordsworth and Coleridge shared a common perception of the natural world as a dynamic ecosystem and a passionate commitment to the preservation of wild creatures and scenic areas. Their 1798 volume was designed as a habitat that would provide a nurturing environment for the diversity of poems contained within it. Coleridge's unique contribution to this collaborative endeavor was his conception of language as a living thing, an integral organic system that can be cultivated by the poet for maximum diversity, either through the coinage of new words or the recovery of archaic ones. This holistic conception of language was clearly indebted to the new understanding of the organism that had emerged from eighteenth-century biology, and it represents a metaphorical extension of the cyclical view of natural process that was expressed in the notion of the economy of nature. For Coleridge, the historical development of language is deeply conditioned by its relation to the natural environment, and his aesthetic principle of organicism likewise entails reference to the linguistic habitat of a poem as an essential determinant of its meaning. "The Rime of the Ancyent Marinere" most fully embodies the poetic praxis envisioned by this organic conception of poetic language; its eclectic use of archaic diction serves to enhance and preserve the lexical diversity of the English language throughout the broad range of its social, geographic, and historical variation. Like Wilhelm von Humboldt, whose seminal work *On Linguistic Variation and Human Development* remains a foundational text in the field of ecolinguistics, Coleridge regarded language not as a product (*ergon*) but an activity (*energeia*).[26] Coleridge's poetic energies were devoted to the development of a distinctive ecolect that might express the proper role of humankind in the economy of nature.

Chapter 2

Wordsworth's Home at Grasmere

Illiam Wordsworth's name is ineluctably associated with the English Lake District, the place where he spent his childhood and adolescence, and to which he returned on a permanent basis in December 1799. Settling into Dove Cottage, Grasmere, with his sister Dorothy, Wordsworth determined to make his home and his poetic career among the lakes and mountains that had first awakened and nourished his childhood imagination. His is a poetry of place, rooted not only in a concrete awareness of geographic location, but also in the significance that attaches to particular places as a result of childhood memory.[1]

Wordsworth's great autobiographical poem, *The Prelude,* provides a narrative account of his intellectual and spiritual development, and its depiction of his childhood in the Lake District has shaped much of what modern readers understand about his rootedness there. However, *The Prelude* was not published until 1850, and it remained a closely guarded manuscript during Wordsworth's lifetime, known only to a small circle of his family and friends. To his contemporaries, Wordsworth was known through the developing canon of his published poetry, starting with two relatively obscure works published in 1793: *An Evening Walk* and *Descriptive Sketches.* With the publication of *Lyrical Ballads* (first published in 1798, with revised editions appearing in 1800 and 1802), and continuing through *The Excursion* (1814) and *Collected Poems* (1815), his international reputation as a poet was assured. Throughout the nineteenth century, Wordsworth was known to readers on both sides of the Atlantic as the most prominent of the "Lake Poets," and the deep-rooted affiliation of his writing with that particular place was further confirmed by the publication of his *Guide to the Lakes,* the best known and most frequently republished of Wordsworth's writings during his lifetime.

In recent decades, however, the grounding of Wordsworth's poetry in a specific locale, and his reputation as a nature poet, has been called into question. Each generation of literary critics, from the New Critics through the post-Structuralists, has discovered new ways of reading Wordsworth's poetry through the lens of its own theoretical preoccupations. Although the continuing exegesis of his work has certainly led to a more thorough understanding of his multifaceted complexity, both as person and as poet, nevertheless something of the radical and elemental simplicity of his poetry has been lost in the process. Accordingly, this chapter will examine some fundamental questions about the meaning of Wordsworth's poetry as it emerges from the lived experience of dwelling in the English Lake District.

The Place of Poetry

William Wordsworth was born on April 7, 1770, at Cockermouth in Cumberland, and his earliest childhood memories (as he recounted them in *The Prelude*) were of the sound of the river Derwent, whose murmurs "from his alder shades and rocky falls . . . sent a voice / That flowed along my dreams" (book 1, lines 272-274).[2] It is perhaps significant that his first memories are of sounds, a speaking-forth of the landscape directly into the "dreams" of the infant, making him an engaged participant in the world that surrounds him, not merely a detached observer. This sense of participation is more concretely evoked in Wordsworth's description of bathing in the river Derwent and sporting along its banks as a five-year-old boy (book 1, lines 291-298). The "voice" of the river speaks out to the child as a companion, or imaginary playmate, in a tone both comforting and mysterious.

The childhood experience of nature was not always so pleasant or reassuring to Wordsworth. *The Prelude* records several occasions when the presence of the natural world appeared ominous and foreboding, most notably the boat-stealing episode, which climaxes in the sudden, terrifying apparition of "a huge peak, black and huge, / As if with voluntary power instinct" (book 1, lines 378-79), and the episode of the drowned man, whose decomposing body suddenly bursts above the surface of the lake "with his ghastly face, a spectre shape / Of terror" (book 5, lines 450-451). The immanence of death, and the sudden eruption of fear into a seemingly placid landscape, is a theme frequently encountered in Wordsworth's description of his childhood. Surely the death of both parents during his

childhood had something to do with Wordsworth's sense of fear and foreboding in the natural world; his mother died when he was only eight years
old, and his siblings were subsequently dispersed to live with various rela-
tives, marking the end of Wordsworth's very close childhood relationship
with his beloved sister Dorothy. His father's death occurred in 1783, when
William was thirteen years old. A painful sense of loss and exile pervades
much of Wordsworth's autobiographical writing, and his childhood sense
of joyful immediacy and participation in the natural world is balanced elsewhere by darker tonalities, and even a morbid fascination with death.

In a note that he dictated to Isabella Fenwick in 1843, Wordsworth
looks back on his childhood awareness of the natural world. He recalls his
morbid fascination with death, and the obstinate denial of his own mortality, in a remarkably candid free-associative commentary:

> Nothing was more difficult for me in childhood than to admit the notion of
> death as a state applicable to my own being. . . . But it was not so much from
> [feelings] of animal vivacity that *my* difficulty came as from a sense of the
> indomitableness of the spirit within me. I used to brood over the stories of
> Enoch and Elijah, and almost to persuade myself that, whatever might
> become of others, I should be translated, in something of the same way, to
> heaven. (*Poetical Works,* 4:463)

The child's stubborn denial of death, and his aspiration to a "heavenly" state
of complete disembodiment, contrasts sharply with his infantile sense of
total bodily immersion in the flow of the river Derwent. Wordsworth goes
on to describe how the entire visible world threatened to vanish into an
"abyss of idealism" at certain moments of his childhood:

> With a feeling congenial to this, I was often unable to think of external
> things as having external existence, and I communed with all that I saw as
> something not apart from, but inherent in, my own immaterial nature. Many
> times while going to school have I grasped at a wall or tree to recall myself
> from this abyss of idealism to the reality. At that time I was afraid of such
> processes. (*Poetical Works,* 4:463)

The modality of visual imagery is part of the problem of "immateriality"
that Wordsworth recalls here; it is only through the immediacy of touch—
the rough stones of a wall, or the furrowed bark of a tree—that the child
can be returned to the presence of the world around him. His fear of being
lost in an "abyss of idealism" is akin to the problem of pure subjectivity
posed by the philosophical idealism of George Berkeley (1685-1753): if

objects have no existence beyond our perception of them, then how can anything be known to exist outside of ourselves? Bishop Berkeley's answer—that God sees everything and thereby guarantees its existence—is unsatisfying to the young Wordsworth, who was coming of age in a secular society where such faith was eroding before the onslaught of Humean skepticism. Only the immediacy of touch, or (as we have seen) the pervasive sound of a natural voice, can recall the child to the "reality" of his existence in a physical body, in a material world.

To the adult Wordsworth, however, such an "abyss of idealism" no longer poses a serious threat to his sense of self-identity. He is troubled, rather, by "a subjugation of an opposite character"—namely, the ineluctable presence of concrete material objects, to the exclusion of the "dreamlike vividness and splendour which invest objects of sight in childhood" (*Poetical Works,* 4:463). Recalling his joy "before the winds / And roaring waters," Wordsworth elsewhere denounces "the bodily eye" as "the most despotic of our senses" (*Prelude,* book 12, lines 95–96 and 128–129). The "despotism of the eye," as Coleridge terms it in the *Biographia Literaria* (1:107), is the inevitable result of an education that stresses the empirical version of reality, predicated upon the mind-body dualism of the Cartesian method. In Wordsworth's view, an excessive reliance on visual data, to the exclusion of more immediate sensory modalities of sound and touch, will result in a "subjugation" of the mind to the cold materiality of external objects. Lost in such a materialistic vision is the "dreamlike" character of childhood perception.

Wordsworth's early poetry, particularly his *Descriptive Sketches,* is weakened by an essentially empirical mode of presentation, with its relentless bifurcation of subject and object. In these early poems of picturesque description, the poet himself is merely a detached observer, not a participant in the scenes that he describes. With the advent of Wordsworth's mature poetic voice, however, that stance of touristic detachment is superseded by poems that dramatize the involvement of the speaker in the places and events that he describes. Particularly in the *Lyrical Ballads,* Wordsworth achieves a sense of participation that enables the reader, as well, to become vicariously invested in the world of the poem. Wordsworth's contributions to *Lyrical Ballads* are not "nature poems," if that term is taken to denote the precise and detailed description of natural objects. Wordsworth's best poems are neither descriptive nor minutely detailed. Rather, they evoke a dynamic world through the vivid sensory imagery of its beholding by an engaged participant. It is a poetry of unmediated experience, not of detached description.[3]

A telling manifesto for this new kind of poetry is "Expostulation and Reply," first published in *Lyrical Ballads* and undoubtedly one of the most familiar poems in the Wordsworth canon. Its very familiarity, however, makes it difficult for us to notice the radical nature of its departure from the prevailing norms of its culture. The first stanzas are spoken in the voice of a schoolmaster, "Matthew," chiding a wayward student:

> "Why William, on that old grey stone,
> "Thus for the length of half a day,
> "Why William, sit you thus alone
> "And dream your time away?" (lines 1-4)[4]

Although this question is evidently intended to be merely rhetorical, a way of rebuking the lazy student for his alleged waste of time, "William" responds as if it were seriously intended to evoke a response. This response is telling, in part, for what it does not say. It does not engage the schoolmaster in a debate concerning the relative merits of books written by "dead men," nor does it defend the value of "looking round" on Mother Earth. To engage the question in those terms would be to concede the validity of the worldview they entail, in which books are the main repositories of knowledge, and sight is the primary modality of perception.

Instead, "William" proposes that there are other ways of knowing, and various non-visual modalities of perception:

> "The eye it cannot chuse but see,
> "We cannot bid the ear be still;
> "Our bodies feel, where'er they be,
> "Against, or with our will." (lines 17-20)

In many ways, this stanza is a *non sequitur*. It bluntly declares that the senses affect us directly and immediately, without the intervention of our conscious will. Such a declaration should not be regarded as merely an assertion of empirical reality, however, since the content of sensory perception may be other than what "science" teaches us. If science is the accumulated knowledge of humankind, as conveyed by books, then the repudiation of book-learning may also connote the rejection of secular humanism as a way of knowing. Since the advent of Renaissance humanism, book-learning (and the fetishization of the printed book as an object of acquisition, textual analysis, and marginal commentary) has impeded our contact with other ways of knowing, ways that precede humanism in the order of history and of experience. Humanism impedes our coming to know our-selves as participants in a living world, a world that we inhabit not only as knowing subjects, but also as organic beings, "mere animals" engaged in the daily tasks of eating, breathing, sleeping, and dreaming.

"William" develops some of these implications in the following stanza:

"Nor less I deem that there are powers,
"Which of themselves our minds impress,
"That we can feed this mind of ours,
"In a wise passiveness." (lines 21–24)

What are these "powers" that impress the mind, regardless of our volition? The poem does not say. Indeed, it leaves the nature of these "powers" deliberately imprecise, and the reader is left to ponder whether these "pow-ers" are meant to be the sort of invisible presences that Immanuel Kant calls the *Ding an sich*—the unknowable object that stands at the source of our perceptions—or whether Wordsworth intends something even more uncanny, such as the pagan nature-spirits that inhabit the world of Coleridge's Ancient Mariner. By its very imprecision, this stanza implies a critique of more precise ways of knowing, including those embodied in the "books" that allegedly contain all that is known, and worth knowing, in heaven and earth. The student's dreamlike states of awareness, by con-trast, are utterly inscrutable, and perhaps finally inexplicable by means of the rational method of scientific inquiry. Such uncanny "powers" can only be approached indirectly and experientially, by a "wise passiveness."

"William" addresses his interlocutor with a further question concerning this state of "wise passiveness":

"Think you, mid all this mighty sum
"Of things forever speaking,
"That nothing of itself will come,
"But we must still be seeking?" (lines 25–28)

The answer to this rhetorical question is rather less evident than most read-ers would suppose. It both echoes and gently caricatures the Protestant work ethic of the schoolmaster, who evidently is in the habit of encour-aging his students to engage in an active "seeking" of knowledge. The stu-dent inquires whether such active "seeking" is really the best way to attain knowledge, especially if the natural world is conceived as a "mighty sum / Of things forever speaking." If things speak directly to us, then we need not seek them out. Yet the tone of this question is hardly self-assured; it implies an openness to experience without predicating what the actual content of that experience may be. It is a meditation on the possibility of conversational exchange with the things that surround us, not a prescription for the results of rational inquiry.

The theme of conversation is further developed in the poem's last stanza, which serves to remind the schoolmaster—and the reader as well—that the most significant conversations occur when we are "alone":

> "—Then ask not wherefore, here, alone,
> "Conversing as I may,
> "I sit upon this old grey stone
> "And dream my time away." (lines 29-32)

The premise that one may "converse" with natural objects, in the absence of any human interlocutor, makes sense only if one accepts the profoundly anti-humanistic implications of this poem. To the daydreaming student, the "old grey stone" provides more engaging companionship than even the most learned and articulate schoolmaster. The tone of the poem is not hostile to humankind—indeed, it addresses "Matthew" as "my good friend"—but it poses a serious question, and implies a serious critique, of the rational, scientific, and humanistic ways of knowing. Like the courtly denizens of Shakespeare's Forest of Arden, "William" renounces the discourse of erudition, and instead discovers "books in the babbling brooks, and sermons in stones."

"Expostulation and Reply" is a remarkably successful poem because it allows both sides of the argument to be heard. If the schoolteacher is made to appear a stern taskmaster, the student is also presented as somewhat defensive and dogmatic in his rejection of book-learning; the poem enables the reader to ponder the limitations of both positions while allowing each to speak for itself. The next poem in *Lyrical Ballads,* entitled "The Tables Turned," addresses some of the same themes, and is even more radically experimental in form. It explores whether a "conversation" is possible between the human mind and the objects of the natural world, and it calls into question the objectivity of our conventional ways of knowing.

The poem's first stanza is addressed to a "friend" who is stubbornly attached to book-learning; this addressee is presumably the schoolteacher "Matthew" of the previous poem. The most significant interlocutors of this poem, however, are the personified presences of the sun, who casts "his first sweet evening yellow" upon the surrounding fields, and the "woodland linnet," whose sweet music conveys more wisdom than is found in any book. The transforming light of the sunset enables the poet to perceive something other than the cold, hard objects of Newtonian science, and the songs of the woodland birds similarly convey something more worthwhile and engaging than mere determinate knowledge. The critique of book-learning is most explicitly conveyed in the poem's penultimate stanza:

> Sweet is the lore which nature brings;
> Our meddling intellect
> Misshapes the beauteous forms of things;
> —We murder to dissect. (lines 25-28)

The "lore" of nature is something other than the factual knowledge obtained by the "meddling intellect," and this poem is vehement in its rejection of such knowledge, especially if it is procured through the death-dealing methods of eighteenth-century natural history, a science that was mainly concerned with the dissection and anatomical description of individual specimens, not with the study of living creatures in their native habitat.

The final stanza of "The Tables Turned" dismisses both "science" and "art," exhorting the reader to engage in a very different kind of seeing and knowing:

> Enough of science and of art;
> Close up those barren leaves;
> Come forth, and bring with you a heart
> That watches and receives. (lines 29-32)

The "barren leaves" of books are implicitly contrasted with the more fecund leaves of the "long green fields"; and the outrageously mixed metaphor of a "heart / That watches" provides another indication of just how far beyond conventional epistemology this poem is prepared to go. As a radical credo of ecological awareness, this poem may seem preachy and even dogmatic in some of its pronouncements; yet its brash assertiveness bespeaks a willingness to run stylistic risks in the service of a larger and more comprehensive vision of human possibility. This poem turns the tables upon the entire Western tradition of scientific knowledge, and it proposes a new role for humankind among the speaking presences of the natural world. The place of poetry, and the task of the poet, is thus inherently dialogical; the poet must seek to engage those inhuman voices in conversation, at some risk to his own sense of identity, self-confidence, and stylistic decorum. To judge by the early reviews, *Lyrical Ballads* broke many rules of good taste, and transgressed against numerous tenets of conventional wisdom.

Departure and Return

Many of the poems in *Lyrical Ballads* are shaped by an underlying narrative of departure and return. This narrative pattern is decisively established by the first poem in the collection, "The Rime of the Ancyent Marinere," whose protagonist sets forth from his native land on a voyage of exploration, returning home after many adventures a changed man. This narrative pattern, whose literary analogues go at least as far back as *The Odyssey*, repeats itself in Wordsworth's poem "The Female Vagrant," which describes how its protagonist lived happily in her rural cottage until she was thrown out into the wider world and carried off to America aboard a British naval vessel. She finally returns home to England, bereft of her family and broken in spirit. A more light-hearted instance of this pattern of departure and return occurs in "The Idiot Boy," which tells how Betty Foy sends her son, Johnny, on horseback into the night to fetch a doctor for her sick neighbor, Susan Gale. Instead of carrying out his appointed mission, however, Johnny wanders aimlessly in the dark forest until, by good luck, the horse brings him safely home. Once again, the wanderer returns home deeply changed by his experience; but in Johnny's case, these changes are entirely beneficial, and even cathartic for the local village community. Susan Gale is miraculously cured of her illness, Betty Foy discovers how deeply she loves her son, and Johnny brings home vivid memories of a strange moonlit forest lurking just beyond the boundaries of the known and familiar world.

In all three of these poems, the resonances of "home" are developed through a series of contrasts with the wild, remote, and often terrifying places encountered on the outward journey. In "The Rime of the Ancyent Marinere," the safe, comfortable setting of the Mariner's hometown, with its kirk, lighthouse, and festive wedding ceremony, is implicitly contrasted with the grotesque imagery of towering icebergs, luminous water-snakes, and an ominous game of dice between Death and Life-in-Death for possession of the Mariner's soul. It is only after he has departed from his home that the Mariner comes to realize the value of everything he has left behind. So too, in "The Female Vagrant," the protagonist recollects her childhood in a cottage by the river Derwent in terms that evidently idealize that experience, presumably as a result of the misery that has occurred since her departure:

> Can I forget what charms did once adorn
> My garden, stored with pease, and mint, and thyme,
> And rose and lilly for the sabbath morn?
> The sabbath bells, and their delightful chime;
> The gambols and wild freaks at shearing time;
> My hen's rich nest through long grass scarce espied;
> The cowslip-gathering at May's dewy prime;
> The swans, that, when I sought the water-side,
> From far to meet me came, spreading their snowy pride. (lines 19-27)

This catalog of remembered sensations, olfactory and auditory as well as visual, reveals how the concept of "home" is ordinarily constructed after one has left it behind; notably absent are any jarring or discordant elements that would lend this imagery the facticity of an actual experience. The concept of "home" tends toward the merely nostalgic in this poem, and the archaic metrical form of the Spenserian stanza also gives this passage a remote, unreal, even mythic quality. Composed in 1793, this is among the earliest works ever published by Wordsworth, and it lacks the precision of imagery and the direct vernacular mode of expression that characterize most of his other contributions to *Lyrical Ballads*. The inverted word order, "From far to meet me came," exemplifies precisely the sort of stilted phraseology that Coleridge would later deplore in the Preface to his "Sheet of Sonnets" (1796); indeed, during their period of close collaboration on *Lyrical Ballads*, Wordsworth may well have learned from Coleridge how to avoid the pitfalls of conventional sonneteers: "their inverted sentences, their quaint phrases, and incongruous mixture of obsolete and spenserian words."[5]

Yet there is good reason to scrutinize the depiction of "home" in "The Female Vagrant," because it does reveal a great deal about Wordsworth's fundamental attitudes and beliefs about the best way of life in a rural community. The stanza just cited describes a broad range of domesticated plants in the speaker's garden, including edible peas, aromatic herbs, and ornamental flowers. She is surrounded by a great variety of tame and wild animals, including the frolicking sheep whose fleece provides a commodity for the local market, the free-ranging hen whose eggs provide daily sustenance, and the wild swans who provide nothing more tangible than friendly companionship. Subsequent stanzas describe how she is accompanied to market by her faithful dog, while her father remains at home to tend their bee-hives, and a "red-breast known for years" conveys a friendly greeting by pecking at her casement window. Their basic subsistence is further eked out by her father's catching fish in a nearby lake; in a note to the poem, Wordsworth describes how "several of the Lakes in the north of England are let out to different Fishermen, in parcels marked out by imaginary lines drawn from rock to rock" (*Lyrical Ballads,* 72n). These "imaginary lines" define an individual's right to take fish from a lake that is the common property of the local village. The most notable feature of the lifestyle depicted in this poem is its reliance on multiple modes of subsistence—vegetable gardening, poultry-farming, sheep-raising, bee-keeping, and fish-ing—which all contribute to the foodstuffs and market commodities produced by this father-and-daughter family unit.

The subsistence mode of agriculture described in this poem appears to be entirely sustainable in the long term, and in fact such a mode of pro-duction, based on a widely varied set of crops rotated annually, eked out by fishing, livestock grazing, and the seasonal gathering of nuts, berries, and firewood from village common areas, had persisted relatively unchanged throughout rural England since the Middle Ages.[6] To be sure, such a mode of existence was far from being the relaxed and idyllic way of life depicted in "The Female Vagrant," particularly in years of drought, pestilence, or crop failure; as previously noted, there is certainly an idealized pastoral quality in the way Wordsworth describes it. Nevertheless, because it was based on a widely variable set of foodstuffs and commodities, such a sub-sistence lifestyle was intrinsically more sustainable and resilient than more modern methods of agriculture, which typically rely upon the intensive cultivation of a single crop, year after year, and provide very little recourse in the event of crop failure. As a mode of subsistence, polyculture is inher-ently more sustainable than monoculture, and it certainly provides a more varied and interesting way of life to the individual farmer. However "unreal" such a lifestyle may appear to the modern reader, we may safely assume that it is, on the whole, accurately drawn from Wordsworth's own memories of rural life as he observed it during his childhood on the banks of the river Derwent. Further instances of Wordsworth's personal knowl-edge of traditional modes of rural subsistence may be adduced from his poem "Nutting," which portrays the guilty pleasures of nut-gathering in the woods, and *The Prelude,* which describes how the young Wordsworth clambered out on cliffs to gather eggs from birds' nests (book 1, lines 327-339).

During the eighteenth century, the traditional methods of subsistence agriculture were gradually being supplanted by more capital-intensive modes of production, and the common areas upon which the local farmers relied for their seasonal grazing and gathering activities were increasingly being withdrawn for exclusive private use by the process of enclosure. These modernizing tendencies in rural areas were greatly accelerated during the 1790s with the advent of the Napoleonic Wars, which drove up the prices of agricultural commodities and made the intensive production of market crops a highly profitable endeavor. In "The Female Vagrant," Wordsworth describes how the incursion of a wealthy landowner, who purchases and encloses all of the surrounding properties, eventually drives out the poem's protagonist and her father from their hereditary lands. This wealthy intruder erects "a mansion proud our woods among" (line 39), and by denying access to these local woods, while also withdrawing the right to fish in local waters, he ultimately succeeds in evicting the father and daughter from their humble cottage. Evidently their traditional rights of access to the lake, woods, and other common areas were not respected by the wealthy intruder, who took "no joy . . . [to] stray / Through pastures not his own" (lines 41–42). Since these common rights are generally matters of local tradition rather than law, the father and daughter have no legal recourse when their rights are usurped by their wealthy neighbor. They are thrown out of their ancestral home and into a wider world of suffering and death.[7]

"The Female Vagrant" is the most overtly political of any of the poems published in *Lyrical Ballads,* and its harsh criticism of wealthy landowners is integral to a larger set of political concerns, which also include a critique of British military adventurism and a deep solicitude for the plight of homeless wanderers. Although these political views are generally regarded as a fairly typical articulation of the ideology of the French Revolution and the Rights of Man, they might also be understood as emerging from a deeper set of beliefs and concerns that remained crucially important to Wordsworth throughout his entire career, even after his youthful enthusiasm for revolutionary politics had been discarded in favor of a more conservative political stance. Despite these changes in his political orientation, Wordsworth remained consistent in his opposition to what we might term the military–industrial complex, especially as it affected the traditional ways of life in rural England. As we shall see later in this chapter, Wordsworth consistently opposed the "development" and "improvement" of rural landscapes, and he remained a staunch defender of sustainable agricultural methods, traditional rural architecture, and all of England's open, scenic, and wild areas, especially in the Lake District. Wordsworth was truly ahead of his time, and radically innovative in his concern for the preservation of traditional rural ways of life, and in his defense of the poor, the homeless, and all the wild creatures that dwell beyond the pale, outside the conventional boundaries of human civilization. In his persistent engagement with these issues, Wordsworth foreshadows some of the most vital concerns of the modern environmental movement.

Several of these environmental issues are addressed in "The Idiot Boy," a poem whose protagonist, like the Ancient Mariner, crosses over the boundary between civilization and wilderness, and returns to tell his tale. Unlike the Mariner, however, Johnny is virtually inarticulate, and his narrative account of his journey through the dark forest provides only a brief glimpse into the actual sensory basis of that experience:

> "The cocks did crow, to-whoo, to-whoo,
> "And the sun did shine so cold."
> —Thus answered Johnny in his glory,
> And that was all his travel's story. (lines 460–463)

Johnny refers here to the hooting of the owls, and the cold light of the moon, both of which are so far outside the realm of his normal experience that he has no proper words for them, and can only describe them metaphorically, in terms of the things he does know: domestic farm animals, and the ordinary light of the sun. Yet by the very act of assimilating the unknown to the known, Johnny bears witness to the uncanny otherness of those wild creatures of the night; the moonlit forest is a realm that truly exists beyond the pale of ordinary experience. Even in his brief description of this encounter with the wild, Johnny conveys the sensory intensity of that realm, using imagery that is auditory and tactile, as well as visual. The cries of the owls, which are also mentioned in the poem's opening stanza, echo in the reader's mind with an enigmatic significance: although these voices are not intelligible, they nevertheless serve to remind us that there is another world out there, outside the boundaries of civilization, human language, and normal perception.

Johnny's return to his native village proves to be cathartic for the entire community. His neighbor, Susan Gale, recovers from an illness that may have been merely psychosomatic in the first place—a cry for help or a call for attention from her heedless neighbors. As soon as she learns how much Betty Foy cares about her, to the extent that she is willing to hazard her only son on a perilous mission to fetch the doctor, Susan finds herself miraculously cured. Betty, in turn, after contemplating the possible death of her son, discovers just how much she loves him, and she greets his return with an ecstatic display of affection, not only for Johnny but also for the faithful steed that brought him back alive. And even Johnny, though seemingly oblivious to the human drama surrounding him, nevertheless brings home vivid memories of his journey through the moonlit forest, and, like the Ancient Mariner, finds within himself "strange power of speech" to convey to his auditors the uncanny intensity of that experience. As a result of Johnny's encounter with the wild, the entire village finds itself healed of its sickness, purged of its indifference to others, and transformed into a more integral and caring human community.

The transformation of human awareness through contact with the wild is the main theme of "Lines Written a Few Miles Above Tintern Abbey," the last poem published in *Lyrical Ballads*. In this poem, Wordsworth describes how he returned to the banks of the Wye River in 1798, after a five-year absence. Located in the southwest part of England, the Wye River was not a pristine wilderness; by the 1790s it had become the site of small-scale industry, such as tanning, charcoal-burning, and iron-smelting, and its waters were heavily polluted by the toxic by-products of these industries. Wordsworth mentions the "wreaths of smoke, / Sent up, in silence, from among the trees" (lines 18–19), evidence of itinerant charcoal-burners engaged in converting wood into charcoal for use in local iron foundries. To be sure, an individual charcoal-burner would have only a small impact upon the forest, but the eventual result of charcoal-burning during the eighteenth century was the complete deforestation of entire districts. Although he certainly notices the gradual industrial despoliation of the landscape, Wordsworth does not dwell upon such unpleasant changes in the land; rather, he focuses upon those aspects of the landscape that have retained their wildness, presenting the appearance of a "wild secluded scene" (line 6) even in the midst of human habitation:

> The day is come when I again repose
> Here, under this dark sycamore, and view
> These plots of cottage-ground, these orchard-tufts,
> Which, at this season, with their unripe fruits,
> Among the woods and copses lose themselves,
> Nor, with their green and simple hue, disturb
> The wild green landscape. (lines 9–15)

These lines stress the fecundity, greenery, and wildness of the landscape on the banks of the Wye, even though it is densely inhabited by people engaged in farming, livestock raising, and cottage industries. It retains its wild character, yet it is not a wilderness.

"Tintern Abbey" stresses the peaceful coexistence of human habitation and wildness in the same landscape, especially by describing the appearance of hedgerows that have reverted to a semi-wild condition:

> Once again I see
> These hedge-rows, hardly hedge-rows, little lines
> Of sportive wood run wild; these pastoral farms
> Green to the very door. . . . (lines 15-18)

Although these hedgerows were originally constructed to serve as fences for livestock, they have become so overgrown that they are now essentially wild, displaying the diversity of flora and fauna that are typically found in woodland. By preserving the biodiversity that once pervaded this region, the hedgerows now function as a remnant habitat, providing refuge for many kinds of wildlife and preserving some vital features of southwest England's primordial ecosystem. Wordsworth depicts the "pastoral farms" of this region as existing in complete harmony with the wild habitat that surrounds them.

Like several other poems in *Lyrical Ballads,* "Tintern Abbey" is centrally concerned with themes of departure and return. Wordsworth is returning to a place that he first visited five years before, and his initial response is one of sheer delight in the evidently unchanged appearance of the landscape. He celebrates the endurance of wild natural beauty, even in the midst of intensive human occupation. The act of returning to a known and familiar landscape, and finding it still essentially intact, provides him with an opportunity to meditate upon the changes that have occurred in his own way of responding to the natural world. Wordsworth describes his response to the landscape during his previous visit as if he were a wild creature running through it:

> . . . when like a roe
> I bounded o'er the mountains, by the sides
> Of the deep rivers, and the lonely streams,
> Wherever nature led; more like a man
> Flying from something that he dreads, than one
> Who sought the thing he loved. (lines 68-73)

Love and fear were inextricably mingled in the poet's initial response to this wild terrain, which he experienced with an intensity that he can barely find words to describe in his later adulthood. The poet goes on to describe the "abundant recompence" that has followed from his loss of those "dizzy raptures": having reached greater maturity, he has discovered "a sense sublime of something far more deeply interfused" (lines 96–97), perhaps another instance of the mysterious "powers" of nature that we previously encountered in "Expostulation and Reply." Even such heightened sensitivity, however, leaves the poet with a sense of regret for the youthful intensity that he has lost. In the closing section of the poem, he turns to his sister Dorothy, who has evidently been standing silently by his side the whole time. He notices "the shooting lights / Of thy wild eyes" (lines 119–120) and exhorts her to sustain the immediacy of her response to the natural world. The word "wild" occurs three times in this final verse paragraph, always in connection with Dorothy's "wild eyes" and "wild ecstacies" in the presence of Nature. Although the poet himself can no longer feel such "ecstacies," the poem clearly places great value upon such a fierce and passionate response to the natural world.

From an ecocritical point of view, "Tintern Abbey" poses several important questions about the right relationship between humankind and the natural world. The opening lines of the poem depict a human community dwelling in harmonious coexistence with nature; the local farmsteads are "green to the very door," and the local farmers have acted to preserve a remnant of the primordial ecosystem of that region by allowing their hedgerows to run wild. Considering the increasingly destructive activities of the nearby charcoal-burners, however, it remains an open question whether such an environmentally benign mode of agriculture can be sustained in the long run. The question of whether wildness can be preserved is also crucial to the central meditative development of the poem, in which Wordsworth depicts his younger self as if he were a wild beast, bounding over the mountains, and he later exhorts Dorothy to preserve her own inner wildness. But again, this poem raises the question of whether such wildness can be sustained in any human relationship with nature. Will Dorothy eventually succumb, as her brother already has done, to the process by which "these wild ecstacies shall be matured / Into a sober pleasure" (lines 139–140)? Looking at *Lyrical Ballads* as a whole, it does appear unlikely that such a state of "wild" awareness can be sustained for long by any individual; only the Idiot Boy emerges at the end of his poem with his appreciation for wild nature entirely intact. The prevailing tone of the collection is tragic; many of the characters in *Lyrical Ballads* are eventually broken, or at least tamed, by their circumstances.

Wordsworth's contributions to *Lyrical Ballads* were intended as experiments in a new kind of poetry, so it is not surprising that they raise more questions than they answer. However, these poems were deeply influential upon all subsequent developments in environmental awareness, both in Britain and America. Their profound questions concerning the possibility of sustainable development remain significant, and hotly debated, up to the present day, and many contemporary participants in that debate would be well advised to consult Wordsworth's poetry for useful insights concerning the close linkages between our inner "wild" nature and our collective behavior, as a society, toward the natural world. Wordsworth himself remained deeply concerned about the future development of the Lake District, particularly as its environmental integrity became threatened by the encroachment of wealth, industry, and modern lifestyles, and his later writings evince a growing understanding of the complex ecological interrelationships between people and the places they inhabit.

The Human Ecology of the Lake District

Wordsworth's interest in the natural world is largely developed in relation to places that have long been inhabited by human communities. Unlike Coleridge or Shelley, he evinces relatively little interest in remote or exotic wilderness areas; the uncharted waters of the South Sea, or the silent glaciers of Mont Blanc, exert very little fascination upon his poetic imagination. Although he traveled extensively through the Alps, and could have written a great deal about that rugged and little-explored terrain, his poetry generally remains closer to home. Though he does occasionally write about other places, the Lake District remains the favored locale for most of his published verse, and it is also the subject of his most popular prose work, the *Guide to the Lakes*. Wordsworth's interest in the Lake District is not just an accident of his birthplace and upbringing; it is also the result of his abiding concern for the issues of sustainability already discussed. As a subsistence farming community that had remained relatively unchanged in its agricultural methods since the Middle Ages, the Lake District presented one of the best examples anywhere in Europe of a community living in sustained and harmonious relationship with its local environment. Moreover, the Lake District still preserved much of its primordial wild character, in both its rugged topography and its indigenous flora and fauna. The local inhabitants have learned how to coexist with many of these wild creatures, and these creatures are frequently encountered in Wordsworth's poetry; we have already noted his affection for wild swans, linnets, throstles, and red-breasts; we have seen how the owls are vitally significant to "The Idiot Boy"; and we might also mention "The Thorn," in which an indigenous thorn-tree, gnarled with age and draped with lichens and moss, plays a central role in the plot. Such non-human beings are vital presences in Wordsworth's poetry, not mere decoration or window-dressing. Indeed, in his *Guide to the Lakes,* Wordsworth laments the extinction of several animal species once indigenous to the area: "Such was the state and appearance of this region when the aboriginal colonists of the Celtic tribes were first driven or drawn towards it, and became joint tenants with the wolf, the boar, the wild bull, the red deer, and the leigh, a gigantic species of deer which has been long extinct."[8] In Wordsworth's view, the extinction of such wild, fierce, and free-ranging creatures must attenuate and impoverish our human experience of the natural world.

Wordsworth may well be regarded as one of the first inventors of "human ecology," if by that phrase we mean the study of the complex relationships between human communities and their dwelling-places. The fullest exemplification of Wordsworth's concept of human ecology occurs in the poem "Home at Grasmere," composed in 1800-1806 but not published until 1888. This long narrative poem describes the arrival of Wordsworth and his sister Dorothy in Grasmere in December 1799, with the intention of settling into Dove Cottage and making it their permanent home. The poem evokes Grasmere as a place of joyful dwelling in harmony with the natural world, and the intensity of the brother-sister bond provides an appealing model for the closeness of the ties they seek to establish with the local village community and the larger non-human community of domestic and wild animals. Although the landscape surrounding Grasmere is not wilderness, there does remain a strong element of wildness in its remnant habitat, and both William and Dorothy bring with them traces of the inner wildness that was depicted in "Tintern Abbey." Karl Kroeber, in a seminal 1974 article on "Home at Grasmere," has gone so far as to assert that Wordsworth perceives the landscape surrounding Grasmere as a wolf might see it—looking at the land with the hungry, roving eyes of a wild predator, not the possessive gaze of a prospective landowner.[9] Certainly it is true that Wordsworth is not your average suburbanite; his response to the landscape is utterly untainted by possession, or resource extraction, or even an aesthetic preference for picturesque views. Rather, it emerges from a far more primordial human set of responses, involving hunger, fear, sexual desire, and intense curiosity about what lies just beyond the next hilltop. None of these motivations fall within the conventional boundaries of eighteenth-century descriptive poetry, and "Home at Grasmere" is a decidedly unconventional poem.

Wordsworth begins the poem by recalling how, as a boy, he first caught sight of the Vale of Grasmere. Approaching Grasmere from the surrounding hills, he suddenly sees the entire landscape in motion:

> . . . who could gaze
> And not feel motions there? He thought of clouds
> That sail on winds; of Breezes that delight
> To play on water, or in endless chase
> Pursue each other through the yielding plain
> Of grass or corn, over and through and through,
> In billow after billow, evermore
> Disporting. (lines 24-31)[10]

Such kinesthetic imagery is not conventionally descriptive, but it conveys something much more immediate than a precise visual image, and it suggests something of the boy's fascination with the *Gestalt* of the whole valley, buffeted by the winds, and the answering motion of the boy's own body as he bounds downhill like an uncaged animal.

As the adult Wordsworth and his sister approach Grasmere in winter, the living landscape speaks to them in several voices:

> . . . The naked Trees,
> The icy brooks, as on we passed, appeared
> To question us. "Whence come ye? to what end?"
> They seemed to say; "What would ye," said the shower,
> "Wild Wanderers, whither through my dark domain?"
> The sunbeam said, "be happy." (lines 165-170)

The wanderers receive mixed signals from the icy landscape; initially forbidding, these messages become more welcoming as the warmth of spring approaches. By addressing them as "Wild Wanderers," the shower lends validity to their inner sense of wildness; they are both interrogated and ultimately validated as wild denizens of the natural world.

As a human ecologist, Wordsworth is especially concerned with the relationship between the village of Grasmere and its surrounding environment. He notes the prevalence of small landowners in the Lake District, holding their farmlands as independent estates, inherited from their forefathers, and therefore free from debt: "He, happy Man! Is Master of the field, / And treads the mountains which his Fathers trod" (lines 382-383). The mountainous environment of the Lake District, in Wordsworth's view, has isolated Grasmere and thereby served during the Middle Ages to protect it from the encroachments of feudal overlords. He notes the ethic of self-sufficiency among the local people, and contrasts the harsh anomie of urban life with the cooperative sense of solidarity among the village inhabitants: "Society is here / A true Community, a genuine frame / Of many into one incorporate" (lines 614-616). Such affiliations are often based on actual kinship relations, although Wordsworth notes that this sense of family solidarity extends beyond humankind to their animal companions: "One family, . . . Human and brute" (lines 619-622). He describes the humble, yet important roles played in this community by beasts of burden: a small gray horse that bears a paralytic man, and an ass that carries a cripple (lines 502-509). And he addresses the entire community of "wild creatures" that share this abode with its human inhabitants: blackbirds, thrushes, owls, and eagles (lines 515-550). The villagers of Grasmere bring to their daily encounters with these wild creatures an instinctive sense of kinship.

Has this human community succeeded in establishing a sustainable relationship with its natural environment? Despite his generally favorable depiction of Grasmere's social structures, Wordsworth finds reason for deep concern. He notes the disappearance of "a lonely pair / Of milk-white Swans" who sojourned for two months in the Lake of Grasmere (lines 238-239). Their absence is unexplained, and Wordsworth fears the worst: perhaps "the Dalesmen may have aimed the deadly tube" and shot the harmless swans (line 266). The probable death of these two swans affects him deeply, not only because of their innocence and trusting nature, but also because, like the killing of the Albatross by the Ancient Mariner, it represents an inscrutable crime against nature. If humans are capable of betraying the creatures that love them, even in the ideal community of Grasmere, then what hope exists for the future of humankind? As he ponders the fate of the swans, "consecrated friends, / Faithful Companions" (lines 261-262), Wordsworth is deeply pessimistic. The only thing that could possibly heal the relationship between the human community and the wild creatures that dwell within it is the power of

> . . . overflowing love,
> Not for the Creature only, but for all
> That is around them, love for every thing
> Which in this happy Region they behold! (lines 286-289)

In Wordsworth's view, such an avowal of love must extend beyond a limited affection for individual creatures, to encompass all living things that dwell in the entire regional ecosystem. This is one of the most expansive affirmations of an environmental ethic to be found anywhere in Wordsworth's writings.

Several of the key concepts of human ecology are further developed in Wordsworth's *Guide to the Lakes,* a work that is still read by many wanderers in the Lake District. He has a great deal to say on the topic of environmental design, advocating the traditional architecture of the Lake District:

> these humble dwellings remind the contemplative spectator of a production of Nature, and may (using a strong expression) rather be said to have grown than to have been erected;—to have risen, by an instinct of their own, out of the native rock—so little is there in them of formality, such is their wildness and beauty. (62)

He deplores the gaudy and artificial constructions of the wealthy landowners who have built homes without regard to the particular character of the place. He likewise deplores the introduction of exotic plants, and advocates instead the cultivation of those species that are native to the region.

Wordsworth concludes his *Guide to the Lakes* by suggesting that the entire area should be regarded as a sort of "national property":

> In this wish [for simplicity and beauty of design] the author will be joined by persons of pure taste throughout the whole island, who, by their visits (often repeated) to the Lakes in the North of England, testify that they deem the district a sort of national property, in which every man has a right and interest who has an eye to perceive and a heart to enjoy. (92)

In this passage, Wordsworth clearly foreshadows the modern concept of a National Park, namely, a scenic area of such unique value to the nation that it should be preserved in perpetuity for the enjoyment of all citizens. His prescient suggestion eventually led to the designation of the Lake District as a National Park, and it also played a significant role in the conception and development of the National Park system in the United States.

In his *Guide to the Lakes,* Wordsworth deplores the social changes that are occurring throughout the Lake District, particularly the economic failure of small farmers, the incursion of wealthy landowners, and the consequent transformation of what was once a thriving village community into a tedious array of fancy estates and vacation homes. He deplores the introduction of industrial machinery, which has deprived the local people of their income from spinning and weaving wool, and further weakened the regional economy. In 1845 he was further outraged at the proposal to build a new railway into the heart of the Lake District. He expressed his outrage in his "Sonnet on the Projected Kendal and Windermere Railway":

Is then no nook of English ground secure
From rash assault? Schemes of retirement sown
In youth, and mid the busy world kept pure
As when their earliest flowers of hope were blown,
Must perish;—how can they this blight endure?
And must he too the ruthless change bemoan
Who scorns a false utilitarian lure
Mid his paternal fields at random thrown?
Baffle the threat, bright Scene, from Orrest-head
Given to the pausing traveller's rapturous glance:
Plead for thy peace, thou beautiful romance
Of nature; and if human hearts be dead,
Speak, passing winds; ye torrents, with your strong
And constant voice, protest against the wrong. (*Guide,* 146)

He went on to develop an extended argument against the railway in two letters that were published in contemporary newspapers. Wordsworth's key arguments against the railway include the predicted incursion of mass tourism or "railway inundations" (160); the tawdry commercialization of the railway terminus through the proliferation of "wrestling matches, horse and boat races without number, and pot-houses and beer-shops" (155); the damage to the integrity of communal village life by interloping "strangers not linked to the neighborhood, but flitting to and fro between their fancy-villas and the homes where their wealth was accumulated" (162); "Utilitarianism, serving as a mask for cupidity and gambling speculations" (162); and the *intrinsic sacred character* of the Lake District: "Sacred as that relic of the devotion of our ancestors [i.e. Furness Abbey] deserves to be kept, there are temples of Nature, temples built by the Almighty, which have a still higher claim to be left unviolated. Almost every reach of the winding vales in this district might once have presented itself to a man of imagination and feeling under that aspect, or, as the Vale of Grasmere appeared to the Poet Gray more than seventy years ago. . . . Were the Poet now living, how would he have lamented the probable intrusion of a railway with its scarifications, its intersections, its noisy machinery, its smoke, and swarms of pleasure-hunters, most of them thinking that they do not fly fast enough through the country they have come to see" (162).

Paul Fry, responding to Jonathan Bate's defense of Wordsworth's desire to preserve the lakes, calls such an attitude "offensive," redolent with "snobbery and exclusiveness" (549) and comparable to the self-satisfaction of the "kayak elite"—"gracefully rugged people" who enjoy the remoteness of wilderness beaches, far from the crude, unwashed multitudes.[11] Fry argues that "red" criticism "is evidently still needed, and that is for the demystification of green criticism" (549). Fry criticizes Bate (and also implicitly Wordsworth) for his opposition to mass tourism: "Keep 'nature' hard to reach, and only the right people will make themselves at home in it, leaving everyone else stranded in environmental limbo" (550). Thus, according to Fry, "red" criticism is needed to reveal the class snobbery and elitism that are supposedly implicit in any call for the preservation of remote and scenic areas.

Certainly Wordsworth is not immune to such "red" criticism; his railway pamphlet is regrettably shrill in its depiction of the ignorance, boorishness, and incurable bad taste of the working classes. Yet Wordsworth took strong exception to the claim that he was merely preserving the remote landscape of the Lake District for a moneyed elite, while callously seeking to exclude the poor: "They actually accuse me of desiring to interfere with the innocent enjoyments of the poor, by preventing this district becoming accessible to them by a railway."[12] The district will remain as accessible as ever to those who are willing to employ appropriate technological means of access, whether on foot or by animal power. The public pathways are open and available to all, no matter what their social class. But in Wordsworth's view, the railway will irrevocably alter the character of the Lake District by connecting it to the urban web of commerce. Now that the whole world is linked by the metal wings of aircraft, the rubber tires of automobiles, and the glass filaments of the internet, it hard for us even to conceive of such "retirement" as Wordsworth advocates here. As we witness the destruction of even the most remote wilderness preserves by a relentless onslaught of all-terrain vehicles, the incursion of a railway appears to be only a mild threat, and might even be regarded as environmentally benign by comparison.

In his resistance to the railroad scheme, Wordsworth is not primarily concerned to exclude the working class. Although modern readers may wince when he depicts the urban "artisans" as lacking in aesthetic appreciation, such a distressing class prejudice must be balanced by his sincere concern for the well-being of the rural poor among whom he lives. It is precisely the incursion of *nouveau riche* exburbanites who care nothing about the local community that Wordsworth most urgently deplores. Indeed, more clearly than many modern preservationists, Wordsworth is keenly aware of the class issues implicit in his stance of resistance to speculative commercial development, and he evinces a subtlety in his understanding of these ecological issues that is not often apparent in the anti-environmental rhetoric of our present era. Wordsworth was prophetic in his understanding that unlimited transportation access, recreational development, and suburban sprawl will ultimately ruin the rural landscape for everyone who inhabits it, both rich and poor.

Chapter 3

The Ecological Vision of John Clare

J ohn Clare (1793-1864) described himself on the title page of his first collection of poems as a "Northamptonshire Peasant," a bold assertion of regional identity that situated his voice in an East Midland county that was becoming increasingly a zone of ecological conflict, marked by unequal struggle between the advocates of parliamentary enclosure and the forlorn adherents of the older, sustainable methods of open-field agriculture. The arguments advanced in favor of parliamentary enclosure during the early nineteenth century will sound familiar to contemporary readers still subjected to the insidious rhetoric of "progress": it was claimed that the enclosure of common fields and "waste" land would rationalize the existing patchwork of land ownership and enhance the productivity of agriculture by providing an incentive for individual farmers to exploit their newly consolidated plots with maximum efficiency. Swamps and marshes would be drained, streams would be rechanneled, forests and scrublands would be cleared, and subsistence farming in general would give way to capital-intensive agriculture. Overlooked in the arcane legal and political process of enclosure were the traditional grazing and gleaning rights of the poor, as well as the environmental impact of this radical change in agricultural methods. Parliamentary enclosure proceeded by legal consensus among various classes of landholders; only a few voices were raised to question the fate of the poor, and virtually nobody questioned the fate of the Earth.[1]

Clare entered this discursive minefield with the publication of his first collection, *Poems Descriptive of Rural Life and Scenery* (1820), which forthrightly denounced the "improvement" of his local environment while evoking with elegiac melancholy the gradual disappearance of the common fields, marshes, and "waste" lands, and the extinction of an entire way of life in harmony with the natural cycles of the day, season, and year.[2] Clare's poems typically represent the landscape through the point of view of a local resident, often a peasant, shepherd, or woodman, or even within the imagined consciousness of a native animal, plant, or waterway. Clare's environmental advocacy is more fully developed in his later collections of poetry, *The Village Minstrel* (1821), *The Shepherd's Calendar* (1827), and *The Rural Muse* (1835), and in his numerous manuscript poems, letters, and journals. Taken together, his works convey a detailed knowledge of the local flora and fauna, an acute awareness of the interrelatedness of all life-forms, and a sense of outrage at the destruction of the natural environment. Clare's poetry engages ecological issues with an intensity and breadth of vision that is largely unprecedented in the Western tradition of nature writing; indeed, Clare's unique accomplishment in combining a deep sensitivity for natural phenomena with forceful environmental advocacy clearly entitles him be regarded as the first "deep" ecological writer in the English literary tradition.

The social and political contexts of Clare's poetry have been thoroughly scrutinized from a variety of critical perspectives. John Barrell has examined in precise historical detail the impact of the Enclosure Acts on Clare's native village and the reflection of that traumatic process in Clare's early poetry. Johanne Clare, in a wide-ranging and sympathetic study of Clare's response to contemporary social issues, elucidates the connection between Clare's evolving articulation of political beliefs and his depiction of natural landscape. Raymond Williams, in a recent edition of Clare's poetry and prose, has made perhaps the most unequivocal plea for Clare as a spokesman for the English working class.[3] However, the truly radical and innovative character of Clare's ecological consciousness still remains obscured by other aspects of his reputation, especially his received image as an uneducated "peasant poet" who perhaps deserves our pity, but who certainly is unworthy of serious intellectual consideration. Yet it is precisely the unconventionality of Clare's poetic vision that prevented his work from being adequately published or recognized in his own lifetime, and that still impedes an adequate critical response to his most unorthodox ideas. One of the most perceptive comments on Clare's reputation is made by Geoffrey Summerfield: "Academics have tended to . . . [consign] Clare to the outer ditches and hedgerows. The poets, however, have always known better: Edward Thomas, Robert Graves, [Edmund] Blunden, James Reeves,

Dylan Thomas, John Hewitt, Theodore Roethke, Charles Causeley, John Fowles, Ted Hughes and Seamus Heaney have all borne witness to his fructifying presence in their lives as readers and writers."[4] Perhaps as a result of Clare's growing reputation as a poets' poet, as well as the ongoing publication of the definitive Oxford edition of his poetry, we are now on the brink of much broader popular and academic awareness of Clare. Yet in order to assess the scope and originality of his poetic achievement, the ecological dimension of his thought needs to be more widely recognized and understood. His poetry provides a powerful and suggestive model for environmental advocacy, while it also carries enormous historical significance as one of the inaugurating moments of ecological consciousness in English literature.

Dwelling Places

John Clare's writing is grounded in the bedrock of his lifelong affection for the land and people of his native village, Helpston (or Help*stone,* as he spelled it, perhaps with punning reference to its solidity as a point of geographic and psychological reference). One of his earliest poems, "Helpstone," appears at the beginning of his first published book, *Poems Descriptive of Rural Life,* thus establishing a frame of reference for the subsequent poems in the collection and bearing witness to the priority that he accorded to his sense of rootedness in the local environment. While deploring the changes that economic "progress" has brought to the village—the wholesale destruction of forests and wetlands, the disappearance of streams, and the enclosure of common fields—Clare still retains his memory of the unspoiled landscape that he knew in his youth, which he evokes in loving detail. He idealizes his own childhood, not in the trite sentimental way that became fashionable in much post-Wordsworthian poetry, but as a means of intensifying the qualities of perception and playful spontaneity that make possible an unselfconscious love for the local environment. Given a choice between the "innocence" of childhood and the painful "experience" of a cold, calculating adulthood, Clare (like Blake) will advocate innocence as a form of protest against organized cruelty and oppression.

In "Helpstone," Clare evokes the "happy Eden of those golden years" of childhood, affirming his solidarity with the plants, animals, insects, and waterways of his "native place." In a typical passage, Clare describes a "vanish'd green,"

Where flourish'd many a bush & many a tree
Where once the brook (for now the brook is gone)
Oer pebbles dimpling sweet went wimpering on
Oft on whose oaken plank I've wondering stood
(That led a pathway o'er its gentle flood)
To see the beetles their wild mazes run
With getty jackets glittering in the sun[5]

Clare's memory of the brook is colored by his present awareness that "now the brook is gone," leaving in its place only the silence and desolation that his poem must seek to replenish through the vigor and specificity of its descriptive language. So the gentle motion of the brook is evoked through the vivid dialect term "wimpering," meaning to ripple or meander, and the submerged metaphor of "dimpling sweet," likening the brook to a smiling human face. The evident anthropomorphism of this latter expression, along with the "getty jackets" of the beetles, may be justified by the implied perspective of childhood; to a young child, all natural objects seem animated, aware, and responsive to its own consciousness. Like imaginary playmates, the beetles dart and frolic in the sun, while the brook confers a gentle, maternal presence. The scene is observed through the eyes of a wondering child, poised precariously on a narrow plank above the stream.

Clare's experience of the local environment is that of a native inhabitant, one who has experienced the landscape with the freshness and vividness of a child and has managed to convey something of that youthful perspective into the poetry of his adulthood. Throughout his career, he explicitly sought to enhance the "locality" of his writing, expressing the apprehension that even in his most extended work to date, an autobiographical poem entitled "The Village Minstrel," he had failed to achieve an adequate intensity of description: "The reason why I dislike it is that it does not describe the feelings of a ryhming peasant strongly or localy enough."[6] Clare is not primarily concerned here with the level of factual detail that we might call "local color"; rather, he is seeking to evoke a more profoundly affective dimension of his poetry, which might be specified as an authentic sense of rootedness in the local environment. What is essential to Clare's sense of locality is not the sheer quantity of factual information on local flora and fauna, but a deeper sense of the relation of all creatures to a habitat in which the human observer is also implicated. The scope and originality of Clare's ecological vision emerges from this commitment to his local environment, a "native place" where the "ryhming peasant" can gain an intimate knowledge of the interrelationship of all life-forms.

Rather than merely loving "Nature" in the abstract, as Wordsworth is prone to do, Clare eagerly participates in the natural process that unfolds around him in the teeming forests, fields, and fens of Northamptonshire.

Clare brings to his poetry a remarkably detailed and accurate knowledge of local wildlife; indeed, he has frequently been described as "the finest naturalist in all of English poetry."[7] Even as a child, he was quite curious about wild birds and animals, and his knowledge greatly increased during his adult life. He was not primarily interested in the taxonomic knowledge provided by the Linnaean tradition of natural history; he knew no Latin and was not especially interested in the "official" Latin terms for genus and species. However, he was able to identify most local flora and fauna by sight, using the vernacular and dialect terms that he had learned from his parents, friends, and fellow laborers, finding these sufficient for his needs and more "natural" than the arcane Latin terms.[8] Unlike most contemporary naturalists, Clare detested the practice of specimen-collecting, preferring to observe birds, and even butterflies, on the wing. Like Gilbert White, he made careful observations of each species' habitat, distribution, behavior, and seasonal variation or migration, recording his extensive observations in a series of journal entries and informal letters to his publisher James Hessey, for a projected *Natural History of Helpstone*. These materials remained unpublished until 1951, when they were collected in *The Prose of John Clare;* they have since been re-edited by Margaret Grainger in *The Natural History Prose Writings of John Clare* (1983), a volume that has added greatly to our understanding of Clare as a close observer of the natural world.

Clare's view of nature departs definitively from the utilitarian view of the natural world that prevailed among many of his contemporaries. While Clare rejoices in the beauty of the Earth, he does not primarily see it as existing for human purposes, and he resists its appropriation for economic use or even aesthetic contemplation. The natural world is not comprised of "resources," or "scenery"; Clare regards himself as a normal participant in the living world around him, just another inquisitive mammal going about its daily activities. As a result, his poems rarely "set the scene" in the approved picturesque manner; he provides an accumulation of close-up details rather than sweeping perspectives.[9] Like Gilbert White, Clare tends to present these details in a rambling, anecdotal fashion that undercuts the expectation of narrative development, effacing indications of chronology or causality in favor of a synchronic moment that reflects the daily and seasonal patterns of agricultural activity and biological existence. Clare often situates his poems in morning or evening, summer or winter, but he rarely provides a precise index of clock-time or calendar-date.[10] The events recounted in his poetry are said to occur frequently or customarily, and several of his poems begin with the phrase "I love to . . ." which likewise indicates frequently repeated activity. This frequentative mode is at odds with the dominant Western cognitive categories of causality and chronology, placing his poetry outside the technological mainstream and within an alternative cultural tradition that is more in harmony with the biotic rhythms of the natural world.

Clare's intense engagement with the natural world, his respect for the local environment as an autonomous realm, and his projection of his experience in a mode of presentation that elides chronological difference, enables his deep insight into the interdependence of all living things, an insight that is virtually unprecedented in the English-speaking world and constitutes the core of his originality as an ecological writer. Clare's vision of the natural world as a diverse array of species living in symbiotic relationship is expressed most clearly in "Shadows of Taste," a poem that serves as an explicit manifesto for his new way of comprehending the local environment. In this poem, he denounces the "man of science" whose mania for specimen-collecting leads to cruelty rather than knowledge: "While he unconsious gibbets butterflyes / & strangles beetles all to make us wise."[11] This "man of science," with his narrowly taxonomic view of nature, is unconscious of the symbiosis of all species in the local ecosystem, an insight that can only be achieved through the observation of living things in their unspoiled natural environment.

This green world, "Natures wild Eden wood & field & heath," is truly accessible only to an observer who respects the integrity of living things in their native habitat, or "dwelling place." Such an observer, says Clare, can attain a holistic perspective:

> He loves not flowers because they shed perfumes
> Or butterflyes alone for painted plumes
> Or birds for singing although sweet it be
> But he doth love the wild & meadow lea
> There hath the flower its dwelling place & there
> The butterflye goes dancing through the air (*Middle Period*, 3:308)

From this essentially ecological perspective, the individual organism is not regarded as valuable for its economic or aesthetic qualities considered in isolation, but for its participation in a larger community of living things. Such a community is a "dwelling place" for many different species. Clare describes one such biological community, a stunted oak tree that supports a thriving assortment of plants and animals:

> He loves each desolate neglected spot
> That seems in labours hurry left forgot
> The warped & punished trunk of stunted oak
> Freed from its bonds but by the thunder stroke
> As crampt by straggling ribs of ivy sere
> There the glad bird makes *home* for half the year
> But take these several beings from their *homes*
> Each beautious thing a withered thought becomes
> Association fades & like a dream
> They are but shadows of the things they seem
> Torn from their *homes* & happiness they stand
> The poor dull captives of a foreign land
>   (*Middle Period,* 3:308-309; emphasis added)

This oak tree is not beautiful in any conventional sense, but its role as a habitat for various species of ivy and birds induces the poet to love and cherish it as a microcosm of the archetypal green world. Clare emphatically regards the stunted oak as a *home* for its inhabitants, an insight that provides a key to his ecological vision, since the word *ecology* is derived from the Greek word οἶκος, meaning *house* or *dwelling-place.* In Clare's view, an organism has meaning and value only in its proper *home,* in symbiotic association with all the creatures that surround and nourish it. Torn from this living context, the organism will fade into a "withered thought," a "shadow" of its former self, devoid of beauty or purpose. The task of the "peasant poet," in Clare's view, is to bear witness to this fragile community of creatures whose very existence depends on the continued integrity of their ecosystem. Such a deep insight into the symbiotic harmony of all living things is unprecedented in the English-speaking world.

Clare's ecological vision is exemplified in many passages that reveal his extensive knowledge of the interaction and mutual dependence of various species in his local region. In "Summer Morning," for instance, he rejects the common view of sparrows as "pests," pointing out that they eat insects and thus provide a long-term benefit to agriculture (*Early Poems,* 1:10). Wrens are similarly observed to hunt for gnats.[12] Here and elsewhere, Clare is intensely aware of predator-prey relationships, describing them with some degree of sympathy for the threatened prey, but without undue sentimentality, clearly aware of the role of predation in maintaining the population balance in natural ecosystems. In a fascinating passage from his natural history letters, he describes how a beetle kills a moth, "butchers" the carcass, then brings several other beetles to feed on the moth, "3 on each side."[13] His prevailing tone is dispassionate, describing the scene in precise detail and speculating that "Insects have a Language to convey their Ideas to each other," but avoiding the sentimental anthropomorphism of many nineteenth-century accounts of predation. A similarly dispassionate tone is apparent in his dramatic description of predators stalking their prey:

> In the barn hole sits the cat
> Watching within the thirsty rat
> Who oft at morn its dwelling leaves
> To drink the moisture from the eves
> The redbreast with his nimble eye
> Dare scarcely stop to catch the flye
> That tangled in the spiders snare
> Mourns in vain for freedom there
>   (*Shepherd's Calendar*, "September," *Middle Period*, 1:131–132)

This passage describes an intricate food chain, with the robin stalking insects but threatened in turn by the cat. Clare evidently sympathizes with the fly mourning in vain for its freedom, but his main interest remains focused upon the ecological balance revealed in this tense interaction of predators and prey. Another scene of predation is depicted in "The Vixen," where several young foxes emerge from their den to "start and snap at blackbirds bouncing bye / To fight and catch the great white butterflye."[14] Once again, Clare avoids judgment of the foxes' or birds' aggressive behavior; they are simply fulfilling their instinctive predatory roles in the natural order.

Clare's attitude toward the killing of wildlife by humans, however, is quite different. In "Summer Evening," he strongly denounces the wanton destruction of sparrows and their nests:

> Prone to mischief boys are met
> Gen the heaves the ladders set
> Sly they climb & softly tread
> To catch the sparrow on his bed
> & kill em O in cruel pride
> Knocking gen the ladderside (*Early Poems*, 1:9)

Elsewhere he describes the gratuitous cruelty of boys who throw stones at birds, destroy wasps' nests, and torment squirrels with sticks.[15] Not only boys are prone to this kind of violence; he deplores the practice of adult mole-catchers who hang dead moles from tree-branches, as if the moles were "traitors."[16] Observing that frogs, mice, hares, and yellowhammers flee in terror from any human approach, Clare concludes that "Proud man still seems the enemy of all."[17] In a well-known poem, "Badger," he depicts with keen sympathy the terrible fate of a badger captured and tormented by a crowd of villagers:

> He falls as dead and kicked by boys and men
> Then starts and grins and drives the crowd agen
> Till kicked and torn and beaten out he lies
> And leaves his hold and cackles groans and dies (*John Clare*, 247)

Clare narrates this episode largely from the point of view of the badger, identifying at a deep emotional level with its role as the helpless victim of human brutality. The poem thus reveals an important strategy in Clare's environmental advocacy: he does not merely pontificate on abstract moral issues, but lends his voice to the powerless victims of human violence and wanton environmental destruction.

Clare's ecological vision is confirmed by his powerful and moving poems in defense of the local environment. He does not base his arguments on economic utility or aesthetic pleasure, but speaks directly for the Earth and its creatures, attributing intrinsic value to all the flora and fauna that constitute the local ecosystem. He makes a desperate and compelling plea for sustainable open-field agriculture, old-style communal village life, and the preservation of "waste" lands, forests, fens, and marshes. He defends the right of individual birds, animals, insects, flowers, and trees to exist and propagate. His denunciation of enclosure arises from his anger at "accursed wealth" and its environmental impact: the cutting of ancient trees, the loss of wetlands and wild open spaces, the privatization and "emparkment" of common land, the erection of "No Trespassing" signs, and even the local incursion of railways.[18] As an environmental advocate, Clare is virtually unprecedented in the extent of his insight into the complex relation between ecological devastation and social injustice. In our own time, only the most radical views of the Deep Ecologists can rival the scope and intensity of Clare's environmental activism.

A Language That Is Ever Green

Throughout his poetic career, Clare struggled to create a language adequate to convey his ecological vision, drawing upon the stylistic and presentational modes of his precursors in topographic poetry and natural history writing while also remaining attuned to the folk traditions of song and ballad that were among his earliest memories of Helpston village life. As a laborer in the fields, a wanderer in the "waste" lands, and an occasional visitor to London after the first appearance of his poetry in print, Clare sought to synthesize diverse traditions and experiences in a hybrid style, intensely personal and yet deeply rooted in the natural world. As he came to understand the extent of human violation, the "war with nature" waged by "interest, industry, or slavish gain" (an unholy trinity of rural capitalism), Clare experimented with forms that might express the environmental impact of enclosure in a direct, immediate fashion.[19] One such experiment is "The Lament of Swordy Well," a stirring poem of environmental protest written to denounce the conversion of a local wetland that Clare had earlier praised for its botanic variety—including rare species of orchids—into a quarry for sand and gravel.[20] His radical innovation in this poem is to allow Swordy Well to speak for itself, thus endowing the silent object of human exploitation with a voice to lament its own destruction, while dwelling elegiacally upon the lost flora and fauna that populated its formerly lush ecosystem. Clare's poem is one of the first and still one of the very few poems to speak for the Earth in such a direct and immediate way, adapting the rhetorical figure of prosopopoeia (attributing voice to inanimate objects) to a contemporary crisis of ecological awareness. The reader of this poem does not immediately realize the identity of the speaker; it is only in the third stanza that the voice pauses to identify itself and to specify the economic determinants of its present predicament:

> Im swordy well a piece of land
> Thats fell upon the town
> Who worked me till I couldnt stand
> And crush me now Im down (*John Clare,* 147)

The destruction of Swordy Well is cannily assimilated to the plight of the laboring class during enclosure; worked harder than ever and unable to sustain itself under the new economic order, Swordy Well (like the indigent laborer) has fallen "upon the town," becoming dependent for its very being upon the grudging and doubtful charity of the parish overseers. The analogy drawn here between the plight of the farm laborers (mercilessly exploited under the Speenhamland system of parish relief) and the environmental destruction of Swordy Well (quarried into a sad remnant of its former self) suggests that both forms of exploitation are the result of a new, inhumane economic order that overlooks long-term local conditions in favor of crassly selfish economic gain.

The voice of Swordy Well boldly denounces the selfish motives underlying its own destruction while propounding the intellectually advanced notion that natural beings have rights analogous to the civil rights that underlie English common law. Clare is certainly among the first to suggest that the Earth itself should have the legal right to redress of environmental grievances:

> Though Im no man yet any wrong
> Some sort of right may seek
> And I am glad if een a song
> Gives me the room to speak
> I've got among such grubbing geer
> And such a hungry pack
> If I brought harvests twice a year
> They'd bring me nothing back (*John Clare,* 148)

Clare uses the graphic vernacular word "grubbing" to point out a resemblance between the money-grubbing capitalists who finance the destruction of the environment and the grimy diggers who must actually carry out the task. The poem bitterly describes how every bit of sand and gravel was carried away "in bags and carts" until "now theyve got the land" that formerly supported "flowers that bloomed no where beside." Now Swordy Well is barren, stripped of its lush flora and fauna:

> My mossy hills gains greedy hand
> And more than greedy mind
> Levels into a russet land
> Nor leaves a bent behind
> In summers gone I bloomed in pride
> Folks came for miles to prize
> My flowers that bloomed no where beside
> And scarce believed their eyes (*John Clare,* 150)

Here again the harsh vernacular word "russet" evokes the death of the Earth, denuded of its foliage and unable to support even a thin covering of grass. The poem ends on a note of gloomy foreboding:

> Yet what with stone pits delving holes
> And strife to buy and sell

My name will quickly be the whole
Thats left of swordy well (*John Clare,* 152)

This prediction is accurate in the sense that "Swordy Well" no longer survives as an English place-name, only as a poem; and it suggests the larger
dimension of Clare's problem in developing a language that might convey
the reality of a diverse ecosystem under threat of destruction. Only by
constructing a linguistic analogue to the natural world can the poet hope
to remedy its loss. Writing for a predominantly urban readership, Clare
seeks to evoke the vividness and concreteness of a green world that is fast
slipping away.

Clare approaches the problem of creating a linguistic analogue to the
natural world by seeking a "language that is ever green," as he terms it in
"Pastoral Poesy":

But poesy is a language meet
& fields are every ones employ
The wild flower neath the shepherds feet
Looks up & gives him joy
A language that is ever green
That feelings unto all impart
As awthorn blossoms soon as seen
Give may to every heart (*Middle Period,* 3:581)

Clare plays throughout this poem on the double meaning he attributes to
the word "poesy": he uses this spelling to signify both "poetry" and "posy,"
both a gathering of words and a bunch of flowers.[21] Here the green language of poetry inspires the same joy in the reader as the wild hawthorn
blossoms that grow unnoticed in the fields. Clare is not merely enacting a
witty pun or a vague sentimental allusion to the "flowers of rhetoric";
rather, he suggests that poetic language must strive to attain the opacity and
concreteness of natural phenomena while also evoking the sincerity of
response that can only emerge from a wild, unpolished idiom. This green
language cannot be affecting or persuasive if it remains an artificial construct, a hothouse plant; it must be the spontaneous product of natural
forces working in tandem with prevailing local conditions.[22]

Clare's developing conception of "a language that is ever green" enabled
him to stubbornly resist all efforts by his friends, patrons, and publishers to
"clean up" his poetic language. Although he possessed several English
grammars, spelling books, and dictionaries (including a copy of Samuel

Johnson's *Dictionary* donated by a well-meaning patron), Clare did not seem to "improve" in his command of grammar, orthography, punctuation, or diction; indeed, as he developed his poetic technique, he tended to diverge more radically from the prevailing norms of standard English usage. His decision to retain certain features of his own regional dialect was motivated in large part by his need to preserve a language that evoked with concrete immediacy the natural phenomena of his native place. The language of his mature poetry, however, is hardly a "pure" example of Northamptonshire dialect, crossed as it is by various streams of established poetic diction, and marked by personal singularities usually dismissed as "idiolect." Clare's mature poetic language should not be regarded merely as a personal style, but as an attempt to improvise a dialect that will adequately convey his unique sense of "locality"; it may therefore be termed an *ecolect,* in the literal sense of a language that speaks for the οἶκος: the Earth considered as a home for all living things. Unlike earlier writers who were known as "peasant poets," but whose poetic idiom quickly became assimilated to the cultural mainstream, Clare found within himself the stubborn strength needed to retain his grip on the language of his local place, and his development of a uniquely local idiom—an ecolect reflecting not only local dialect but also local environmental conditions—provides a suggestive model for future ecological writers.[23] Clare's historical priority in generating a poetic ecolect suggests that modern ecological consciousness did not emerge gradually from an antecedent configuration of scientific concepts, but constitutes a radically new conceptual paradigm that demands a distinctive form of expression.

The linguistic basis of Clare's ecological vision is perhaps best exemplified in a collection of poems entitled *The Midsummer Cushion,* which Clare transcribed into a manuscript volume in 1831-32, but which remained unpublished as an integral collection until 1979.[24] The title of this collection alludes to "a very old custom among villagers in summer time to stick a piece of greensward full of field flowers & place it as an ornament in their cottage," thus suggesting that the volume is conceived as a microcosm or miniature version of the surrounding ecosystem.[25] Each poem in the collection, by implication, would constitute a discrete organic unit, a linguistic analogue of the individual plant or flower transplanted from the wild natural environment. Clare elsewhere makes this premise explicit, asserting that "I found the poems in the fields, / And only wrote them down."[26] In this way Clare re-literalizes the prevailing Romantic metaphor of organic unity, thereby declaring his intention to gather the wild flowers of "poesy" in a collection that reflects the vital disorder of the natural world, rather than imposing a cold, rational arrangement. *The Midsummer Cushion* thus elaborates Clare's vision of a wild, unenclosed landscape in which all creatures mingle and enact their own destinies, largely free of human intervention or control. The unbridled luxuriance of Clare's poetry in this volume most fully realizes the implications of his ecological paradigm, defying any rational principle of order (one poem, "The Wryneck's Nest," actually appears twice), but to some extent embodying a process of symbiotic association, so that the poems are distributed among local thematic and formal networks, each one finding its "niche" within the larger textual environment of the collection.[27]

Within *The Midsummer Cushion,* Clare's ecological vision is manifested in a wide variety of poems on particular species of plants and animals, especially in a series of poems on birds' nests. These bird's-nest poems exemplify not only Clare's sense of the bird's adaptation to its particular environmental niche, but also Clare's struggle to create a language adequate to the expression of the bird's distinctive way of life. He often employs onomatopoeia to represent the birds' songs, while he uses regional dialect to designate the features of their habitat that are unique to the local area. One of the most successful of these bird's-nest poems is "The Pewits Nest," in which the speaker wanders across the seemingly barren landscape of a fallow field, then suddenly notices the bird:

> Here did I roam while veering overhead
> The Pewet whirred in many whewing rings
> & 'chewsit' screamed & clapped her flapping wings
> To hunt her nest my rambling steps was led
> Oer the broad baulk beset with little hills
> By moles long formed & pismires tennanted
> As likely spots—but still I searched in vain
> When all at once the noisey birds were still
> & on the lands a furrowed ridge between
> Chance found four eggs of dingy dirty green
> Deep blotched with plashy spots of jockolate stain
> Their small ends inward turned as ever found
> As though some curious hand had laid them round
> Yet lying on the ground with nought at all
> Of soft grass withered twitch & bleached weed
> To keep them from the rain storms frequent fall (*Middle Period,* 3:472–473)

Clare coins the onomatopoetic word "chewsit" to represent the pewit's cry, while he uses the vividly kinesthetic dialect word "whewing" to describe its veering, erratic flight. He situates the bird in its local habitat, a "furrowed ridge" near a "broad baulk" or grass strip at the margin of a fallow field. Despite its barren appearance, this habitat is a rich biological community inhabited by moles, pismires, and "noisey birds"; it is "waste" land only by modern economic standards.[28] The pewit's "nest"—not really a nest but only a bare patch of ground—also exemplifies this paradoxical bounty within apparent poverty, since it lacks the soft, warm grasses used by other birds, yet serves as an adequate home for the pewit's "dingy dirty green" eggs. What looks at first like an anthropocentric critique of the bird's improvidence becomes instead a recognition of its ability to thrive in adversity, lashed by frequent storms on the cold, barren earth. Its eggs are blotched with "plashy spots of jockolate [chocolate] stain" that mimic the wet, marshy ground of the Helpston area, thus serving as protective camouflage.[29] Neither the bird nor its eggs are "beautiful" in any conventional sense, but they are elegantly adapted to their environment, and the poem's blunt, astringent language seems equally well adapted to the depiction of such creatures, eking out a frugal existence on the margins of agricultural "progress."

The ecological basis of Clare's linguistic practice furnishes a powerful and suggestive model for contemporary ecological writing. Clare's regional dialect is an intentional feature of his poetry that contributes to his sense of rootedness in a particular landscape and his profound alienation from contemporary notions of technological "progress" that tended to destroy the land and its peasant-farming community. Just as he resisted the neatness and artificial ordering of landscape that resulted from the violence of enclosure, so too he increasingly rejected the efforts of his editors to tidy up his manuscripts. By refusing to punctuate his poems or conform to "refined" standards of diction, grammar, and spelling, he created an "unenclosed" verse that provides a linguistic analogue to the free, unenclosed landscape that it seeks to conserve and perpetuate. Clare's poetic language thus serves as the basis for a compositional praxis that emerges from a deep understanding of the harmony of all creatures with their natural environment. Clare's *ecolect*—his development of an alternative "language that is ever green" to express his ecological vision—offers an increasingly influential model for the current generation of ecological writers.

The Unfrequented Sky

Clare's meticulous description of local flora and fauna in their natural habitat is conveyed in the "green" language of pastoral poesy, based on his

native Northamptonshire dialect with its colorful deviations from the lexicon and grammar of standard English. The sonnet "Sand Martin" is fairly
typical of Clare's mature linguistic practice, especially in its use of the vivid
dialect word "flirting" (meaning to flit or flutter) and its refusal of any
punctuation except the dash:

> Thou hermit haunter of the lonely glen
> & common wild & heath—the desolate face
> Of rude waste landscapes far away from men
> Where frequent quarrys give thee dwelling place
> With strangest taste & labour undeterred
> Drilling small holes along the quarrys side
> More like the haunts of vermin than a bird
> & seldom by the nesting boy descried
> Ive seen thee far away from all thy tribe
> Flirting about the unfrequented sky
> & felt a feeling that I cant describe
> Of lone seclusion & hermit joy
> To see thee circle round nor go beyond
> That lone heath & its melancholly pond (*Middle Period,* 4:309-310)

Although it is not overtly concerned with traditional pastoral themes, this
sonnet may nevertheless be considered as a displaced version of pastoral.
Like most pastoral poems, this one is quite simple in its setting and subject
matter, comprising nothing more than an evocation of this bird's unusual
way of life in a remote "waste" area. Yet it clearly exemplifies the pastoral
process of "putting the complex into the simple" (as William Empson
described it),[30] since it addresses some complex issues having to do with
the relation between human society and the wild creatures that inhabit the
"wild" or "waste" areas outside the domain of civilization. In contrast with
the neoclassical mode of pastoral, which entailed a somewhat snobbish
depiction of the lives of simple shepherds, this poem is a more sympathetic
meditation on the actual existence of a bird. It resists a crude anthropomorphism, and it respects the difference that separates human from non-
human beings, at the same time that it evokes a deep sense of identity
between the speaker, himself a loner who feels excluded from the haunts
of men, and the bird, which likewise partakes of a hermit-like seclusion.
This sense of a shared identity is expressed in the poem's first word, "thou,"
which establishes a fraternal bond between man and bird, rather than
adopting an objectifying or descriptive stance, as a naturalist typically
would.

Clare's poetic style may seem awkward to anyone trained in the more genteel modes of literature, and not merely because of his use of occasional dialect words. In this poem, the repetition of certain key words seems tautological to a reader accustomed to the rhetorical technique of elegant variation. Within this short poem, the words "hermit," "haunt," "lone," "heath," and "quarrys" are all repeated, and the word "frequent" is echoed in the word "unfrequented." Such repetition seems aesthetically justified, however, by a doubling of poetic perspective; everything in the poem is described from both a human and a non-human point of view. Thus the bird is described as a "hermit" in the first line, but by the end of the poem the speaker has come to feel a "hermit joy" in the bird's presence. The "frequent quarries," created by human commerce, give way to "the unfrequented sky," the sole haunt of the solitary bird. The word "quarry" derives etymologically from the French word *carré,* meaning "square," but the bird's motion at the end of the poem is a "circle," thus contrasting the rectilinear forms of human industry with the sweeping and cyclical curves of the natural world. The destructive aspect of human activity enters the poem most overtly through the "nesting boy," whose effort to seek out and destroy the sand martin's nest is rarely successful because of the bird's shy reclusiveness. Like the poet himself, the bird remains "far away from all thy tribe"; he is a loner, a solitary wanderer on the "desolate face" of the Earth.

Intrinsic to this poem is a sense of displacement; the bird creates a "dwelling place" by drilling a hole into the wall of a remote quarry that is not its natural home, but an abandoned site of human industry. So too Clare in this period had been forced out of his home in Helpston and was living rather miserably in a cottage provided by his aristocratic patrons.[31] In this sonnet, as indeed in most of his poems about birds and animals, Clare is pondering the affinity between his own situation, as a failed poet and social outcast, and the situation of the bird, particularly a bird so isolated even from its own kind. So too in his poems about gypsies, Clare is often given to meditate on their stubborn ability to survive in niches that have been forsaken as useless by the rest of humankind. Clare is keenly aware of the desperate and demeaning effects of poverty, but he lacks faith in glib solutions that entail "progress" and economic growth; rather, he sees poverty as ideally a form of spiritual discipline, a way of encouraging us to live within our means and to adopt a less greedy and exploitive relation to the Earth and its natural resources. Rather than digging more quarries, we should learn from the ways of the sand martin to reclaim the habitat we have already destroyed.

Clare's poetry does repay close reading. Far from being a sentimental appropriation of a bird or a landscape for human purposes, this poem meditates upon the very possibility of a meaningful relationship between humans and the world of living creatures that surrounds them. Clare acknowledges the otherness of the bird but does not dismiss it as unknowable. The nesting boy exemplifies the human desire to appropriate and exploit wild defenseless creatures; Clare respects the bird's peculiar choice of a dwelling place and sees it as a plausible solution for his own complex dilemmas, his own doomed quest for a place he could call home. If Clare's contemporaries had often treated him and his entire social class as "vermin," it allows him to achieve a more distanced perspective upon what it means to be human, and upon what reality may exist outside of social relationships; and in this sense there may be a much more real sense of affinity between Clare and the bird than there is between Clare and the rest of humankind. If the human "tribe" is embarked on a rectilinear path of conquest over nature, Clare will follow a different course, circling round the same place until it truly becomes a home to him. Any place, no matter how desolate, known intimately enough, can become a miniature analogue of the Earth itself. Clare's pastoral poetry attempts to locate itself in this microcosmic world, making a home on the outer margins of what can be comfortably known or said. It allows us an awkward but authentic vision of what kinds of dwelling may be possible for humankind in a post-industrial landscape.

Chapter 4

The End of Nature: Environmental Apocalypse in William Blake and Mary Shelley

Global apocalypse is a theme with a long history in Western literature, going back at least as far as the catastrophic flood depicted in Genesis and the fiery doom foretold in the Book of Revelation. But the dawn of the Industrial Revolution marked the first time that such apocalyptic events were imaginable as the result of normal human activity, rather than an inscrutable act of God. In the early years of the nineteenth century, as the manufacturing cities of England disappeared into a thick haze of photochemical smog, it became possible to imagine that new technologies of mass production might alter the climate and eventually destroy the Earth's ability to sustain life.

This chapter examines the theme of environmental apocalypse in the English Romantic period, seeking to understand why such a vital moment in the intellectual history of the environmental movement has been undervalued by what Karl Kroeber has termed "Cold War Criticism," a term intended to suggest the unfortunate elision of environmental contexts in the epistemological battles of literary criticism that emerged amidst the adversarial politics of the post–World War II era.[1] Although the apocalyptic theme has long been regarded as integral to the Romantic World Picture, particularly in major studies of William Blake by Harold Bloom, Joseph Wittreich, and Morton Paley, yet the environmental implications of this theme have been overlooked or undervalued by several generations of literary critics.[2] This chapter works toward a revisionary understanding of the apocalyptic narratives of the Romantic period, first examining how Blake's poetry from the *Songs of Experience* to *Jerusalem* engages in a sustained and bitter critique of the material conditions of production—the "dark Satanic Mills" that constituted the coal-fired industrial base of Britain's mercantile empire.[3] This chapter will also consider the novels of Mary Shelley, particularly *The Last Man,* as narratives of environmental apocalypse, deeply concerned with the possible destruction of the Earth's capacity to sustain human life.

Dark Satanic Mills

London in 1800 was the hub of a vast mercantile empire and the largest city in Europe, with a population well over one million people.[4] No longer exempt from the economic pressures of urban life, the English countryside was radically transformed by the city's inexhaustible demand for food and other commodities, leading to the development of capital-intensive methods of agriculture, deep-pit coal mining, and the construction of turnpikes, canals, and railways to haul an ever-increasing quantity of goods to market. Within the city of London, William Blake witnessed the congestion, noise, pollution, and spread of contagious disease that inevitably resulted from unchecked population growth in a dense urban area. London in Blake's time was an unplanned conglomeration of houses and factories, without safe drinking water or adequate sanitation, whose crumbling bridges and muddy streets were laden with filth, vermin, and disease.

Blake's poem "London" (circa 1794) evokes the bleak, polluted urban environment that resulted from the unrestricted burning of coal, the discharge of raw sewage into the Thames, and the inexorable spread of contagious disease. Blake writes:

I wander thro' each charter'd street,
Near where the charter'd Thames does flow.
And mark in every face I meet
Marks of weakness, marks of woe.

In every cry of every Man,
In every Infant's cry of fear,
In every voice, in every ban,
The mind-forg'd manacles I hear. (lines 1–8)

Blake's nightmare depiction of London's "charter'd streets" lends particular emphasis to the psychologically oppressive aspects of the urban landscape. The original purpose of the Royal Charters, legal documents creating the various boroughs of London Town, was to enumerate and protect the civil liberties of the inhabitants; but in Blake's view, these documents had become instruments of political tyranny and social oppression, allowing the unchecked growth of industrial capitalism with its attendant wage-slavery, the "mind-forg'd manacles" that bind the laborer to an inhuman machine. Even a free-flowing river, the Thames, becomes "charter'd," bound and constricted in its flow by the legal designation (or "chartering") of its banks and the damming of its tributaries for the production of water power. The South Bank of the Thames, where Blake lived during most of the 1790s, was a major leather manufacturing district and a significant source of foul-smelling effluent into the Thames, which also received large amounts of raw sewage and industrial wastes from London's rapidly expanding population. Such an unhealthy urban environment, combined with poor nutrition and inadequate health care, led to extremely high rates of infant mortality. The "Infant's cry of fear" is a plausible response to such a dreary and pathological urban environment.

Blake's "London" goes on to evoke the horrendous conditions of child labor, prostitution, venereal disease, and air pollution that pervade the city:

How the Chimney-sweeper's cry
Every blackning Church appalls,
And the hapless Soldier's sigh
Runs in blood down Palace walls.

But most thro' midnight streets I hear
How the youthful Harlot's curse
Blasts the new-born Infant's tear
And blights with plagues the Marriage hearse. (lines 9-16)

The elegant architecture of London, including the neoclassical white marble facade of St. Paul's Cathedral (used in the design for *Jerusalem,* plate 57, as an emblem of the city of London), is literally "blackning" as a result of industrial pollution, especially the smoke of coal-fired steam engines pouring into the atmosphere at rapidly increasing rates during Blake's lifetime. In 1784, the world's most powerful steam engine was installed in London, just south of Blackfriars Bridge. Designed by Michael Boulton and James Watt, the Albion Mill was intended to demonstrate the vast potential of steam power for industrial processes, and its enormous machinery became an instant tourist attraction, celebrated by Erasmus Darwin in his *Botanic Garden* (1791), a work for which Blake provided several illustrations.[5] The first canto of Darwin's poem personifies this prodigious 200-horsepower steam engine as a "giant-birth" who "wields his large limbs, and nodding shakes the earth," and Darwin elsewhere evokes the "Giant-Power" of the Albion Mill as it grinds wheat into flour:

> There the vast mill-stone with inebriate swirl
> On trembling floors his forceful fingers twirl,
> Whose flinty teeth the golden harvests grind,
> Feast without blood! and nourish human-kind.
>   (*Botanic Garden,* canto 1, lines 275-278)

When the Albion Mill burned down in March 1791, Darwin added a lamenting footnote to his poem: "The Albion Mill is no more; it is supposed to have been set on fire by interested or malicious incendiaries, and is burnt to the ground. Whence London has lost the credit and advantage of possessing the most powerful machine in the world!"[6]

Darwin's celebration of the new-fangled Albion Mill expresses the prevailing view of the dominant social classes of his time, but it ignores the dissenting views of the "malicious incendiaries" who evidently regarded this new machine as a threat to their livelihood. According to Blake's most recent biographer, Peter Ackroyd:

> Some believed [the destruction of the Albion Mill] to have been arson, and the rejoicing millers on Blackfriars Bridge made no secret of their feelings. "Success to the mills of ALBION," one placard was inscribed, "but no Albion Mills." The factory was destroyed, and remained as a black ruined shell until 1809—Blake passed it every time he walked into the City, with the hills of Highgate and Hampstead in the distant smoky air.[7]

In February 1791, Blake had moved into the Hercules Buildings in Lambeth, just south of the Albion Mill along Blackfriars Road. When Blake speaks of "Albion fallen upon mild Lambeths Vale" (*Jerusalem,* plate 20), he may well have in mind the blackened ruins of the Albion Mill.[8]

Although the Albion Mill was destroyed, many other steam engines continued to operate in and around London, blackening the atmosphere and transforming the urban manufacturing economy from the human scale of artisans' workshops to the vast industrial wasteland of factories, loading docks, and warehouses that still dominate the South Bank of the Thames. By 1800, London rivaled any of England's northern industrial cities in the number of steam engines installed; over 100 steam engines were at work in London's flour mills, breweries, tanneries, and other large-scale industrial operations.[9] It is in this context that we should understand Blake's prophetic vision of the "dark Satanic Mills" that would eventually come to dominate "England's green & pleasant Land" (*Milton,* plate 1).

England in 1800 faced some crucial decisions concerning its future development, although few people at the time realized that such decisions were being made, or that the increasing pace of the Industrial Revolution was anything other than inevitable. Those who resisted the invisible hand of progress, sometimes through violent acts of destruction (such as the burning of the Albion Mill, along with frame-breaking and other acts of industrial sabotage), were generally regarded as dangerous Luddites and their voices excluded from the political process. Blake's voice was among those excluded, as he strove to express his deep concerns about the social and environmental effects of uncontrolled large-scale industrial development. Blake's critique of industrial capitalism, and his depiction of its ultimate consequences, is most fully and coherently expressed in his two major prophetic books, *Milton* (composed circa 1800-04) and *Jerusalem* (composed circa 1804-07). Both of these long narrative poems use the prophetic past tense to describe England's present predicament, with particular emphasis on the grim industrial landscape that was inexorably forming around Lambeth, on the South Bank of the Thames, where Blake lived from 1791 to 1800.

Farther to the south of London, primeval oak forests were being cut down, peeled of their bark, and reduced to charcoal for use in foundries, steam-engines, and other industrial processes. Blake may well have witnessed the destruction of these ancient "Oak Groves," their branches piled into glowing heaps by charcoal-burners, as he walked through the Surrey hills, in the outskirts of London just south of Lambeth:

The Surrey hills glow like the clinkers of the furnace: Lambeth's Vale
(Where Jerusalem's foundations began; where they were laid in ruins,
Where they were laid in ruins from every Nation, & Oak Groves rooted)
Dark gleams before the Furnace-mouth, a heap of burning ashes.
   (*Milton,* plate 6)

This passage powerfully evokes the devastation of the surrounding countryside as London's increasing appetite for fuel and raw materials led to the destruction of ancient forests, including the "Oak Groves" that were formerly sacred to the Druids. As Blake surveyed the Surrey hills from a distance at night, they must have glowed with scattered sparks of orange fire "like the clinkers of the furnace."

In London itself, Blake observed the rapid growth of industries that required vast quantities of raw materials. The metalworking industry grew substantially in London during the Napoleonic Wars to meet an urgent demand for military weapons, including some ominous new technologies of mass destruction: submarines, steel cannon, and explosive artillery shells.[10] "Loud groans Thames beneath the iron Forge," writes Blake, "to forge the instruments / Of Harvest: the Plow and Harrow to pass over the Nations" (*Milton,* plate 6). On the outskirts of London, numerous coal-fired brick kilns were working at peak capacity to supply building materials for the new industrial infrastructure. In *Vala or the Four Zoas* (composed circa 1797-1803), Blake describes the harsh conditions of labor in these brick kilns, which were operating at peak capacity, around the clock:

> The King of Light beheld her [Vala] mourning among the Brick kilns, compelled
> To labour night & day among the fires. Her lamenting voice
> Is heard when silent night returns & the labourers take their rest:
>
> 'O Lord, wilt thou not look upon our sore afflictions
> Among these flames incessant labouring? Our hard masters laugh
> At all our sorrow.' (*Four Zoas,* page 31)[11]

In Blake's view, one of the most significant consequences of the Industrial Revolution is the harsh and dehumanizing conditions of labor, as highly skilled self-employed artisans were replaced by unskilled laborers (often women and children) working at repetitive tasks in factories. Even such a seemingly benign technology as a steam-powered flour mill is destructive in its effects on the people who are compelled to work in such a noisy, dangerous, and dehumanizing environment: "The living & the dead shall be ground in our rumbling Mills / For bread of the Sons of Albion" (*Jerusalem,* plate 38). The workers in such "rumbling Mills" are ground down by the monotony of their tasks, and in some cases killed outright by industrial accidents. In the early days of the Industrial Revolution, workers were all too often injured and killed by fires and explosions, or yanked to a terrible death in the whirring belts and gears of enormous machines.

Blake is quite vehement in his denunciation of these infernal machines. In one of his earliest illuminated works, *There is No Natural Religion* (1788), he asserts that "the same dull round even of a universe would soon become a mill with complicated wheels." Blake is thinking here not only of the dehumanizing effects of industrial machines, but also of the broader and more insidious effects of a mechanical model of the universe, based on the mathematical Newtonian laws of motion. This mechanical model, along with the empirical scientific worldview of Bacon and Locke, provides the essential intellectual infrastructure for the Industrial Revolution, and Blake regards the "universities of Europe" as the main source of this pervasive, dehumanizing ideology:

> For Bacon & Newton, sheathd in dismal steel, their terrors hang
> Like iron scourges over Albion; Reasonings like vast Serpents
> Infold around my limbs, bruising my minute articulations.
>
> I turn my eyes to the Schools & Universities of Europe
> And there behold the Loom of Locke whose Woof rages dire,
> Washd by the Water-wheels of Newton. (*Jerusalem,* plate 15)

In Blake's view, the new technologies of mass production are themselves the result of a misguided and fundamentally erroneous way of understanding the natural world; he utterly rejects the inductive method of reasoning that underlies the Enlightenment worldview, and he advocates instead a characteristically Romantic way of knowing that is visionary, synchronic, holistic, and utopian. Blake's major prophetic works emerge from his radical rejection of classical Newtonian physics and his quest for an alternative means of discovering and expressing truth.[12]

Although he rejects the vast, inhuman technologies that were coming to dominate the new industrial landscape, Blake is certainly not opposed to all forms of technical innovation. He was himself a talented metalworker who invented a new method of engraving copper plates to produce his illuminated works.[13] Indeed, in *Jerusalem,* Blake distinguishes between the "Cruel Works" of heavy industry and the smaller, more human scale of alternative "Edenic" technologies:

> . . . Black the cloth
> In heavy wreathes folds over every Nation. Cruel Works
> Of many Wheels I view, wheel without wheel, with cogs tyrannic
> Moving by compulsion each other: not as those in Eden: which
> Wheel within Wheel in freedom revolve, in harmony & peace.
> (*Jerusalem,* plate 15)

Blake here develops a contrast between the vast, inhuman scale of factories "of many Wheels" (such as the textile mills of Birmingham that were literally blanketing world markets with cheap, mass-produced cloth) and the smaller, more intricate and ingenious machines that bear within them the promise of individual freedom. Although Blake does not specify precisely what sort of machines he has in mind here, his general insight nevertheless brilliantly foreshadows the work of E. F. Schumacher, whose book *Small Is Beautiful* provides a classic account of the value of human-scale technology for sustainable economic development.[14]

Later in *Jerusalem,* Blake describes how the "simple workmanship" of the hourglass, plowshare, and waterwheel have been "broken and burned with fire" in England's headlong rush to develop ever larger and more powerful machines:

> And all the Arts of Life they changed into the Arts of Death in Albion.
> The hour-glass contemned because its simple workmanship
> Was like the workmanship of the ploughman, & the water-wheel
> That raises water into cisterns, broken & burned with fire
> Because its workmanship was like the workmanship of the shepherd.
> And in their stead, intricate wheels invented, wheel without wheel
> To perplex youth in their outgoings, & to bind to labours in Albion.
>   (*Jerusalem,* plate 65)[15]

The keyword here is "workmanship." Repeated three times, this word denotes the expert knowledge of the self-employed artisan who takes pride in the product of his labor, and thereby partakes of the "Arts of Life." Blake himself, an expert practitioner in the trade of printing and engraving, was intimately familiar with a mode of production that used simple hand tools and hand-powered printing presses to create a finely wrought artifact. His essential insight is that "workmanship" makes labor interesting and worthwhile to the individual worker, lending even to simple tasks the value of life-enhancing craftsmanship. These "Arts of Life" are contrasted with the "Arts of Death," by which Blake means not only the new military technologies of mass destruction, but also the emerging heavy industries whose workers are assigned tedious, repetitive tasks, becoming mere cogs in the vast machine.

Blake is not only concerned with the misery and abasement of the human spirit that inevitably results from the deployment of heavy industry in urban areas. He is also aware that these coal-fired industries entail a serious potential for environmental damage. Blake is certainly ahead of his time in foreseeing the possibility of global environmental change as a result of large-scale industrial pollution; even the best scientific minds of the early nineteenth century regarded environmental pollution as only a local problem and a minor nuisance. Humphry Davy, the discoverer of oxygen and England's leading scientific authority on the chemistry of atmospheric gases, stated in a public lecture of 1802 that the burning of fossil fuels could have no appreciable effect on the atmospheric supply of oxygen, because the amount of oxygen consumed was so small in relation to the total amount. Davy stated that there is "no difference of Oxygen in cities, Woods, or Sea shore—The quantity consumed by fires [is] incalculably small compared with the sum total."[16] It was inconceivable to Davy that human industry could have any significant impact on the global atmosphere.

Two hundred years later, as we contemplate the very real effects of global warming as a result of the unrestricted burning of fossil fuels, Blake's dire warning about the environmental consequences of heavy industry seems all too prophetic. In one of the most lyrical and evocative passages in *Jerusalem,* Blake describes how the entire natural world has been devastated by the relentless turning of the "Starry Wheels":

> Hoarse turn'd the Starry Wheels, rending a way in Albion's Loins
> Beyond the Night of Beulah. In a dark & unknown Night,
> Outstretch'd his Giant beauty on the ground in pain & tears:
> His Children exil'd from his breast pass to and fro before him
> His birds are silent on his hills, flocks die beneath his branches
> His tents are fall'n! his trumpets, and the sweet sound of his harp
> Are silent on his clouded hills, that belch forth storms & fire.
> His milk of Cows, & honey of Bees, & fruit of golden harvest
> Is gather'd in the scorching heat, & in the driving rain:
> Where once he sat he weary walks in misery and pain:
> His Giant beauty and perfection fallen into dust:
> Till from within his witherd breast grown narrow with his woes,
> The corn is turn'd to thistles & the apples into poison:
> The birds of song to murderous crows, his joys to bitter groans!
> The voices of children in his tents, to cries of helpless infants!
> And self-exiled from the face of light & shine of morning,
> In the dark world a narrow house! he wanders up and down,
> Seeking for rest and finding none! and hidden far within,
> His Eon weeping in the cold and desolated Earth.
>   (*Jerusalem,* plates 18-19)

Blake's depiction of the "desolated Earth" is a comprehensive catalog of environmental damage: the skies over England are darkened with smoke, birds have fallen silent, flocks have died, harvests have failed, apples are poisoned, and the Earth's climate is marked by scorching heat and devastating storms. Albion, the giant personification of England, is "self-exiled" by the devastation of his homeland; his children cry helplessly, and his Eon (or female companion) weeps as she beholds such terrible destruction. This disaster has not occurred as the result of external forces or enemy action; England has been destroyed by its own industrial activity, the "Starry Wheels" of complex machines, and infernal iron-forges and coal-mines "that belch forth storms & fire."[17] Only too late does Albion realize that his relentless drive to industrialize, along with his incessant wars of imperial conquest, have resulted in the desolation of the entire Earth.

The Great City of Golgonooza

Blake differs from many of his Romantic contemporaries in his attitudes concerning the relative value of urban and rural life. Although he is extremely critical of London, he does not advocate an escape into the unspoiled countryside, or to the wildlands of North America, as many of his contemporaries had done. (Wordsworth and Clare extolled the value of rural life; Coleridge and Southey tried to organize an exodus of radical Pantisocrats to the American Wilderness; and Joseph Priestley actually did emigrate to rural Pennsylvania after his home in Birmingham was looted by a reactionary mob.) To be sure, in 1783 Blake did publish some rather tepid and conventional poems in praise of pastoral life, and in September 1800 he moved to the rural village of Felpham, on the south coast of England, at the personal request of his patron; but his experience of provincial life proved to be extremely uncongenial, and Blake returned to London in September 1803, thenceforth to become an inveterate urbanite.[18] Blake's preference for urban existence was, of course, partly a consequence of his trade as a printmaker; only in London could he find clients and markets for his professional work. But there is something even more fundamentally revealing about Blake's character in his stubborn attachment to London; evidently the social and cultural stimulus offered by urban life far outweighed its negative aspects.

One important consequence of Blake's preference for urban life is his resistance to conventional pastoral or georgic imagery as an alternative to the bleak cityscape of London. Rather than advocate pastoral escapism, his great prophetic books offer a local solution to the problems of city life. Both *Milton* and *Jerusalem* offer a utopian vision of urban renewal, by which London is transformed into the great city of Golgonooza (*Jerusalem*, plate 98). Golgonooza, the City of Art, is largely a visionary construct; Blake imagines London as it might be transformed and humanized by the creative energy of Los, who serves as a mythic counterpart to the struggling artist. Los builds Golgonooza in Ulro, a dark realm of chaos and death "where Souls incessant wail" (*Milton,* plate 26); its purpose is to provide a place of refuge for spirits fleeing that grim place of darkness and despair.

Blake's concept of Golgonooza is most fully developed in the first book of *Milton* (plates 24-29), where Los and his sons collaborate to form an entire universe on a human scale. "Los is by mortals nam'd Time" (*Milton,* plate 24), and the city of Golgonooza is steeped in temporality, "Minutes & Hours, / And Days & Months & Years & Ages & Periods: wondrous buildings" (*Milton,* plate 28). Golgonooza is home to the lark, a traditional emblem of poetic fancy, and the wild thyme, a humble plant that serves as "Los's Messenger to Eden" (*Milton,* plate 35). Golgonooza provides a home for a great diversity of creatures of all shapes and sizes, from "the Mole clothed in velvet" to "the Serpent clothed in gems & gold" (*Milton,* plate 27). Blake's emphasis on biodiversity suggests that Golgonooza is a sort of Ecotopia: a place where people can live in harmony with their environment, using appropriate human-scale technology to create an urban dwelling-place that nourishes the creative spirit of all residents.[19] In place of London's enormous factories and powerful steam-engines, Golgonooza has smaller, hand-operated machines, including a loom where women weave "clothing with joy & delight" (*Milton,* plate 28) and a wine-press where the sons and daughters of Luvah "tread the grapes / Laughing & shouting" (*Milton,* plate 27). This wine-press is also "the Printing-Press / Of Los; and here he lays his words in order above the mortal brain" (*Milton,* plate 27). Everyone in this City of Art is engaged in acts of creation, using human-scale technologies and natural, organic materials. They do not follow hourly schedules or external deadlines, but work in a field of wild time (the "Wild Thyme" of *Milton,* plates 35 and 42) according to the inherent cycles and rhythms of their own creative endeavor.[20]

Like all human creations, Golgonooza is imperfect and fallible; its inhabitants are still subject to death, disease, and painful errors. In Blake's cosmogony, Golgonooza remains quite distinct from Jerusalem, the City of God, which can exist only by an act of divine creation. Yet Golgonooza provides an appealing analogue for a modern Ecotopia precisely because Blake imagines it as a purely human construct, something we can achieve by our own conscious effort. Rather than wallow in defeatism or escapism, Blake chooses to imagine London as it might become through the work of ordinary human beings. In Blake's view, there is no limit to what the human imagination can create; indeed, one of the most appealing passages in *Milton* describes how the "Sons of Los" build the overarching sky as a dwelling-place for human beings:

> The Sky is an immortal Tent built by the Sons of Los
> And every Space that a Man views around his dwelling-place,
> Standing on his own roof, or in his garden on a mount
> Of twenty-five cubits in height, such space is his Universe.
> And on its verge the Sun rises & sets; the Clouds bow
> To meet the flat Earth & the Sea in such an ordered Space.
>   (*Milton*, plate 29)

Clearly there is no need to escape from the city to the countryside, because anyplace we find ourselves, even the chaotic streets of London, can become "an ordered Space" through the work of the human imagination.[21]

Such a vision of urban renewal might well be criticized as idealistic, even naive. How could the urban industrial landscape be affected, let alone transformed, by the artistic vision of a single individual? Blake's prophetic books provide no blueprint, no plan of action; they are purely "visionary" in that negative sense. And to be sure, his writings had relatively little influence in their own time.

But perhaps Blake was ahead of his time. After 200 years of industrial "progress," and in the wake of some serious environmental disasters, we have grown less trusting of large-scale technological or economic "fixes" to the chronic problems of the inner city. If the modern cityscape can be renewed, Blake's vision of Golgonooza may actually prove to be a more practical model than even the most detailed blueprints offered by professional city planners, because Blake attends carefully to the limitations of large-scale technology, and because he gives free rein to the limitless possibilities of the human spirit. According to Donna Meadows, "if there is a solution to the world's environmental problems, that solution is more likely to come from a poet than from a physicist."[22] William Blake may well prove to be the poet that we needed all along, the bard of Ecotopia, home to the lark and the wild thyme.

The Last Man

Blake was not alone in his concerns about the destructive effects of heavy industry, advanced military technology, and British imperial adventurism on the global environment. The novels of Mary Shelley, particularly *The Last Man,* provide further evidence that the destruction of the Earth's capacity to sustain human life was a vital concern of the English Romantic writers. In *The Last Man,* published in 1826, Shelley portrays an empty world in which mankind has perished as the result of a mysterious plague.[23] The novel provides no medical explanation for the spread of this fatal disease, and its mystery is an intrinsic part of its terror. Its geographical point of origin is clear; it arises in the Orient as a particularly virulent strain of an endemic disease, and it spreads to the West after a war of liberation is fought by the Greeks against the Turks. The leader of the Greeks is an Englishman, Lord Raymond, transparently modeled after Lord Byron, who likewise perished while leading an army of Greek "freedom fighters" against the evil Turkish empire. However, Mary Shelley re-imagines the death of Lord Byron, who in real life perished miserably from a tropical fever; in this novel the heroic Lord Raymond goes out in a blaze of glory as he single-handedly assaults the city of Constantinople on his black stallion and accidentally sets off an enormous explosion that levels the entire city, in an eerie foreshadowing of modern technologies of mass destruction (156). Throughout the novel, up to the very moment of his death, Lord Raymond epitomizes the arrogant masculine quest for world domination, and his dangerous charisma stands in stark contrast to the ineffectual Adrian, modeled upon Percy Shelley, who preaches an ecological ethic of non-violence, vegetarianism, and harmony with nature. The insufferably scrupulous Adrian rides a white horse as an emblem of his pacifism, and twice in the novel he manages to separate two warring factions and pacify them through the spellbinding power of his eloquence (235, 299).

Despite his high moral standards and his incessant didacticism, Adrian remains defenseless against the plague, which advances relentlessly across Asia, America, and Europe until eventually it reaches England, where it devastates the entire population. Only humans are affected by the disease; the beauty of nature is unaffected, and Shelley's narrator emphasizes the lushness of the vegetation and the abundance of the wildlife that thrives in the absence of humankind:

> Summer advanced, and, crowned with the sun's potent rays, plague shot her unerring shafts over the earth. The nations beneath their influence bowed their heads, and died. The corn that sprung up in plenty, lay in autumn rotting on the ground, while the melancholy wretch who had gone out to

gather bread for his children, lay stiff and plague-struck in the furrow. The
green woods waved their boughs majestically, while the dying were spread
beneath their shade, answering the solemn melody with inharmonious cries.
The painted birds flitted through the shades; the careless deer reposed unhurt
upon the fern—the oxen and the horses strayed from their unguarded sta-
bles, and grazed among the wheat, for death fell on man alone. (216)

The plague is personified here as a female being, as if Mother Nature herself were taking revenge upon "man alone" for his impious desecration of
the very sources of life. As the plague advances implacably across England,
it leaves only a small band of survivors. This "failing remnant" (330) gradually succumbs until the novel's narrator, Lionel Verney, emerges as the sole
survivor amid the ruined grandeurs of Rome in the year 2100. He is left
alone in this barren post-apocalyptic landscape to ponder the death of
humankind.

What is the significance of this plague that destroys all of humanity?
Although its ultimate origin is obscure and perhaps intentionally unknowable, nevertheless the novel clearly establishes that the harsh conditions of
warfare are somehow responsible for the plague's transformation from a
locally endemic disease into a lethal pandemic. It has become a critical
commonplace to compare the plague in this novel with the recent world-
wide spread of the AIDS virus, although I believe a more accurate analogy
could be drawn to the global epidemic of influenza after World War I,
which killed millions of people already weakened by the prevailing unsan-
itary conditions and wartime food shortages.[24] So too, in *The Last Man,*
there is a distinct cause-and-effect relationship between the terrible conditions of warfare and the development of a virulent strain of disease that
can wipe out entire populations.

However, Mary Shelley's understanding of disease is not based on modern germ theory, but on the theory of *miasma.* Rather than spreading by
direct personal contact, the plague in her novel is spread through the
atmosphere, the very air we breathe.[25] This spreading miasma is exacerbated by a warming of the Earth's climate that increases the plague's viru-
lence. In an uncanny foreshadowing of modern anxiety about global
warming, Shelley's narrator describes the alienating effect of an unnaturally
warm environment:

It was no consolation, that with the first winds of March the lanes were filled
with violets, the fruit trees covered with blossoms, that the corn sprung up,
and the leaves came out, forced by the unseasonable heat. We feared the

balmy air—we feared the cloudless sky, the flower-covered earth, and delightful woods, for we looked on the fabric of the universe no longer as our dwelling, but our tomb, and the fragrant land smelled to the apprehension of fear like a wide church-yard. (211)

Such feelings of alienation from the natural world seem quite familiar in our own time, as the Earth's temperature rises inexorably and the air and water are laden with invisible toxins. Thus Bill McKibben's *The End of Nature* (1990) argues that by altering the Earth's climate, human beings are ending the very idea of wildness. Not only are we threatening the long-term survival of our own species; in his view, nature as something separate from human activity has already ceased to exist.[26]

In the passage just cited, Mary Shelley examines what is meant by our "dwelling" in the global ecosystem, a context that is often taken for granted in the critical analysis of other, seemingly more immediate literary, historical, or ideological contexts. Does humankind possess the power to alter the Earth beyond recognition, to make it the "tomb" of our dreams and desires? Only at the dawn of the Industrial Revolution, at the threshold of an unprecedented increase in Britain's coal-fired production capacity, did such thoughts become thinkable. As the manufacturing cities of England disappeared into a thick haze of photochemical smog, it became possible to imagine that human activity might alter the climate and eventually destroy the Earth's ability to sustain human life. Shelley's use of the term "dwelling" points to her essentially ecological understanding of the relationship between human beings and the green world of field and forest that nourishes us. Earth is the οἶκος, or *dwelling-place,* for all living things, an insight that constitutes the conceptual core of modern ecological thought.

The Last Man may thus be regarded as a novel of environmental apocalypse, a direct precursor of modern science-fiction novels that depict an Earth depopulated by environmental catastrophe, such as George Rippey Stewart's *Earth Abides,* as well as a forerunner of nonfiction works that warn of the dire consequences of our misplaced faith in technology, such as *Silent Spring.*[27] Like Rachel Carson and many other contemporary environmental writers, Mary Shelley evinces a strong awareness of gender issues that might legitimately be termed "ecofeminist," since her apocalyptic vision of a ruined Earth emerges from a sustained critique of the patriarchal institutions that have dominated science, technology, politics, and economics since the dawn of Western civilization. *The Last Man* bears witness to the catastrophic results of a plague unleashed by the age-old masculine quest for world domination. Similarly, in *Frankenstein* (1818), the transgression of a mad (male) scientist into the traditionally female domain of generation and nurturance leads to the inadvertent creation of a violent, uncontrollable "new species," a "monster" who combines an all-too-human propensity for violence with superhuman intelligence, strength, and endurance. *Frankenstein* foreshadows the nightmare potentiality of genetic engineering in our own time, particularly in such recent scientific innovations as the creation of synthetic organisms, from Supermice to Terminator Seeds, whose ultimate effects upon the terrestrial ecosystem are impossible to predict.

Both Mary Shelley and William Blake are deeply troubled by the possibility that a global environmental disaster may result from the uncontrolled development of advanced technologies, particularly the growth of heavy industry and the deployment of military weapons of mass destruction. Blake's prophetic vision of the "dark Satanic Mills," despite its unflinching depiction of the human consequences of such reckless innovation, is accompanied by a utopian alternative to such destructive technologies: the great city of Golgonooza. Mary Shelley's *The Last Man* offers a less qualified depiction of the consequences of human intervention in global ecosystems, since it predicts the imminent extinction of all humankind. Such global annihilation, often regarded as a mere poetic fiction, bears a more urgent burden of possibility in our own era, when the inexorable destruction of the ozone layer and the accumulation of greenhouse gases threaten to make the Earth unable to sustain human life. Both Blake's visionary protest against the Industrial Revolution and Shelley's prediction of a global pandemic offer informative parallels to contemporary ecological concerns.

Were the English Romantic writers proto-ecological thinkers, as Karl Kroeber has suggested?[28] Do ecological concepts provide a useful framework for the analysis of their work? To argue in the affirmative, one would have to go beyond the trite observation that much Romantic writing celebrates the beauty of nature. Nor is it necessary to assimilate all aspects of their work to the twentieth-century science of ecology or to a distinctively modern set of concerns about environmental pollution. Yet the urgency of these concerns in our own time has helped us to see that much of their writing emerges from a desperate sense of alienation from the natural world, and expresses an anxious endeavor to re-establish a vital, sustainable relationship between humankind and the fragile planet on which we dwell. At the dawn of the third millennium, there is growing public realization that no simple technological solution can ever be devised for such intractable problems as global warming; a more systematic approach, involving fundamental changes in the modern consumer lifestyle, will be needed to address the imminent threat of global environmental catastrophe. A re-examination of the environmental concerns of the English Romantic period can provide a fresh perspective from which to view our own situation, and may well suggest possibilities of remedial intervention and progressive social action that are presently outside the mainstream of political and literary discourse.

Chapter 5

Ralph Waldo Emerson: Writing Nature

The son of a Boston Congregationalist minister, Ralph Waldo Emerson (1803-1882) did very little to distinguish himself in his first 30 years, and he showed every sign of following dutifully in his father's footsteps. He attended Boston Latin School, Harvard College, and Harvard Divinity School, he married a well-to-do merchant's daughter, and in 1829 he became pastor of Boston's Second Unitarian Church. Inwardly, however, Emerson was torn by doubts and dissatisfactions with orthodox Christian piety, exacerbated by inconsolable grief at the sudden death of his wife, Ellen Louisa Tucker, from tuberculosis at the age of 19. In 1832 he resigned from the Unitarian ministry, unable to reconcile his own conscience with "the dead forms of our forefathers."[1] Henceforth he would seek his own path of inquiry, beyond the boundaries of conventional religious belief.

Emerson spent a year traveling on the Continent and in England, where he met with several leading literary figures of the Romantic period, including William Wordsworth, Samuel Taylor Coleridge, and Thomas Carlyle. Of these three figures, Coleridge was the most directly influential upon the subsequent development of Emerson's thought. Coleridge's emphasis upon the intuitive ability of human reason to discover spiritual truth, as well as his evident affection for "all creatures great and small," struck resonant chords within Emerson's troubled, questing intellect.

Upon his return to America, Emerson found an ideal outlet for his eloquence in the Lyceum movement, a loose coalition of grassroots organizations that sponsored educational programs of visiting lecturers. Starting in 1833 and continuing for several decades, Emerson found a meaningful and socially prominent role for himself as a traveling speaker throughout New

England, holding audiences spellbound with his thoughtful, provocative lectures. Emerson used these occasions to refine and develop his ideas on a vast range of topics, and many of his most successful lectures were subsequently published, thereby establishing him as America's leading public intellectual.[2] His first significant publication was a slim, anonymous volume entitled *Nature* (1836), a redaction of several lectures into the form of an extended manifesto. This groundbreaking essay is the single most influential American statement of the Transcendentalist idea of nature. Emerson argues that we need not derive our knowledge of the world only from dusty books. Rather, through our own immediate experience of the natural world, we can "enjoy an original relation to the universe" (7). This emphasis on the primacy of individual experience, later developed in such essays as "Self-Reliance," is one of the most vital and recurrent themes in Emerson's writing, and it provided inspiration to numerous American writers in the Transcendentalist tradition, from Henry David Thoreau and Walt Whitman through John Muir and Mary Austin.

The twentieth century was considerably less receptive to Emerson's intellectual legacy. The Modernist movement, with its emphasis on skepticism and irony, provided an uncongenial literary atmosphere for Emerson's expansive optimism, while the relentless advance of scientific materialism has made it increasingly difficult for Emerson's distinctively American brand of Transcendental philosophy to be accorded a sympathetic hearing. F. O. Matthiessen's *American Renaissance* (1941), a vast, groundbreaking, and still largely definitive study of the Transcendentalist literary tradition in America, evinces a typical hostility to Emersonian idealism.[3] Matthiessen claims that Emerson "felt himself secure in the realm of the higher laws. To-day he has been overtaken by the paradox that 'The Over-Soul' generally proves unreadable" (3). Matthiessen objects to Matthew Arnold's view of Emerson as "the friend and aider of those who would live in the spirit": "Sixty years later such a judgment helps us not at all. We have witnessed altogether too many vague efforts to 'live in the spirit,' following in the ruck of transcendentalism and disappearing in the sands of the latest theosophy" (5). The underlying indictment of Emerson is clear: as an idealist philosopher of nature, Emerson is vague, dogmatic, and unreadable. Although Matthiessen devotes several chapters to a careful close reading of Emerson's work, this analysis consists mainly in a tortuous attempt to extricate a kernel of Modernist aesthetic rigor from the ruins of Emerson's Transcendentalism.

In a more recent study, *The Idea of Wilderness: From Prehistory to the Age of Ecology* (1991), Max Oelschlaeger presents an even harsher view of

Emerson's accomplishment. Oelschlaeger states that Emerson "is viewed [today] more as a popularizer of European ideas than as a progenitor of a unique philosophy. . . . Emersonian transcendentalism is moribund" (133). Oelschlaeger goes on to present a lengthy catalogue of Emerson's short-comings as a philosopher of nature:

> For Emerson consciousness is nothing more than a vehicle to carry him toward a pre-existing conclusion. *Nature* is not a philosophical inquiry but a literary exercise designed to rest a pre-established belief in God on rational, rather than scriptural, footing. For Emerson a wilderness odyssey is an occasion for the individual mind first to discover a reflection of itself (nature as a system of laws, concepts, and commodities) and then to confirm God's existence. . . . The position is conventionally anthropocentric and androcentric, enframed by a Baconian-Cartesian perspective: nature is mere putty in human hands, bestowed by God upon his most favored creation, *man* (135).

In Oelschlaeger's view, Emerson is chiefly important as a precursor to Thoreau, who had the good sense to discard Emerson's misty-eyed Transcendentalism in favor of a more rugged engagement with the brute material facts of nature. Such a harsh view of Emerson's intellectual legacy is entirely typical of twentieth-century critics, and in this case it emerges either from a failure to understand, or from a refusal to engage seriously with, Emerson's most seminal and influential ideas.

Yet, paradoxically, Emerson remains the single most widely quoted American author in the English-speaking world. Every year, like clockwork, a half-dozen of his most inspirational apothegms are trundled out for countless commencement speeches at college campuses throughout the United States. The vibrant, provocative character of his essays has become dulled by excessive familiarity. Emerson is one of the best known, and least understood, of American authors. He is utterly inaccessible to readers who dwell within the prevailing worldview of scientific materialism except as a kind of toothless grandfather figure to be publicly revered on all solemn civic occasions, and privately mocked for his naive optimism, his vague theosophy, and his ineffectual idealism.

Stanley Cavell, a keenly incisive and largely sympathetic critic of American Transcendentalism, remarks: "I take it for granted that the thinking [of Emerson and Thoreau] is unknown to the culture whose thinking they worked to found (I mean culturally unpossessed, unassumable among those who care for books, however possessed by shifting bands of individuals)."[4] The ideas of Emerson have not taken hold in contemporary American society because they frequently cannot be seen for what they are. Throughout his essays, Emerson elaborates a radical critique of the most fundamental and pervasive of American ideologies: the macroeconomic model of free-market capitalism and its microeconomic counterpart, rampant commodity fetishism. Emerson's *Nature* presents a very different understanding of "Commodity," grounded in an ecological understanding of the relationship between humankind and the natural world. This ecological worldview was derived in large part from Emerson's acquaintance with, and critical response to, the writings of Samuel Taylor Coleridge.

An Encounter with Coleridge

Emerson was an avid reader of Coleridge's works during his years of study at Harvard Divinity School; in November 1826 he borrowed the *Biographia Literaria* (1817) from the Harvard College Library.[5] As Emerson struggled with his own crisis of faith, Coleridge's *Biographia* may well have offered an attractive way out of the seemingly insuperable obstacles that beset his effort to reconcile human reason with traditional modes of religious belief. Coleridge's critique of the mechanistic philosophy of Associationism, and his presentation of a Transcendentalist alternative (largely derived from the German philosophers Immanuel Kant and Friedrich Schelling), evidently appealed to Emerson as offering a path beyond the intransigent dualities of reason and faith, science and poetry. In the climactic chapter 13 of the *Biographia,* entitled "On the Imagination, or esemplastic power," Coleridge struggles to reconcile the apparent duality of subject and object (a legacy of the Cartesian philosophy, which posited the complete separation of body and mind). From this strenuous "transcendental deduction" emerges Coleridge's famous definitions of Primary and Secondary Imagination, which especially appealed to Emerson because they offered a dynamic resolution of the impasse between human creative activity and the vast, inscrutable forces of divine Creation.

Coleridge defines the Primary Imagination as "the living Power and prime Agent of all human Perception, and as a repetition in the finite mind of the eternal act of creation in the infinite I AM."[6] As a faculty of perception, the Primary Imagination is always unconsciously at work in every human mind, actively projecting a world of external objects. This phenomenal world is not "given" for Coleridge; it must be constructed by the human mind out of the raw material of sensation. Merely by the act of perception, the "finite mind" creates a world, and in this way it repeats the original creation of the universe out of chaos by "the infinite I AM." The

Secondary Imagination is "an echo of the former," a voluntary creative process that can only occur in the self-conscious mind of the poet. According to Coleridge, "it dissolves, diffuses, dissipates, in order to re-create,"[7] first breaking the objects of perception into their basic elements, then seeking to recombine these elements in poetic discourse. On a more fully conscious level than the Primary Imagination, the Secondary Imagination produces a linguistic analogue of the divine act of creation, using words to shadow forth a microcosm.

Coleridge's definitions of Primary and Secondary Imagination allow poets to participate in the vast, world-making forces of divine Creation while still retaining their innate spontaneity and free will. In the sixth chapter of *Nature*, Emerson proposes his own definition of Imagination, as "the use which the Reason makes of the material world" (34), thus emphasizing the poet's ability to "transfigure" the objects of nature (35). Emerson further elaborates these Coleridgean concepts in the first chapter of *Nature*, where he argues that "the lover of nature is he whose inward and outward senses are still truly adjusted to each other; who has retained the spirit of infancy even into the era of manhood." This latter phrase is directly paraphrased from the *Biographia Literaria*, chapter 4, in which Coleridge claims that the character and privilege of genius is "to carry on the feelings of childhood into the powers of manhood."[8] Emerson's characteristically Romantic emphasis on infancy as a time of spontaneous, unselfconscious creativity also owes a great deal to Wordsworth's "Ode: Intimations of Immortality," which describes a six-year-old child as an "Eye among the blind" with unique powers of perception.[9] More generally, Emerson's fascination with the unconscious, intuitive roots of human creativity, and his vigorous effort to reconcile the "inward and outward senses," is built upon a dialectical method of intellectual inquiry that he learned in large part from Coleridge.

Emerson first encountered Coleridge's *Aids to Reflection* in 1827, and in a notebook entry of that year, he copied out the memorable phrase "All things strive to ascend & ascend in their striving."[10] Two years later, the first American edition of *Aids to Reflection* (Burlington, Vermont, 1829) was published with an introduction by James Marsh, followed by Marsh's edition of *The Friend* (Burlington, Vermont, 1831). Marsh's eloquent prefaces to these works were widely influential among the community of New England intellectuals who had forsaken conventional forms of religious belief.[11] To Emerson in particular, these American editions of Coleridge's works awakened his imagination to new possibilities of religious experience. In January 1830, Emerson mentions that he had read "Coleridge's

Friend with great interest; Coleridge's *Aids to Reflection* with yet deeper."[12]
In January 1830, Emerson became a subscriber to the Boston Athenaeum
Library, and the first book he ever borrowed from that extensive collection
was Coleridge's *Sibylline Leaves* (London, 1817), a comprehensive collection
of Coleridge's poetry that included, most notably, "The Rime of the
Ancient Mariner" with marginal glosses. In October 1834, Emerson bor-
rowed Coleridge's *On the Constitution of Church and State* (London, 1830)
from the Boston Atheneum.[13] Emerson eventually obtained many of
Coleridge's works for his personal library, including editions of *The Friend*
(London, 1818), *The Statesman's Manual* (Burlington, Vermont, 1832),
Biographia Literaria (New York and Boston, 1834), *Specimens of the Table-Talk*
(New York, 1835), *Letters, Conversations, and Recollections* (London, 1836),
and *Literary Remains* (London, 1836-39).[14] Such a comprehensive personal
collection bespeaks the fascination that Coleridge's works held for Emerson during the 1830s, when he was constructing the essential framework
of his distinctively American philosophy of nature.

Emerson visited Coleridge at Highgate in 1833, and his record of that
encounter provides an opportunity to fathom the intensity of Emerson's
personal response to Coleridge's intellectual legacy. Emerson made extensive notes of this visit in his journal,[15] and he elaborated these notes into a
retrospective narrative that he published 23 years later, as chapter 1 of *English Traits* (1856). Emerson opens his published account with the following
reflection: "The young scholar fancies it happiness to live with people who
can give an inside to the world, without reflecting that they are prisoners,
too, of their own thought, and cannot apply themselves to yours" (767).
Emerson's youthful sense of longing for an authentic relation to the world,
and his lingering disappointment in the reality of contact with the leading
intellects of Britain, pervade his description of his encounters with
Coleridge, Wordsworth, and Carlyle. None of these intellectual heroes can
possibly live up to the exalted expectations of the questing American
youth, and the prevailing theme of this chapter is one of disillusionment,
tinged with the ironic awareness that Emerson himself, a quarter-century
later, has now attained the popular heroic status of a Victorian Sage on
both sides of the Atlantic.

Emerson's 1833 encounter with Coleridge proves frustrating for both
parties. In Emerson's published narrative, Coleridge is enveloped by an air
of decadence; he is barely out of bed by one o'clock, and "he took snuff
freely, which presently soiled his cravat" (771). Coleridge is also belligerent,
denouncing "the folly and ignorance of Unitarianism" and attacking the

"unreasonableness" of Emerson's close friend, William Ellery Channing. When Emerson declares that he too has been "born and bred" a Unitarian, Coleridge scornfully replies, "Yes, I supposed so" (771). Yet still there remains a gleam of the underlying charisma that endowed Coleridge with the reputation of a prophetic or *magus* figure among the younger generation of British intellectuals: "he appeared, a short, thick old man with bright blue eyes and fine clear complexion" (770).[16] Avoiding the temptation to engage in religious controversy, Emerson compliments Coleridge on the success of his American publications, particularly *Aids to Reflection,* which has attracted "many readers of all religious opinions" (772), and Coleridge ends the interview on a conciliatory note by reciting some lines of his poetry.

This narrative account is notable for its uneventfulness—for what does not occur. Evidently the visit consisted mainly of Coleridge lecturing his visitor in a monologue "which was often like so many printed paragraphs in his book," and there was little opportunity for Emerson to share his own ideas with his philosophical mentor. Emerson regrets that "the visit was rather a spectacle than a conversation, of no use beyond the satisfaction of my curiosity. He was old and preoccupied and could not bend to a new companion and think with him" (773). Emerson's disappointment, and even latent contempt for Coleridge, is unmistakable here.

Yet there must be some compelling reason behind Emerson's decision to recall this visit in such minute detail more than two decades later. One incidental detail of the interview may provide a clue. Coleridge described how a picture-dealer once mistook a painting by the contemporary American artist, Washington Allston, for the work of an old master. The dealer only realized his mistake when, "still talking with his back to the canvas, [he] put up his hand and touched it, and exclaimed, 'By Heaven! this picture is not ten years old:'—so delicate and skilful was that man's touch" (772-773). Coleridge's friend Washington Allston was also part of Emerson's circle in Cambridge, Massachusetts (Allston's first wife, Ann, was the sister of William Ellery Channing), and there is evidently some ambivalence in Coleridge's praise for this American artist as comparable to an "old master." Is Allston's painting a skillful evocation of venerable techniques, or just a clever fake? Can the American artist achieve an original relation to the European tradition, or is he merely an imitator of past greatness?

The question of creative originality, especially for Americans, is central to many of Emerson's essays, from *Nature* through "Self-Reliance" and "The Poet." Throughout these essays, Emerson declares the American writer's independence from the formalism and decadence of the Old World. By covertly acknowledging the issue of creative autonomy in this account of his visit to Coleridge, Emerson countenances the terrifying possibility that all of his own published work is merely a clever imitation of his transatlantic forebears. Yet this Oedipal encounter with Coleridge, recounted years later, also functions as a kind of public exorcism. Emerson wrestles with his imaginary father figure, survives Coleridge's denunciation of his "ignorance and folly," and eventually carries away the "delicate and skilful" touch of his father's blessing. The deep psychological resonance of this encounter is apparent.

In a subsequent chapter of *English Traits,* Emerson presents a more balanced appraisal of Coleridge's lifetime accomplishment as a man of letters:

> Coleridge, a catholic mind, with a hunger for ideas, with eyes looking before and after to the highest bards and sages, and who wrote and spoke the only high criticism in his time,—is one of those who save England from the reproach of no longer possessing the capacity to appreciate what rarest wit the island has yielded. Yet the misfortune of his life, his vast attempts but most inadequate performings, failing to accomplish any one masterpiece, seems to mark the closing of an era. Even in him, the traditional Englishman was too strong for the philosopher, and he fell into *accommodations:* and, as Burke had striven to idealize the English State, so Coleridge 'narrowed his mind' in the attempt to reconcile the gothic rule and dogma of the Anglican Church, with eternal ideas. (901–902)

While Emerson differs with Coleridge on fundamental matters of religious doctrine, he nevertheless reveals a profound respect for Coleridge's "hunger for ideas" and places him among "the highest bards and sages." Elsewhere Emerson explains why he values Coleridge's work so highly: "The ambition of Coleridge in England embraced the whole problem of philosophy; to find, that is, a foundation in thought for everything that existed in fact" (1155).

Emerson admires the acumen and energy that Coleridge brought to his lifelong effort to reconcile the inward world of *thought* with the outward world of *fact*. Although he rejects Coleridge's Anglican orthodoxy, Emerson nevertheless adopts him as a central role model. Emerson inherits from Coleridge a style of inquiry, and a hunger for synthesis, that will summon him forth upon his own intellectual adventure.

Writing *Nature*

Emerson's *Nature* embarks upon a bold and somewhat quixotic attempt to remake American culture. It offers a bold critique of the emerging industrial economy and the pervasive consumer culture that was rapidly growing throughout New England. As a witness to the Industrial Revolution, Emerson was intensely aware of the astonishing advances that science and technology were making in his own lifetime. In 1871 he summed up the amazing discoveries of the modern age: "In my lifetime have been wrought five miracles,—namely, 1, the Steamboat; 2, the Railroad; 3, the Electric Telegraph; 4, the application of the Spectroscope to astronomy; 5, the Photograph;—five miracles which have altered the relations of nations to each other."[17] Emerson was correct in his assessment of the historical significance of these inventions, which did actually result in a dramatic change in the "relation of nations to each other," and which would also result in the devastation of the terrestrial environment in ways that Emerson could not possibly have imagined. The tone of this journal entry is entirely positive, and likewise in *Nature* he is generally optimistic about the future of humankind. Indeed, Emerson never expresses any concern about the large-scale environmental effects of human industrial activity. He proposes a definition of "Nature" that emphasizes its invulnerability to human alteration:

> *Nature,* in the common sense, refers to essences unchanged by man: space, the air, the river, the leaf. *Art* is applied to the mixture of his will with the same things, as in a house, a canal, a statue, a picture. But his operations taken together are so insignificant, a little chipping, baking, patching, and washing, that in an impression so grand as that of the world on the human mind, they do not vary the result. (8)

Emerson's tone here is irrepressibly optimistic: the world cannot possibly be affected by human industrial activity, because such activity is so insignificant in scale. It is simply inconceivable to Emerson that human industry might alter the very fabric of the global environment, fouling the air, polluting the rivers, and poisoning the leaves. He is oblivious to the possibility of global environmental change as the consequence of human action.[18]

However, it would be a mistake to suppose that Emerson is completely unaware of the deleterious effects of the Industrial Revolution. He is mainly concerned about the harmful effects of rampant commodity fetishism upon the human spirit. Emerson most memorably expressed his aversion to the mindless accumulation of material possessions in an ode to William Henry Channing: "Things are in the saddle, / And ride mankind."[19] In chapter 2 of *Nature,* entitled "Commodity," Emerson provides a trenchant critique of the consumerist culture that was already coming to dominate the American cityscape. He rather tendentiously defines "Commodity" in a way that excludes the products of modern industry and encompasses only those natural resources that are free and renewable:

> Under the general name of Commodity, I rank all those advantages which our senses owe to nature. . . . The misery of man appears like childish petulance, when we explore the steady and prodigal provision that has been made for his support and delight on this green ball which floats him through the heavens. What angels invented these splendid ornaments, this ocean of air above, this ocean of water beneath, this firmament of earth between? this zodiac of lights, this tent of dropping clouds, this striped coat of climates, this fourfold year? Beasts, fire, water, stones, and corn serve him. The field is at once his floor, his work-yard, his play-ground, and his bed. (12)

In this passage, Emerson evokes all the global "commodities" that can never be owned by individuals, or even by nations, as private property: air, ocean, stars, climates, seasons. He thereby implicitly rejects the crude capitalist model of commodity as the consumption of natural resources, and explores instead what a modern ecologist might term "coevolution": the mutual adaptation of organisms to their environment, and the Earth's corresponding adaptation to the organisms that inhabit it. According to this ecological view, the individual organism, regarded by conventional science as existing in a relationship of causality with its environment, needs to be completed by what Kant calls the category of "community": the simultaneous mutual conditioning of many agents in a total system.[20] Whether this mutual adaptation is conceived in cybernetic terms of "feedback loops," or through Wordsworth's more ineffable notion that "the external World is fitted to the Mind" ("Home at Grasmere," 821), Emerson's concept of "Commodity" clearly foreshadows the Gaia Hypothesis, whereby "this green ball which floats him through the heavens" is a single self-reproducing organism, modified over billions of years by living things as a habitat for their own survival.[21]

Emerson's conception of the entire terrestrial globe as a complex dynamic ecosystem is more fully developed in the following passage from "Commodity":

> Nature, in its ministry to man, is not only the material, but also the process and the result. All the parts incessantly work into each other's hands for the profit of man. The wind sows the seed; the sun evaporates the sea; the wind blows the vapor to the field; the ice, on the other side of the planet, condenses rain on this; the rain feeds the plant; the plant feeds the animal; and thus the endless circulations of the divine charity nourish man. (12)

Once again, Emerson reappropriates the terminology of the marketplace to support his emerging conception of the global ecosystem. By "the profit of man" Emerson means instruction, not mere financial gain. He asserts that "the endless circulations of the divine charity nourish man" not only by growing edible crops, but also by providing mankind with the edifying spectacle of the wind, the weather, and the seasons. All of these interrelated natural cycles provide food for thought, nourishment to the awakened intellect.

Emerson's understanding of nature might indeed be regarded as anthropocentric, since all of the world's activity is seen to revolve around the human species as a privileged observer. But Emerson does not thereby fall under the same indictment as those ruthless despoilers of the American landscape who were hunting the buffalo, the wolf, and the grizzly bear into virtual extinction. Emerson's vision of America is pastoral and Arcadian; like Thomas Jefferson, he imagines a rural landscape inhabited by small farmers whose work is in harmony with the land and the seasons, and whose sense of community is expanded to include "the waving of the boughs in the storm" (11) and the presence of wild creatures that dwell in the surrounding forests. Emerson's taste for the wild has not often been remarked, but the theme of *wildness* runs almost as strongly through his work as it does in Thoreau's. For Emerson, wildness is a spontaneous quality of human perception, not just an attribute of the thing perceived: "In the presence of nature, a wild delight runs through the man, in spite of real sorrows" (10). Indeed, in his introduction to *Nature,* Emerson advocates the wilderness as a place where he can dwell most truly in harmony with his surroundings:

> I am the lover of uncontained and immortal beauty. In the wilderness, I find something more dear and connate than in streets or villages. In the tranquil landscape, and especially in the distant line of the horizon, man beholds somewhat as beautiful as his own nature. (10)

Emerson develops his conception of wilderness more fully in the essay "Spiritual Laws," published in *Essays: First Series* (1841). He argues that human language, because of its "rigid names," is inadequate to capture the "fluid consciousness" of a mind attuned to the presence of wild nature: "We judge of a man's wisdom by his hope, knowing that the perception of the inexhaustibleness of nature is an immortal youth. The wild fertility of nature is felt in comparing our rigid names and reputations with our fluid consciousness" (308). For Emerson, as later for Thoreau, the "wild fertility" of nature offers a challenge to the human imagination and a rebuke to the fixity of conventional names and logical categories.

Emerson's interest in nature is not mercenary or material; it is spiritual and symbolic. The fourth chapter of *Nature,* "Language," develops his understanding of the relationship between words and "natural facts." Emerson advances three main propositions:

1. Words are signs of natural facts.
2. Particular natural facts are symbols of particular spiritual facts.
3. Nature is the symbol of spirit. (20)

These three propositions no longer command universal assent in the secular and skeptical modern age, when the term "spirit" can only be employed in quotation marks by academic writers. Yet Emerson's argument is worthy of serious attention as an early American example of *ecolinguistics,* a discipline that analyzes the structure and historical development of language in its environmental context. Emerson is particularly fascinated by the etymology of words that express "a moral or intellectual fact," arguing that every such word "if traced to its root, is found to be borrowed from some material appearance" (20). He cites several examples:

> *Right* means *straight; wrong* means *twisted. Spirit* primarily means *wind; transgression,* the crossing of a *line; supercilious,* the *raising of the eyebrow.* We say the *heart* to express emotion, the *head* to denote thought; and *thought* and *emotion* are words borrowed from sensible things, now appropriated to spiritual nature. (20)

In most of these examples, an abstract noun is shown to have its origin in the name of a concrete material object. Although Emerson does not specify the etymologies of *thought* and *emotion,* he undoubtedly has particular etymologies in mind. The etymology of *emotion* would be quite evident to any educated person of his time; the word is derived from the Latin roots *ex* + *movere,* meaning "to move forth." The implied etymology of *thought* would not have been so obvious to Emerson's readers, partly because the Germanic roots of English words were not well understood, even by well-educated people, in his day; and also because the word *thought* does not in fact derive from a concrete noun.[22] But Emerson may have intended an etymology proposed by the English linguist Horne Tooke, who derived the word *think* from the word *thing*.[23] If Horne Tooke's etymology is the one that Emerson has in mind here, then by implication *thoughts* are the traces left by *things* on the human mind, and the historical derivation of the word *thought* provides a clue to the origin of *thinking* as a human activity. Emerson does suggest that there is a close connection between *thoughts* and *things* at the origin of language, and in the process by which language is acquired by children:

> Most of the process by which this transformation is made, is hidden from us in the remote time when language was framed; but the same tendency may be daily observed in children. Children and savages use only nouns or names of things, which they convert into verbs, and apply to analogous mental acts. (20)

According to Emerson, the "names of things" are applied by children and "savages" to "analogous mental acts," thus providing a window into "the remote time when language was framed." The process of language acquisition by children provides evidence for the origin of language: linguistic ontogeny recapitulates phylogeny. Such an intense curiosity about the primitive origins of language is entirely characteristic of the English Romantic writers, particularly Wordsworth, Coleridge, and Shelley, but Emerson gives these traditional inquiries an ecolinguistic turn by devoting his attention to the various ways in which the historical development of language is conditioned by our terrestrial environment.

Throughout the chapter on "Language," Emerson examines how the entire human repertoire of abstract concepts is derived from concrete natural phenomena. Borrowing from Coleridge a Romantic conception of the symbol, he argues that "every natural fact is a symbol of some spiritual fact."[24] He provides several examples:

> An enraged man is a lion, a cunning man is a fox, a firm man is a rock, a learned man is a torch. A lamb is innocence; a snake is subtle spite; flowers express to us the delicate affections. Light and darkness are our familiar expression for knowledge and ignorance; and heat for love. Visible distance behind and before us, is respectively our image of memory and hope. (20-21)

Emerson is not merely arguing that nature provides handy images for preexistent mental concepts; rather, he suggests that these concepts, and the words that express them, are originally derived from human experience in the natural world. The underlying paradigm at work here is one of *coevolution* (although not in a Darwinian sense): Emerson seeks to demonstrate that natural phenomena and the human repertoire of concepts mirror each other because each has developed in response to the other.[25] (This process might be described as a feedback loop that results in a good "fit" between human language and the phenomenal world.) The human mind not only *attributes* significance to natural objects; it is also capable of *deriving* significance from these objects:

> Have mountains, and waves, and skies, no significance but what we consciously give them, when we employ them as emblems of our thoughts? The world is emblematic. Parts of speech are metaphors, because the whole of nature is a metaphor of the human mind. The laws of moral nature answer to those of matter as face to face in a glass. (24)

Emerson is exploring the significance of the fact that there exists a virtually exact correspondence between natural phenomena (mountains, waves, and skies) and the cognitive repertoire that is mapped out in human language. In this sense, "the whole of nature is a metaphor of the human mind." He goes on to suggest that "there is a necessity in spirit to manifest itself in material forms," and thus material objects may be considered as *scoriae* (scars or traces) of "the substantial thoughts of the Creator" (25).

But why should this be the case? Is there some underlying reason for the evident "harmony" between words and things? Emerson shies away from easy answers to this question; indeed, he acknowledges that the words we use to resolve this question are themselves metaphorical:

> This doctrine is abstruse, and though the images of "garment," "scoriae," "mirror," &c., may stimulate the fancy, we must summon the aid of subtler and more vital expositors to make it plain. . . . A life in harmony with nature, the love of truth and of virtue, will purge the eyes to understand her text. By degrees we may come to know the primitive sense of the permanent objects of nature, so that the world shall be to us an open book, and every form significant of its hidden life and final cause. (25)

Emerson concedes that the words we use to describe the "fit" between human cognition and natural phenomena are themselves unstable, shifting, and derived from the very phenomena that we wish to describe. For this reason, it is hard to gain sufficient "leverage" to grapple with the problem.

Emerson's proposed solution, that there is a "Creator" who generates appearances in accord with our mind's ability to perceive them, is not likely to find many adherents in the contemporary world. But his statement of the essential problem, and his keen awareness of the obstacles that any candid investigator will face in coming to terms with it, remains definitive for all subsequent inquiry.

Emerson makes a fundamental advance in the domain of ecolinguistics by his acknowledgment of the fact that human language has evolved in a world of natural phenomena. For this reason, our conceptual repertoire is not the purely abstract construct of the autonomous intellectual agent posited by Kant and Descartes; rather, it is the linguistic toolbox of organic beings in daily contact with mountains, waves, and skies. Nor is this conceptual repertoire a static and eternal set of divine Ideas; it is constantly changing and evolving in response to new environmental stimuli. Emerson elucidates the process by which powerful minds generate new concepts:

> The poet, the orator, bred in the woods, whose senses have been nourished by their fair and appeasing changes, year after year, without design and without heed,—shall not lose their lesson altogether, in the roar of cities or the broil of politics. Long hereafter, amidst agitation and terror in national councils,—in the hour of revolution,—these solemn images shall reappear in their morning lustre, as fit symbols and words of the thoughts which the passing events shall awaken. At the call of a noble sentiment, again the woods wave, the pines murmur, the river rolls and shines, and the cattle low upon the mountains, as he saw and heard them in his infancy. And with these forms, the spells of persuasion, the keys of power are put into his hands. (23)

With this eloquent evocation of the process of linguistic evolution, Emerson places himself firmly in the position of advocating a dynamic approach to the problem of *adequation* between words and things. We were not born knowing how to express the concepts that structure the possibility of engagement with our surroundings; rather, new concepts are born in the struggle of human language to encompass new images, new contingencies of perception in the phenomenal world.

Emerson's dynamic conception of the relation between language and cognition is expressed in a memorable paragraph that concludes the chapter "Language":

> A new interest surprises us, whilst, under the view now suggested, we contemplate the fearful extent and multitude of objects; since "every object

rightly seen, unlocks a new faculty of the soul." That which was unconscious truth, becomes, when interpreted and defined in an object, a part of the domain of knowledge,—a new weapon in the magazine of power. (25)

This description of the process by which knowledge is generated out of experience is intrinsically ecological, since it draws upon the relationship between the inquiring intellect and the "fearful extent and multitude of objects" among which it finds itself. Emerson derives from Coleridge's *Biographia Literaria* the notion that "truth soon changes by domestication into power," and from *Aids to Reflection* he gleans the apothegm that "every object rightly seen, unlocks a new faculty of the soul."[26] This latter phrase epitomizes the innovative ecolinguistic approach that Emerson has developed to investigate the problem of human cognition. Our daily encounter with the world elicits a shock of recognition; the human mind is surprisingly well-equipped to cope with objects that we have never seen before. Merely by writing about nature, Emerson is writing *Nature* as a linguistic toolbox for inquiring spirits.

A Transparent Eye-Ball

Throughout his essays, Emerson employs the faculty of sight as something more than a simple analogy for the faculty of human reason. One of the most memorable passages in *Nature* describes an epiphanic moment of encounter with the natural world:

> Crossing a bare common, in snow puddles, at twilight, under a clouded sky, without having in my thoughts any occurrence of special good fortune, I have enjoyed a perfect exhilaration. I am glad to the brink of fear. In the woods, too, a man casts off his years, as the snake his slough, and at what period soever of life, is always a child. In the woods, is perpetual youth. Within these plantations of God, a decorum and sanctity reign, a perennial festival is dressed, and the guest sees not how he should tire of them in a thousand years. In the woods, we return to reason and faith. There I feel that nothing can befall me in life,—no disgrace, no calamity, (leaving me my eyes,) which nature cannot repair. Standing on the bare ground,—my head bathed by the blithe air, and uplifted into infinite space,—all mean egotism vanishes. I become a transparent eye-ball; I am nothing; I see all; the currents of the Universal Being circulate through me; I am part or particle of God. (10)

The signature motif of a transparent eye-ball is one of the best-known images in all of Emerson's writing, and it has sometimes been taken out of context to suggest that Emerson somehow relies exclusively upon the faculty of sight to provide inspiration and insight into the inner workings of the natural world. Taken in context, however, it is quite evident that Emerson intends the image of the transparent eye-ball in a much more comprehensive way; indeed, he deplores the barren facticity that inhabits most "normal" adult perception:

> To speak truly, few adult persons can see nature. Most persons do not see the sun. At least they have a very superficial seeing. The sun illuminates only the eye of the man, but shines into the eye and heart of the child. The lover of nature is he whose inward and outward senses are still truly adjusted to each other; who has retained the spirit of infancy even into the era of manhood. (10)

For Emerson, the act of seeing is not merely informative, but transformative. It enables the "eye and heart of the child" to be opened, illuminated, and gradually instructed by the appearances of nature. So too, the "transparent eye-ball" of Emerson as it crosses the bleak common at the center of Concord, or roams free in the surrounding woods, derives more than crude sensory data from the encounter. In a subsequent chapter of *Nature*, the implications of such "transparency" are more fully described: "For the universe becomes transparent, and the light of higher laws than its own, shines through it" (25). For Emerson, the figure of "transparency" is bound up with the enduring philosophical question of how the "inward and outward senses are adjusted to each other." Only in certain rare visionary moments can such an "adjustment" of inner and outer senses seem transparent or obvious; at other times even the most transcendental writer must struggle to find the connection between outward phenomena and the inner domain of self-consciousness, the "ME" and the "NOT-ME" (8).

The famous motif of the transparent eye-ball emerges from Emerson's struggle to resolve the intractable dualism of body and mind that Western philosophy inherited from Descartes. In his effort to overcome this dichotomy, and to discover "the analogy that marries matter and Mind" (26), Emerson delved deeply in the prose works of Coleridge, finding there the tools he needed to develop an alternative conception of the place of humankind in the phenomenal world. Most important to Emerson's philosophical quest were Coleridge's *Aids to Reflection* and *The Friend,* both of which engage in an extended critique of Descartes and the entire philosophical tradition that underlies the classical methods of Western science. Coleridge heaps scorn upon "the utter emptiness and unmeaningness of the vaunted Mechanico-corpuscular Philosophy" (*Aids to Reflection,* 398), and he offers an alternative worldview that offered precisely the intellectual framework and the specialized terminology that Emerson needed to articulate his own distinctively Transcendental conception of Nature.

One of the most important ideas that Emerson derived from Coleridge was the distinction of Reason and Understanding (which Coleridge had derived in turn from Kant and Schelling). In a chapter of *The Friend* entitled "Reason and Understanding," Coleridge develops an elaborate distinction between these two faculties of human cognition. He defines the Understanding as a mental faculty "by which we generalize and arrange the phenomena of perception: that faculty, the functions of which contain the rules and constitute the possibility of outward Experience" (1:157). Reason, on the other hand, is "the mind's eye" (1:158), a phrase that Coleridge derives from Shakespeare's *Hamlet* (I.ii.150). Coleridge is well aware of the intellectual history of the eye as an image for various modes of cognitive experience. In his "Essays on the Principles of Method," appended as a conclusion to the 1818 edition of *The Friend,* Coleridge describes his lifelong aspiration "to attain that *singleness of eye,* with which *the whole body shall be full of light*" (1:512), citing a phrase from the New Testament (Matthew 6.22). Such "singleness of eye" will assist in resolving the fundamental question that haunts Coleridge as much as it will later haunt Emerson:"Whether there be a correspondent reality, whether the Knowing of the Mind has its correlative in the Being of Nature" (1:512). The difficult passage between Knowing and Being can only be navigated with the aid of Reason, regarded by Coleridge in more than a merely figurative sense as "the mind's eye."

In developing his conception of Reason, Coleridge emphasizes the quality of *transparency* that distinguishes it from the closely related faculty of Understanding. Coleridge develops this distinction by means of an analogy between a piece of steel (the Understanding) and a piece of plate glass (the Reason):

> We will add one other illustration to prevent any misconception, as if we were dividing the human soul into different essences, or ideal persons. In this piece of steel I acknowledge the properties of hardness, brittleness, high polish, and the capability of forming a mirror. I find all these likewise in the plate glass of a friend's carriage; but in addition to all these, I find the quality of *transparency,* or the power of transmitting as well as reflecting the rays of light. (1:157; emphasis added.)

The quality of transparency is thus an essential feature that distinguishes the faculty of Reason from the more mundane and autonomic faculty of Understanding. Coleridge elsewhere uses the concept of transparency to describe the ecstatic vision of an illiterate person who has just learned to read the Bible: "The words become *transparent,* and he sees them as though he saw them not" (1:513; emphasis added). Not only the Bible, but also the Book of Nature can elicit such ecstatic vision. In his "Sonnet to the River Otter," Coleridge evokes the perspective of a child who looks through clear water to see the "bedded sand that vein'd with various dyes / Gleam'd through thy bright *transparence!*" (10-11; emphasis added). In this sonnet, the quality of transparence enables the hidden dimension of natural objects to emerge into human awareness, specifically the intense awareness of a child peering into the shimmering depths of a wild, free-flowing river.[27]

In *Aids to Reflection,* Coleridge contrasts the astonishing powers of the human eye, considered as an integral part of the body, with the repulsive appearance of an eye as it might appear as a detached organ during an autopsy:

> Look steadily at it—as it might lie on the Marble Slab of a dissecting Room. . . . Behold it, handle it, with its various accompaniments or constituent parts, of Tendon, Ligament, Membrane, Blood-vessel, Gland, Humors; its Nerves of Sense, of Sensation, and of Motion. Alas! All these names, like that of the Organ itself, are so many Anachronisms, figures of Speech, to express that which has been: as when the Guide points with his finger to a heap of stones, and tells the Traveller, "That is Babylon, or Persepolis."—Is this cold Jelly "the Light of the Body?" Is this the Micranthropos in the marvellous Microcosm? (396)

With a disgusting emphasis on physiological detail, Coleridge asserts that the detached human eye is nothing but a mass of "cold Jelly." Only by considering its function as a living organ can we begin to understand its role within the integral structure of the human organism. Coleridge uses the example of the human eye to demonstrate his more general point about the dynamic nature of organic structures:

> But the particles that constitute the *size,* the visibility of an organic structure are in perpetual flux. They are to the combining and constitutive Power as the pulses of air to the Voice of a Discourser; or of one who sings a roundelay. The same words may be repeated; but in each second of time the articulated air hath passed away, and each act of articulation appropriates and

gives momentary form to a new and other portion. As the column of blue smoke from a cottage chimney in the breathless Summer Noon, or the stedfast-seeming Cloud on the edge-point of a Hill in the driving air-current, which momentarily condensed and recomposed is the common phantom of a thousand successors;—such is the flesh, which our *bodily* eyes transmit to us. (397-398)

Coleridge eloquently evokes the process by which a living organism can replace every cell of its material body and yet retain the same identity, the same living structure. Human bodies, in this respect, are like standing waves on the flowing surface of a river. The inherent dynamism of this view of organic structure is fundamentally in accord with twentieth-century biology, and it offered Emerson a plausible alternative to the prevailing Cartesian view of animals as mindless machines, moving by clockwork like wind-up toys. Coleridge's *Aids to Reflection* thus provided Emerson with a suggestive model for the way that the human organism (and specifically, the human eye) could interact with its surroundings while yet retaining a distinct sense of individual autonomy.

Emerson's "transparent eye-ball" coalesces these disparate Coleridgean themes into a single resonant image. In the context of Emerson's own struggle to devise an alternative to the dominant ideology of American capitalism, this image provided him with an effective means to articulate the distinctive quality of his own vision of the ideal relationship between people and their dwelling-places. Emerson's vision is post-humanistic in the sense that it does not take for granted that "man is the measure of all things" or that the world exists merely for human consumption. Rather, Emerson seeks to articulate ways in which a dynamic and sustainable relationship can be attained between human beings and the landscapes they inhabit. As "a transparent eye-ball" roaming the forests and fields of his native ground, Emerson projects himself as an Everyman figure, possessing a heightened awareness to which any of his readers might aspire. "Crossing a bare common, in snow puddles, at twilight, under a clouded sky," this protagonist loses his individual selfhood, only to discover a much more expansive sense of identity: "I am nothing; I see all; the currents of the Universal Being circulate through me; I am part or particle of God" (10). More than merely a vague mystical utterance, this famous passage articulates a deep sense of kinship between individual human beings and the "currents of the Universal Being" that circulate through them. By attributing the immanence of such divine energies to the natural world, Emerson seeks to redeem the American landscape from the merely utilitarian conception of its possibilities that was rampant in his own time (and still endures today). If Emerson's views seem quaintly ineffectual to modern readers, it is largely a consequence of the continuing cultural dominance of secular humanism, even among the most sophisticated intellectuals of our own time.

Transcendentalism and Its Discontents

Contemporary reviewers of Emerson's *Nature* were shocked by its impiety. They frequently complained of its obscurity, and they deplored Emerson's steadfast resistance to the onward march of "human progress." In a fairly typical review essay of 1838, for example, Samuel Gilman dismissed Emerson as

> a writer, who seems to entertain no clear and definite principles,—who bewilders his hearers amidst labyrinths of beautiful contradictions; who floats around among beautiful and impalpable abstractions, and who is but the second or third hand receiver of ideas and visions, that have already been more than once exploded in the course of human progress, and could never get a foothold in this matter-of-fact world.[28]

Worse than this, Emerson even had the audacity to mention "sex."[29] Modern readers are repelled by other aspects of the essay: its circumlocutions, its grandiloquence, its recondite allusions, and its outdated science. Worst of all, to a modern reader, is its frequent appeal to the immanent divine energy of the natural world. This latter aspect of Emerson's *Nature* is known as its "Transcendentalism" and is dreaded by all American college students. When these students have been particularly obstreperous, they are required to write a 1,000-word essay on the puzzling question, "What is Transcendentalism?" They knot their brows, they festoon their papers with lengthy quotations, and still they cannot get it right.

Emerson could not quite get it right, either. (This should be comforting news to many American college students.) Although Emerson derived his understanding of the term "transcendental" mainly from Coleridge (with a little help from Carlyle), who in turn derived it from Immanuel Kant, each of these writers shaped and adapted the term to suit their own particular purposes, and by the time it reached Emerson it was bent almost completely out of its original shape. For Kant the term "transcendental" referred to the *a priori* categories of the human understanding, which are presupposed by all experience; for Schelling it referred more ambitiously to the dialectical process by which the Absolute is manifested in nature and history. Coleridge adopted Kant's usage, but gave it a linguistic turn: Coleridge revised Kant's doctrine of time and space (the "transcendental aesthetic") by pointing out that even these supposedly immediate intuitions are actually constituted by the structure of language.[30] Carlyle, in contrast, emphasized the heroic role of the human will in the emergence of transcendental ideas, in a foreshadowing of Friedrich Nietzsche's ominous Will to Power.

Emerson had very little direct access to the German transcendental philosophers, and he probably misunderstood (or willfully misappropriated) what he learned from Coleridge and Carlyle. In Emerson's various attempts to define Transcendentalism, it often sounds more like a choice of lifestyle than a well-defined ideology. Moreover, Emerson was only one of a large, contentious group of American Transcendentalists, each of whom had a distinct conception of what the term ought to mean. Like many other literary movements, Transcendentalism was defined more clearly by an intuitive sense of group membership than by a rigorous or even definable set of philosophical tenets.

And yet there is something appealing about Emerson's attempts at a definition. Setting aside any attempt at logical rigor, he embraces the rough-hewn spontaneity of the American marketplace of ideas, tossing out a welter of evocative and gnomic utterances in the hope that some of them will stick in the reader's consciousness. In this respect, his published essays recapitulate the rhetorical structure of his public lectures, where the performative aspect of each sentence and paragraph mattered more than the logic of transition among topics or the overall coherence of the argument. Emerson's well-known statement that "A foolish consistency is the hobgoblin of little minds" (265) should be understood in this context. Apparently contradictory utterances may nevertheless lead the listener (or reader) to a deeper understanding, partly because language is inadequate to the task of expressing higher truth, and also because the truths of Reason are dialectical and therefore incapable of expression except through paired sets of opposing assertions (or logical antinomies).

Emerson labors to define his philosophical stance most engagingly in "The Transcendentalist," a lecture read at the Masonic Temple in Boston, in January 1842. Emerson expounds the Transcendental moralism of the German philosophers Jacobi and Fichte from Coleridge's translation, and he correctly attributes the origin of the term "transcendental" to Immanuel Kant, explaining that Kant demonstrated "that there was a very important class of ideas, or imperative forms, which did not come by experience, but through which experience was acquired; that these were intuitions of the mind itself; and he denominated them *Transcendental* forms" (198). Emerson makes the important qualification that "there is no pure Transcendentalist" (199), no cult of true believers, just an inquiring community of seekers after truth. Emerson is averse to dogmatism of any kind. The stance of the Transcendentalist is for Idealism against Materialism, but beyond that basic outlook there remains much leeway to develop an original response to the panoply of experience in the phenomenal world.

Emerson further elucidates the importance of nature to the Transcendentalists:

> Nature is transcendental, exists primarily, necessarily, ever works and advances, yet takes no thought for the morrow. Man owns the dignity of the life which throbs around him in chemistry, and tree, and animal, and in the involuntary functions of his own body; yet he is balked when he seeks to fling himself into this enchanted circle, where all is done without degradation. Yet genius and virtue predict in man the same absence of private ends, and of condescension to circumstances, united with every trait and talent of beauty and power. (198)

Emerson claims that human consciousness is "balked" when we try to enter fully into the "dignity of life" that surrounds us, because our self-awareness makes it difficult, or even impossible, to experience this world in the same integral way that we could when we were children, or as animals can in their normal activities. Indeed, Emerson exalts the unselfconsciousness of animals as they exist in their habitats:

> We have had many harbingers and forerunners; but of a purely spiritual life, history has afforded no example. . . . Only in the instinct of the lower animals, we find the suggestion of the methods of it, and something higher than our understanding. The squirrel hoards nuts, and the bee gathers honey, without knowing what they do, and they are thus provided for without selfishness or disgrace. (197-198)

Emerson's post-humanistic stance is quite apparent here. He rejects the Cartesian view of animals as unthinking machines, and he avoids the common dismissal of their mental life as merely instinctual. Both squirrels and bees gather resources for the future, but in Emerson's view, they do so without calculation or planning. For this reason he presents the squirrel and bee as instances of a "purely spiritual life" that is lived without selfishness, disgrace, or mercenary forethought. By living in the pure immediacy of the present moment, such animals can provide humans with exemplary modes of existence in harmony with the natural world. In this sense, Transcendentalism is a mode of ecological thought. It beholds the Earth as a community of living things, and it advocates an open, inquiring mode of awareness for all human beings. Nature exists for its own purposes, and if approached in a spirit of humility, it can teach us lessons. Nature does not exist merely for the purpose of human consumption.

Emerson's fundamental importance to the formation of an authentically ecological conception of the natural world has been obscured by generations of commentators who refuse to take seriously his challenge to conventional ways of understanding the place of humankind in the natural world. If such learned critics as F. O. Matthiessen and Max Oelschlaeger regard American Transcendentalism as "moribund," and if they dismiss Emerson's essays as vague, dogmatic, and unreadable, it is perhaps the unfortunate consequence of their own dogmatism, their own reluctance to critically examine the culturally dominant premises of scientific materialism. Oelschlaeger characterizes Emerson's position as "conventionally anthropocentric and androcentric, enframed by a Baconian-Cartesian perspective: nature is mere putty in human hands, bestowed by God upon his most favored creation, *man*" (135). But this description of Emerson's outlook is fundamentally inaccurate. Emerson does not regard man as the measure of all things, nor does he accept the materialist worldview that is the legacy of Bacon and Descartes. Rather, he advocates a post-humanistic philosophy that makes Nature, rather than the quaint traditions of human culture, the source of all worthwhile knowledge and the repository of all enduring ethical values.

Emerson's philosophical outlook has been widely misunderstood, and frequently ignored, because it poses a direct challenge to the normal American way of doing business. In "Thoughts on Modern Literature," an essay published in *The Dial* (October 1840), Emerson frankly admits that his personal views are anathema to business-as-usual:

> A selfish commerce and government have caught the eye and usurped the hand of the masses. It is not to be contested that selfishness and the senses write the laws under which we live, and the street seems to be built, and the men and women in it moving not in reference to pure and grand ends, but rather to very short and sordid ones. . . . But we say that these low customary ways are not all that survives in human beings. (1158)

Emerson is well aware that Transcendentalism represents a radical departure from the ordinary ways of American life. He further acknowledges that this outlook is still inchoate, an aspirational alternative to a "selfish commerce and government" that is gradually emerging into consciousness as the result of extended contact with "the presence of nature":

> There is that in us which mutters, and that which groans, and that which triumphs, and that which aspires. There are facts on which men of the world superciliously smile, which are worth all their trade and politics, the impulses, namely, which drive young men into gardens and solitary places, and cause extravagant gestures, starts, distortions of the countenance, and passionate exclamations; sentiments, which find no aliment or language for themselves on the wharves, in courts, or market, but which are soothed by silence, by darkness, by the pale stars, and the presence of nature. (1158)

Although such youthful enthusiasm may be easily mocked and satirized, there is no denying the exultant tone of Emerson's early essays. His philosophical outlook is intentionally provisional, unsystematic, because it is still a work-in-progress, open to subsequent development in the light of later experience. In a memorable phrase, he declares that all of American literature is in the "optative mood":

> Our American literature and spiritual history are, we confess, in the optative mood; but whoso knows these seething brains, these admirable radicals, these unsocial worshippers, these talkers who talk the sun and moon away, will believe that this heresy cannot pass away without leaving its mark. ("The Transcendentalist," 199-200)

Transcendentalism is a "heresy" because it calls into question all of the fundamental premises of "common sense" upon which American commerce and government are based. It is essentially an ecological worldview because it uses "Nature" as the sole criterion by which to judge the utility and ethical value of all human activity.

If Emerson's views are to be accurately understood, and their relevance to the development of ecological thought adequately assessed, then the Transcendentalist philosophy will need to be regarded as something substantive and effectual, not mere otherworldliness. In "Thoughts on Modern Literature," Emerson characterizes the most admirable part of Goethe's outlook as "deep realism":

> With the sharpest eye for form, color, botany, engraving, medals, persons, and manners, he [Goethe] never stopped at surface, but pierced the purpose of a thing, and studied to reconcile that purpose with his own being. What he

could so reconcile was good; what he could not, was false. Hence a certain greatness encircles every fact he treats; for to him it has a soul, an eternal reason why it was so, and not otherwise. This is the secret of that *deep realism,* which went about among all objects he beheld, to find the cause why they must be what they are. (1162; emphasis added)

Such "deep realism" is quite similar in its outlook and methodology to the "true and original realism" advocated by Coleridge.[31] It examines the conceptual basis for all phenomena, resisting merely conventional explanations and traditional understandings. In this sense it is indeed a "radical" outlook.

As he developed his mature philosophy of nature, Emerson became ever more fully aware of the dynamic and cyclical processes that underlie the appearances of the natural world. In his essay on "Nature" in *Essays: Second Series* (1844), Emerson expresses his sense of the cyclical process that underlies all appearances:

The divine circulations never rest nor linger. Nature is the incarnation of a thought, and turns to a thought again, as ice becomes water and gas. The world is mind precipitated, and the volatile essence is forever escaping again into the state of free thought. (555)

For Emerson the stance of idealism did not lead away from concrete experience; rather, it provided him a way of conceptualizing the way that matter can exist in a dynamic state, through the exchange of information. Organisms are not static forms, but bundles of organized chemical processes fueled by the pure energy of light. Emerson's best treatment of ecological process occurs in an essay on "Farming" published in 1858:

Science has shown the great circles in which Nature works; the manner in which marine plants balance the marine animals, as the land plants supply the oxygen which the animals consume, and the animals the carbon which the plants absorb. These activities are incessant. Nature works on a method of *all for each and each for all.* The strain that is made at one point bears upon every arch and foundation of the structure. There is a perfect solidarity.[32]

Emerson evinces a thoughtful understanding of the carbon cycle as an instance of the way that organisms cycle nutrients through their bodies in a vast, interdependent ecosystem that encompasses both the terrestrial and the marine environment. Such a detailed and rigorous understanding of the ecosystem concept is entirely compatible with Emerson's Transcendentalist outlook; indeed, such holistic thought became more accessible to him because he was well-versed in the Romantic tradition and its ecological understanding of the natural world. Emerson melded the available scientific theories into a distinctive worldview, itself an evolving bundle of concepts rather than a rigid dogma, still generally known (and widely misunderstood, even by ostensibly sympathetic readers) as American Transcendentalism.

Emerson's most sympathetic reader, and his most independent-minded American disciple, was Henry David Thoreau, the subject of my next chapter. Although Thoreau periodically denounced certain of the more ethereal elements of Emerson's philosophy, he nevertheless possessed a clear and unrivaled understanding of the ecosystem concept, and he amplified Emerson's post-humanistic outlook to such an extent that Emerson himself was forced to disavow the misanthropic tendencies of his errant disciple. With their commonalities and their differences, Emerson and Thoreau represent the divergent possibilities of ecological thought in America at the mid-nineteenth century.

Chapter 6

Henry David Thoreau:
Life in the Woods

Born in Concord, Massachusetts, Henry David Thoreau (1817-62) came of age in an era of flourishing national self-confidence and booming commercial prosperity. His father was the proprietor of a pencil factory, a moderately successful enterprise that provided the means for his son to attend the prestigious Concord Academy and Harvard College. A slightly better-than-average student, Thoreau was invited at his graduation from Harvard in 1837 to give a commencement address on "The Commercial Spirit of Modern Times." He shocked his audience by denouncing the mindless pursuit of affluence, advocating instead a lifelong "Sabbath of the affections and the soul,—in which to range this widespread garden, and drink in the soft influences and sublime revelations of nature."[1] Thoreau heeded his own advice and never held a steady job or pursued a professional career, opting instead to earn what little he needed to support himself through occasional odd jobs, which included land surveying, carpentry, gardening, and house-sitting for his closest friend, Ralph Waldo Emerson. Thoreau aspired to become a published author, and his reluctance to pursue a conventional career stemmed in part from his need to carve out time and space for his writing. His ultimate retreat from the world occurred in 1845-47, when he persuaded Emerson to let him build a cabin on some land that he owned on the shores of Walden Pond, a deep, clear, spring-fed lake just two miles south of Concord. During the 26 months that Thoreau lived at Walden Pond, he wrote the two books that were published in his lifetime. The first of these, *A Week on the Concord and Merrimack Rivers* (1849), was harshly reviewed by contemporary critics, who found it tedious and digressive, and who were incensed by the book's overt disdain for conventional Christian piety. A financial failure, it sold only 200 copies, and the remaining 700 copies were eventually returned to the author. Thoreau remarked sardonically, "I have now a library of nearly nine hundred volumes, over seven hundred of which I wrote myself" (*Journal*, 5:459).[2]

Thoreau spent the next few years carefully revising his next work, *Walden; or, Life in the Woods*, which was eventually published in 1854. More than just a factual account of life in the woods, *Walden* is now justly regarded as a classic of American nature writing. As a parable of human experience, it offers an extended meditation on the value of a simple lifestyle, along with profoundly insightful observations of the natural world that foreshadow many aspects of modern ecological thought. *Walden* also marks Thoreau's discovery of his own personal voice: pithy and concise, sometimes playful and ironic, yet always as pellucid as the waters of Walden Pond. Drawing upon the vigorous, bantering, telegraphic rhythms of the American vernacular, *Walden* provided a robust model of prose style for future generations of American writers.

Thoreau suffered from tuberculosis for much of his adult life, and he died of this incurable disease in 1862, at the age of 45. Emerson's famous eulogy on Thoreau, while praising his rare qualities as a writer and observer of the natural world, nevertheless expresses regret that Thoreau failed to realize his full potential:

> With his energy and practical ability he seemed born for great enterprise and for command: and I so much regret the loss of his rare powers of action, that I cannot help counting it a fault in him that he had no ambition. Wanting this, instead of engineering for all America, he was the captain of a huckle-berry party.[3]

There is some justice in Emerson's reluctant criticism of his departed friend; Thoreau certainly had no ambition for "great enterprise" as the term was understood by his contemporaries. Yet Thoreau was hardly a passive observer of the political scene; he was actively involved in the Abolitionist movement, he once harbored a fugitive slave, and he became an ardent advocate for John Brown's hapless insurrection against the institution of slavery. Thoreau aggressively resisted business-as-usual, and he dedicated his life to the discovery of a viable alternative to the increasing economic hegemony of heavy industry in American life. Indeed, by serving as "the captain of a huckleberry party," Thoreau was in fact "engineering for all America" in the sense that he was developing an alternative model for sustainable economic development. Disregarded in his own time, either as an ineffectual schemer or as an annoying gadfly, Thoreau is now regarded as one of the most original and significant contributors to the American tradition of environmental writing.[4]

Like Emerson, Thoreau was well versed in the works of the English Romantic poets. His personal library included *The Poetical Works of Coleridge, Shelley, and Keats, Complete in One Volume* (Philadelphia, 1832), an affordably priced compendium that was rather dismissively reviewed by Emerson in *The Dial*.[5] Also in Thoreau's personal library were two volumes of Wordsworth's poetry: the *Complete Poetical Works* (Philadelphia, 1837) and *The Prelude* (London, 1850). Thoreau was familiar with the works of several other British Romantic writers, including Robert Burns, Walter Scott, Lord Byron, William Hazlitt, Thomas De Quincey, and Felicia Hemans. Thoreau's journals reveal his close scrutiny of works by Wordsworth and Coleridge during the years 1840-42, when Thoreau was most closely associated with Emerson and caught up in the intellectual ferment of Transcendentalism. His journals cite Wordsworth's poems "Resolution and Independence" in June 1840; "Ode: Intimations of Immortality" in January 1841; and "My Heart Leaps Up When I Behold" in March 1842. He mentions Wordsworth's poem "Goody Blake and Harry Gill" in *Walden* (522), and "The World is Too Much With Us" in *The Maine Woods* (731). Thoreau's journals and reading lists also display an extensive familiarity with Coleridge's prose works. He was reading Coleridge's *Letters, Conversations, and Recollections* in July 1837, *Table Talk* in December 1839, *The Statesman's Manual* in January 1841, *Confessions of an Inquiring Spirit* in April 1841, and *Hints toward the Formation of a More Comprehensive Theory of Life* in 1848.[6] In February 1841 Thoreau cites an apothegm from Coleridge's *Aids to Reflection* on the love of God: "He that loves, may be sure he was loved first."[7] Although such pious sentiments are uncharacteristic of Thoreau's later writings, they nevertheless attest to his thoughtful and sympathetic scrutiny of the English Romantic tradition as it emerged into the discursive community of Transcendentalism.

However, Thoreau is more than just a pallid version of Emerson, and his strenuous efforts to devise "an original relation to the universe" eventually led him to break decisively from the doctrines of his mentor. Thoreau's first book, *A Week on the Concord and Merrimack Rivers,* represents a divergence from the more ethereal aspects of Transcendentalism, as Thoreau seeks a solid grounding in experience for his ideas about the natural world. Yet despite his divergence from Emerson, Thoreau remains solidly within the tradition of English Romanticism, particularly in his reliance on an internalized convention of quest-romance.[8] Moreover, despite his characteristic reluctance to acknowledge the influence of any English writer, it is possible to trace the seminal importance of the English Romantics to the development of Thoreau's deep ecological conception of the natural world. Such a conception is already apparent in his first published book.

"Who hears the fishes when they cry?"

Although it is somewhat rambling and disorganized, *A Week on the Concord and Merrimack Rivers* remains one of the most significant expressions of Thoreau's ecological awareness. The underlying narrative possesses an archetypal simplicity. It tells the story of a one-week journey taken by Thoreau and his brother John in their homemade boat, the *Musquetaquid*, in August 1839. Their boat was an amphibious contraption, made with a detachable set of wheels for portages, along with two sets of oars and "several slender poles for shoving in shallow places."[9] Although the portage-wheels were never actually used, they were carried along for the entire journey, and they may have been modeled after a similar device used by Lewis and Clark to portage their boats around the Great Falls of the Missouri River.[10] Like those intrepid explorers, Henry and John Thoreau were embarked upon an audacious journey to the far northwest. The two brothers succeeded in tracing the entire course of the Merrimack River, from its junction with the Concord River near Lowell, Massachusetts, upstream to its distant headwaters in the mountains of New Hampshire. Along the way their boat passed through numerous locks where they saw heavy-laden canal boats and booming industrial towns, and on occasional side-trips they visited rural villages and farmsteads. Every night they camped out on islands and in forests, cooking their meager provisions over an open fire, sleeping on buffalo hides, far from any sign of civilization.

Writing *A Week on the Concord and Merrimack Rivers* became a labor of love for Thoreau after the untimely death of his brother from tetanus in January 1842. Ensconced alone in his hut at Walden Pond, Thoreau elaborated the simple narrative of their journey upriver with lengthy digressions on various topics, some only tangentially related to the main story. Yet the underlying narrative development remains intact, and it provides a firm backbone from which Thoreau appends personal reminiscences, nature lore, local history, and social commentary. The journey itself is archetypal; throughout the book, Thoreau frequently alludes to the mythical voyages of Odysseus, Aeneas, and the Argonauts. Like all of those questing heroes in their wooden boats, Henry and John Thoreau travel outward to the farthest boundaries of human knowledge, then seek to return home. Linking his journey to more recent historical narratives, Thoreau alludes to the voyages of discovery made by Christopher Columbus, James Cook, John Ledyard, James Clark Ross, and numerous other European explorers.[11] Although his own journey upriver is quite modest by comparison with these famous men, Thoreau feels an authentic sense of participation in the thrill of discovery. Indeed, he claims that his own discoveries will have more lasting significance than those of the famous explorers because they uncover a more hidden terrain: an inward dimension of human experience, revealed only in contact with the wild. Thoreau develops this argument most fully in the "Conclusion" to *Walden:* "Nay, be a Columbus to whole new continents and worlds within you, opening new channels, not of trade, but of thought" (578).

Thoreau's inward quest implicitly links his journey with another fictional genre, the quest-romance, which was familiar to him from Spenser's *Faerie Queene* (a work frequently cited in *A Week*).[12] More contemporary examples of the quest-romance genre included key works of the English Romantic poets, such as Shelley's *Alastor*, Keats's *Endymion,* and Coleridge's "Rime of the Ancient Mariner." In all of these instances, the Romantic version of quest-romance is distinguished by its internalized aspect: the questing hero goes forth, not to fight dragons, but to discover himself. *A Week on the Concord and Merrimack Rivers* bears an especially marked resemblance to Coleridge's "Rime of the Ancient Mariner." Both works narrate the protagonist's journey into unknown waters and back home again. Both protagonists encounter and kill an innocent bird; in Thoreau's case, it is a pigeon that he roasts for dinner. "It is true, it did not seem to be putting this bird to its right use to pluck off its feathers, and extract its entrails, and broil its carcass on the coals" (181). Like the Ancient Mariner, Thoreau feels deep remorse for killing the bird, and over the course of his journey he discovers a renewed sense of kinship with all living things. His journey up the Merrimack River ultimately takes him into a realm far beyond human ken: "Wandering on through notches which the streams had made, by the side and over the brows of hoar hills and mountains, across the stumpy, rocky, forested, and bepastured country, we at length crossed on prostrate trees over the Amonoosuck, and breathed the free air of Unappropriated Land" (257). Thoreau finally succeeds in reaching the Unappropriated Land, an unbounded realm of freedom, because he has discovered his own inner wildness, his kinship with all living things. Although it is probably just a generic analogue, not an intentional model, "The Rime of the

Ancient Mariner" closely resembles *A Week* because both are Green parables; they both examine the ethical consequences of crossing the boundary between civilization and the wild.

Thoreau's discovery of his own human nature is unfolded over the course of the journey. As he reaches Billerica, near the bottom of the Concord River, he reflects that "the era in which men cultivate the apple, and the amenities of the garden, is essentially different from that of the hunter and forest life" (45). Looking at the "dead stream" (50) caused by the dam at Billerica, and reflecting on the "meek aspect" of the villagers, Thoreau declares himself exempt from the "organized political government" (45):

> I am convinced that my genius dates from an older era than the agricultural. I would at least strike my spade into the earth with such careless freedom but accuracy as the woodpecker his bill into a tree. There is in my nature, methinks, a singular yearning toward all wildness. (45)

Hearing the call of the wild, Thoreau discovers within himself a deep sense of sympathy for all of the river's living creatures, and he devotes almost an entire chapter to a description of the dozen or so species of fish that inhabit its waters. Going beyond the simple taxonomic description of each fish, he describes its behavior, habitat, and predator/prey relationships with other species. Not merely a detached scientific observer, Thoreau affectionately describes how he befriended the sunfish: "I have stood thus over them half an hour at a time, and stroked them familiarly without frightening them, suffering them to nibble my fingers harmlessly" (24).

Later in this chapter, Thoreau deplores the devastation of the shad fishery that resulted from the construction of Billerica Dam. This passage is remarkable, not only for its prescient understanding of the destructive effects of water-power dams upon migratory fish, but also for its sympathetic evocation of this situation from the fishes' point of view:

> Shad are still taken in the basin of the Concord River at Lowell. . . . Still patiently, almost pathetically, with instinct not to be discouraged, not to be *reasoned* with, revisiting their old haunts, as if their stern fates would relent, and still met by the Corporation with its dam. Poor shad! where is thy redress? When Nature gave thee instinct, gave she thee the heart to bear thy fate? . . . I for one am with thee, and who knows what may avail a crow-bar against that Billerica dam? . . . Away with the superficial and selfish philanthropy of men,—who knows what admirable virtue of fishes may be below low-water-mark, bearing up against a hard destiny, not admired by

that fellow-creature who alone can appreciate it! Who hears the fishes when they cry? (31-32)

Thoreau objects to the Billerica dam, not only for its measurable economic effects, but even more for its transgression upon a watery realm where wild creatures once roamed free. He is among the first American writers to denounce the damming of wild and scenic rivers, in an era when heavy industrial development was virtually unquestioned by anyone. By inquiring "Who hears the fishes when they cry?" he evokes the intrinsic value of these rivers to the fish that inhabit them, not merely to the humans who derive economic value from the fishery or aesthetic value from the scenery. By adopting such a non-human perspective, Thoreau affirms that nature possesses intrinsic value, distinct from any utilitarian value that it may have for human beings. This non-human perspective marks Thoreau as America's first Deep Ecologist, a "fellow-creature" of the sunfish and the shad.

As a Deep Ecologist, Thoreau recognizes the vital importance of material existence, the very flesh of our living bodies, in the formation of our conceptual world. For this reason, he objects to any idealization of human art (or of human language) that would render it as a pure abstraction devoid of material embodiment. He criticizes Aristotle for making precisely this sort of mistake:

> Aristotle defined art to be Λόγος τοῦ ἔργου ἄνευ ὕλης, *The principle of the work without the wood;* but most men prefer to have some of the wood along with the principle; they demand that the truth be clothed in flesh and blood and the warm colors of life. (294)

Thoreau rejects the possibility of a purely conceptual artwork; all human art must have a material embodiment. By translating the Greek word ὕλη (*hyle*) as *wood*, rather than using the more standard English equivalent, *matter*, Thoreau emphasizes the intrinsic concreteness of all human language.[13] Beneath Aristotle's abstract concept of *matter* (ὕλη) lurks the concrete substance *wood*. All words find their etymology in concrete material objects, a point upon which Thoreau evidently agreed with Emerson. From this premise, Thoreau further concludes that human cognition is ineluctably *material,* "clothed in flesh and blood and the warm colors of life."[14] Since words are derived from things that we can see and touch, all human thoughts are necessarily grounded in material substances. All flesh is grass. All thinking is *wood.*

Elsewhere in *A Week,* Thoreau plays upon this verbal association, or interlingual pun, between *matter* (ὕλη) and *wood*. Describing how he and his brother built their boat, he acknowledges that the design was far from perfect:

> However, as art is all of a ship but the wood, and yet the wood alone will rudely serve the purpose of a ship, so our boat, being of wood, gladly availed itself of the old law that the heavier shall float the lighter, and though a dull water-fowl, proved a sufficient buoy for our purpose. (15)

Here again, the *art* of the vessel is inseparable from its actual substance, the *wood* from which it is made. It is the *wood* that floats upon the water, clumsily to be sure, but still more serviceably than even the most ineffably ideal abstraction. A purely conceptual boat will never float, no matter how well designed. Parting company with Kant, Emerson, and their followers in the tradition of transcendental idealism, Thoreau declares himself to be firmly nailed down to the world of material objects. Not a crass materialist, he nonetheless celebrates the phenomenal richness of human experience—the exuberant physicality of life in the *woods*.

Life in the Woods

Thoreau subtitled his great work *Walden; or, Life in the Woods,* and the locative expression "in the woods" recurs with resonant force throughout the work. He embarks upon the narrative proper with a simple descriptive phrase, "down to the woods":

> Near the end of March, 1845, I borrowed an axe and went down to the woods by Walden Pond, nearest to where I intended to build my house, and began to cut down some tall arrowy white pines, still in their youth, for timber. (354)

The location of his house, and the very material of it, is *wood,* cut by his own hand. The cutting of wood constitutes an essential part of the narrative, and for Thoreau the trees are imbued with distinct personality; they are not mere commodities. They are tall, arrowy, vibrant, youthful. Subsequently, in a chapter on "House-warming," Thoreau advocates the attribution of a sacred character to trees, in keeping with the ancient Roman tradition of sacred groves:

> I would that our farmers when they cut down a forest felt some of that awe
> which the old Romans did when they came to thin, or let in the light to, a
> consecrated grove, (*lucum conlucare,*) that is, would believe that it is sacred to
> some god. (521)

Thoreau's deep ecological worldview is once again apparent; the cutting of
trees should be accompanied by the recognition of their intrinsic sacred
character, as it was in ancient times. As a reader of John Evelyn's *Sylva*
(1664), Thoreau was well versed in the classical tradition of sacred groves.[15]
Even in the modern industrial age, the economic value of wood remains
higher than virtually any other commodity:

> It is remarkable what a value is still put upon wood even in this age and in
> this new country, a value more permanent and universal than that of gold.
> After all our discoveries and inventions no man will go by a pile of
> wood. . . . It is now many years that men have resorted to the forest for fuel
> and the materials of the arts; the New Englander and the New Hollander,
> the Parisian and the Celt, the farmer and Robinhood, Goody Blake and
> Harry Gill, in most parts of the world the prince and the peasant, the scholar
> and the savage, equally require still a few sticks from the forest to warm them
> and cook their food. (521-522)

Especially in the winter months, when fuel is essential, wood becomes a
commodity more precious than any other, and Thoreau reminds his readers that wood is also indispensable as "the materials of the arts." Wood as
raw material for art, and for industry, serves to remind us of our ineluctably
physical existence, even after "all our discoveries and inventions." Thoreau
refers to Wordsworth's poem, "Goody Blake and Harry Gill," in which
Goody's poaching of sticks from a hedge leads to her arrest by the greedy
and selfish Harry Gill. Thoreau evidently did not read this poem as a lesson about social class, but rather as a parable on the injustice of all private
property ownership. In his view, all woodlands should be the common
property of humankind, not the private property of anyone in particular.
In a journal entry of 1838, Emerson noted Thoreau's penchant for cutting
"fishpoles in the woods without asking who has a better title to the wood
than he."[16] Like Goody Blake, Thoreau often helped himself to "a few
sticks from the forest" in defiance of established property rights.

Wordsworth's poetry remained an important point of reference
throughout Thoreau's career. The Intimations Ode was a touchstone for all
American Transcendentalists, and Thoreau was particularly intrigued by

Wordsworth's exploration of the subtle links between landscape and childhood memory. In a meditative journal entry, Thoreau refers to this poem with particular admiration, and he echoes its Platonic postulate of the soul's pre-existence:

> Methinks my present experience is nothing; my past experience is all in all. . . . As far back as I can remember I have unconsciously referred to the experiences of a previous state of existence. "For life is a forgetting," etc. Formerly, methought, nature developed as I developed, and grew up with me. My life was ecstasy. In youth, before I lost any of my senses, I can remember that I was all alive, and inhabited my body with inexpressible satisfaction; both its weariness and its refreshment were sweet to me. This earth was the most glorious musical instrument, and I was audience to its strains. . . . For years I marched as to a music in comparison with which the military music of the streets is noise and discord. I was daily intoxicated, and yet no man could call me intemperate. With all your science can you tell how it is, and whence it is, that light comes into the soul? (*Journal,* 2:306-307)

Thoreau refers here to Wordsworth's memorable line from the Intimations Ode, "Our birth is but a sleep and a forgetting" (line 58), and he takes the Platonic doctrine of pre-existence as a jumping-off place for his own meditation on the significance of childhood memory. In this journal passage, Thoreau also echoes a phrase from "Tintern Abbey": "For nature then . . . / To me was all in all" (lines 73-76). Like Wordsworth, Thoreau finds that his childhood memories of the natural world have an intensity that far exceeds "the light of common day" (line 77). Building upon Wordsworth's lyrical evocation of a time when the Earth was "apparelled in celestial light" (line 4), Thoreau brashly flings forth the rhetorical question, "whence it is, that light comes into the soul?" The imagery of celestial light will be a recurrent element in Thoreau's evocation of the intense beauty of the natural world.

Yet Thoreau resists the seductive power of Wordsworth's influence, and he expresses keen skepticism toward the more tepid, civilized, Old World aspects of Wordsworth's poetry. As previously discussed in the introduction (above, page 3), Thoreau's essay "Walking" categorically dismisses the entire English literary tradition: "English literature, from the days of the minstrels to the Lake Poets . . . breathes no quite fresh, and in this sense, wild strain. It is an essentially tame and civilized literature" (676). A more pointed critique of Wordsworth occurs in a journal entry of July 9, 1851:

Coming out of town . . . when I saw that reach of the Charles River just above the depot, the fair, still water this cloudy evening suggesting the way to eternal peace and beauty, whence it flows, the placid, lake-like fresh water, so unlike the salt brine, affected me not a little. I was reminded of the way in which Wordsworth so coldly speaks of some natural visions or scenes "giving him pleasure." (*Journal*, 2:295)

Although such evocations of "pleasure" occur frequently in Wordsworth's poetry, Thoreau may well have in mind a specific phrase from the Intimations Ode: "Earth fills her lap with pleasures of her own" (line 78). In context, Wordsworth is describing the process by which the Earth, "even with something of a Mother's mind," weans the child from "the glories he hath known" (lines 79–80). Thoreau's critique of Wordsworth evidently emerges from his resistance to Wordsworth's assimilation of the Platonic doctrine of the soul's pre-existence to the traditional Christian belief in heaven as an "imperial palace" (line 85) that stands utterly disjunct from the natural world. Thoreau is unwilling to accept the implication that Earth's pleasures are only second-best, a sort of consolation prize offered to the infant who still vaguely yearns for his heavenly home. Thoreau was ineluctably hostile to organized religion, and he rejects the Christianizing tendencies of the Intimations Ode because he regards the Earth as our unique and ineluctable home. Indeed, as a committed secularist, and despite his Transcendentalist tendencies, Thoreau embraces the Earth as the only true dwelling-place for all humankind. "Here or nowhere is our heaven" (*A Week*, 308).

Thoreau most fully develops this sense of intrinsic earthiness in *Walden*, affirming that the human body is partly composed of earth: "Shall I not have intelligence with the earth? Am I not partly leaves and vegetable mould myself?" ("Solitude," 432). Like the biblical Adam, who was made of red clay, Thoreau affirms his kinship with the soil. Humans are humus! Later in *Walden*, the melting sand of the railroad bank in springtime sprouts into lobes, leaves, and proto-vegetal fronds in its unquenchable aspiration to mimic living forms. For Thoreau, the entire natural world possesses immanent vitality and creative energy. Heaven is here before us, in the grass beneath our feet. In Thoreau's pantheistic worldview, there is no need for an absentee watchmaker God or a heavenly realm of disembodied spirits.

In "Spring," Thoreau waxes lyrical in his evocation of the vital energies of nature:

As it flows it takes the forms of sappy leaves or vines, making heaps of pulpy sprays a foot or more in depth, and resembling, as you look down on them, the laciniated lobed and imbricated thalluses of some lichens; or you are reminded of coral, of leopards' paws or birds' feet, of brains or lungs or bowels, and excrements of all kinds. It is a truly *grotesque* vegetation, whose forms and color we see imitated in bronze, a sort of architectural foliage more ancient and typical than acanthus, chiccory, ivy, vine, or any vegetable leaves. (565)

Thoreau celebrates the inherent dynamism, the joyful exuberance, and the utter contingency of this "sandy rupture": "I am affected as if in a peculiar sense I stood in the laboratory of the Artist who made the world and me,—had come to where he was still at work, sporting on this bank, and with excess of energy strewing his fresh designs about" (566). "No wonder that the earth expresses itself outwardly in leaves, it so labors with the idea inwardly. The atoms have already learned this law, and are pregnant by it" (566). The underlying evolutionary process at work here is essentially Lamarckian, not Darwinian. Like Jean Baptiste de Lamarck (1744-1829), the great French biologist and evolutionist, Thoreau regards the entire material world as pervaded by a vital force that tends incessantly to generate ever-more-complex living forms.[17]

The genre of *Walden* is more georgic than pastoral. It provides the reader with a practical set of instructions on how to make a living through agricultural work. Thoreau's cultivation of the earth is also a meditative and spiritual practice, and it involves more than just the production of crops, considered either as subsistence or as a commodity. Thoreau is seeking to bring himself into closer communication with the Earth and its creatures; he is "making the earth say beans instead of grass" (447). As Stanley Cavell points out, the hoeing of beans is also, for Thoreau, a metaphor for writing.[18] He describes himself as a "plastic artist": "Early in the morning I worked barefooted, dabbling like a plastic artist in the dewy and crumbling sand" (447). The troubling sense of doubleness, or alienation, that he mentions earlier in *Walden* (429) is here overcome by a confident assertion that his individuality is merged back into the living earth itself: "It was no longer beans that I hoed, nor I that hoed beans" (449). His connection with the Earth and its creatures is reaffirmed by the daily task of hoeing, which thereby takes on a ritual aspect. Indeed, Thoreau laments the loss of the ancient pagan festivals "by which the farmer expresses a sense of the sacredness of his calling, or is reminded of its sacred origin" (454). And he acknowledges that the success of a farm is not measured by its productivity alone. "These beans have results which are not harvested by me. Do they not grow for woodchucks partly? . . . Shall I not rejoice also at the abundance of the weeds whose seeds are the granary of the birds?" (455). Rather than declare war upon the "pests" and "vermin" that ravage his crop, Thoreau acknowledges that his humble bean-field is part of a larger ecosystem, a web of life from which it takes and to which it returns nutrients. During the two years he spent at Walden Pond, Thoreau educated himself in ways of farming that make less of an impact upon the land, particularly by renouncing the use of horse-drawn implements and artificial fertilizers. He sought to develop a technique of farming that is simple, sustainable, and in harmony with the local ecosystem, and in this sense he is a true pioneer of the organic farming movement in America.

In "Economy," Thoreau gives an account of the foodstuffs he purchased or grew by his own labor, but this chapter leaves out of account the foods that he gathered from the wild, entirely outside the cash economy. Yet in a real sense these foods were important to him, both for dietary and for spiritual reasons, and as they are mentioned in the later chapters of *Walden* they fill out the picture of Thoreau's relationship to the place where he dwells. Much more than the occasional dinner he may have eaten at Emerson's house, these wild foodstuffs gave Thoreau a balanced diet and a primitive, pre-agrarian sense of participation in the web of life in the woods. "Who estimates the value of the crop which Nature yields in the still wider fields unimproved by man? . . . in all dells and pond holes in the woods and pastures and swamps grows a rich and various crop only unreaped by man" (448). By seeking edible plants in these "unimproved" areas, and by fishing in local ponds, Thoreau not only supplemented his diet with a variety of natural foods rich in vitamins, minerals, and fiber; he also found a way to resolve the stark dichotomy of subject and object, the inner and outer worlds that had persisted in the discourse of Western philosophy since Descartes. The act of eating, in an utterly concrete sense, overcomes the disjunction of self and other by assimilating the other to the self. By paying careful attention to the phenomenology of eating, Thoreau discovered a way to heal his own sense of doubleness or alienation from the natural world.

The immediate neighborhood of his hut on Walden Pond provided Thoreau with a copious bounty of herbal remedies and edible wild plants:

> In my front yard grew the strawberry, blackberry, and life-everlasting, johns-wort and goldenrod, shrub-oaks and sand-cherry, blueberry and ground-nut. Near the end of May, the sand-cherry, (*Cerasus pumila,*) adorned the sides of the path with its delicate flowers arranged in umbels cylindrically about its

short stems, which last, in the fall, weighed down with good sized and hand-
some cherries, fell over in wreaths like rays on every side. I tasted them out
of compliment to Nature, though they were scarcely palatable. (413)

This passage indicates that Thoreau nibbled on virtually any plant that he
found in his vicinity, even those that were "scarcely palatable," out of
curiosity, keen appetite, and an eagerness to discover a broad repertoire of
wild foodstuffs. Even the wild plants or "weeds" growing in his cornfield
provide a "satisfactory" meal: "I have made a satisfactory dinner, satisfactory
on several accounts, simply off a dish of purslane (*Portulaca oleracea*) which
I gathered in my cornfield, boiled and salted" (371). Thoreau is attracted by
the "beauty and fragrance" of grapes growing wild in the meadows: "In
October I went a-graping to the river meadows, and loaded myself with
clusters more precious for their beauty and fragrance than for food. . . . I
collected a small store of wild apples for coddling, which the proprietor
and travellers had overlooked. When chestnuts were ripe I laid up half a
bushel for winter" (512). And he avows a sense of kinship with the Native
Americans who harvested many of the same wild foodstuffs: "I discovered
the ground-nut (*Apios tuberosa*) on its string, the potato of the aborigines,
a sort of fabulous fruit" (512). In each of these instances, Thoreau's discovery of an edible wild plant enables him to attain a more comprehensive
understanding of his local environment, to explore his kinship with the
wild, and to break down cognitive barriers between self and other.
Through the simple act of eating, he seeks to rebuild a concrete sense of
relationship with the natural world.

In addition to gathering wild edible plants, Thoreau also experimented
with various sorts of animal food. He went fishing in local ponds, and on
one occasion he devoured a woodchuck that was plundering his bean-
field:

Once I went so far as to slaughter a woodchuck which ravaged my bean-
field,—effect his transmigration, as a Tartar would say,—and devour him,
partly for experiment's sake; but though it afforded me a momentary enjoyment, notwithstanding a musky flavor, I saw that the longest use would not
make that a good practice, however it might seem to have your woodchucks
ready dressed by the village butcher. (369)

Elsewhere in *Walden,* Thoreau describes his powerful feelings of aggression
when he encountered a woodchuck, perhaps the same one that was rav-
aging his crops: "I caught a glimpse of a woodchuck stealing across my

path, and felt a strange thrill of savage delight, and was strongly tempted to seize and devour him raw" (490). Such a primitive expression of blood-lust provides Thoreau with a momentary "thrill," but eventually it leads him to question whether it is wise or ethically defensible to include animal flesh in his diet. He explores this question in the chapter "Higher Laws," contextualizing it with reference to both Western and Hindu traditions of vegetarianism. He adopts a nuanced position, advocating the value of hunting in the education of young boys, yet deploring the needless killing of animals, either for sport or for profit, by grown men. With clarity and intellectual honesty, Thoreau acknowledges his own experience and proclivities as "a carnivorous animal," and he admits that "for my part, I was never unusually squeamish; I could sometimes eat a fried rat with a good relish" (495). Yet he affirms, "whatever my own practice may be, I have no doubt that it is a part of the destiny of the human race, in its gradual improvement, to leave off eating animals" (494). Like his Romantic precursors William Blake and Percy Shelley, Thoreau advocates vegetarianism, not only as a practical mode of subsistence, but also as a means of imaginative and spiritual "improvement."[19] By eating wild foods, Thoreau gains access to the wild mind:

> Who has not sometimes derived an inexpressible satisfaction from his food in which appetite had no share? I have been thrilled to think that I owed a mental perception to the commonly gross sense of taste, that I have been inspired through the palate, that some berries which I had eaten on a hillside had fed my genius. (496)

In such passages, Thoreau is exploring the possibility of a new epistemological basis for human perception. The "despotism of the eye" may be overcome, and the Cartesian separation of humankind from its dwelling-place in the natural world may be healed, by attending to the sense of taste. He is "inspired through the palate" to behold the Earth and its creatures with renewed intensity, exploring uncharted realms of sensory experience that lurk beyond the ordinary categories of visual perception.

Thoreau's most lyrical passages describe the purity and refreshment of the water he drank from Walden Pond. "The pond was my well ready dug" (468), and by drinking its waters, Thoreau continues the process of self-purification that lends him the nickname of "Hermit" in "Brute Neighbors" (501). Like Wordsworth, he takes an austere pride in being a water-drinker, and he shuns any stronger beverage. He bathes daily in Walden Pond, a baptismal ritual that he terms a "religious exercise": "I have been as sincere a worshipper of Aurora as the Greeks. I got up early and bathed in the pond; that was a religious exercise, and one of the best things which I did" (393). His daily immersion in the waters of Walden Pond enables him to achieve a greater degree of self-awareness than he ever could have attained in the busy, fretful world of human society. His retreat into hermitlike reclusion brings him into contact with the elemental basis of all existence, the very being of the Earth itself. He evokes the timeless nature of Walden Pond, whose "water laves the shore as it did a thousand years ago" (471). As a steadfast companion, the pond takes on certain qualities of sentient being: "It is earth's eye; looking into which the beholder measures the depth of his own nature" (471). Simply by living in close proximity to the pond, Thoreau is able to continue his internalized quest for the truth of his own being. Using his skills as a professional surveyor, he mapped the outline and measured the depth of the entire pond, thereby refuting the prevailing local belief that the pond was "bottomless." By producing a map of Walden Pond (550), Thoreau also "measures the depth of his own nature" (471), and he thereby calls into question the prevailing Romantic and Transcendentalist dogma of an unbounded, autonomous selfhood. Like Walden Pond, the individual self is not "bottomless," but finite and bounded by the material world in which it resides. "I can assure my readers that Walden has a reasonably tight bottom at a not unreasonable, though at an unusual, depth" (551). Just as the pond is paved with "smooth rounded white stones" (465), so too the human mind is grounded in a hard material substrate, the rocky integument of the Earth itself.

For Thoreau, the correspondence between the pellucid waters of Walden Pond and the depth of his own intellect is not merely metaphorical. Rather, such a correspondence has substantial reality; it is *symbolic* in the strong (Coleridgean) sense of that term. Thoreau affirms, "I am thankful that this pond was made deep and pure for a symbol" (551). The pond is indeed a symbol in the sense that Coleridge uses that term in *The Statesman's Manual;* Thoreau would agree with Coleridge that a symbol "always partakes of the Reality which it renders intelligible" (*Lay Sermons,* 30). But he would disagree with Coleridge's subsequent assertion that a "material symbol" serves to represent "the pure untroubled brightness of an IDEA" (*Lay Sermons,* 50). Thoreau often expresses skepticism toward any such assertion of a purely transcendent realm: "Here or nowhere is our heaven" (*A Week,* 308). In Thoreau's view, the symbolic attributes of Walden Pond do not arise from its participation in a transcendental Idea, but are inherent in its very existence as a material object. Thus the melting of the pond in springtime unleashes the immanent "joy" of its watery being: "It is glorious to behold this ribbon of water sparkling in the sun, the bare face of the pond full of glee and youth, as if it spoke the joy of the fishes within it, and of the sands on its shore" (570). Both the pond and the human beholder are ineluctably grounded in the material world, and their acts of signification arise from a speaking-forth of their temporal existence. Language is a liquid medium; words are watery.

By affirming such a this-worldly metaphysic, Thoreau undercuts the *a priori* Ideas upon which such Romantic writers as Coleridge and Emerson had grounded their conception of language. Thoreau explores an alternative way of understanding language, which embodies his sense of the ineluctable temporality of human existence: "Time is but the stream I go a-fishing in. . . . I would drink deeper; fish in the sky, whose bottom is pebbly with stars" (400). By invoking the wonder and mystery of a world whose temporal unfolding is utterly contingent, Thoreau bespeaks the ungroundedness of a human language that lacks any fixed points of reference, any transcendental currency of "Ideas." Such a dynamic conception of language is what he calls "tawny grammar."

Tawny Grammar

Thoreau evokes the concept of "tawny grammar" in his essay "Walking":

> There are other letters for a child to learn than those which Cadmus invented. The Spaniards have a good term to express this wild and dusky knowledge, *Grammatica parda,* tawny grammar, a kind of mother-wit derived from that same leopard to which I have referred. (681)

This conception of a wild language, supple and spotted as a leopard, emerges from Thoreau's extended meditation on the role of symbolic discourse in a world where concepts have no fixed points of reference, no grounding in transcendental Ideas. In such a world, human language is endlessly mutable, as free and wild as a leopard: "Here is this vast, savage, howling mother of ours, Nature, lying all around, with such beauty, and such affection for her children, as the leopard" (680). Thoreau contrasts the stasis, complacency, and book-learning of modern urban society with the unfettered, transformative modes of expression that are found among the indigenous peoples of North America. He notes that "an Indian had no given name at first, but earned it, and his name was his fame; and among some tribes he acquired a new name for every new exploit" (679). Thoreau is fascinated by the possibility of a language in which even proper names are mutable and reflect the character of those who bear them. He imagines that even modern citified Americans may acquire such "original wild names" in rare moments of "passion or inspiration": "We have a wild savage in us, and a savage name is perchance somewhere recorded as ours" (680). As we have seen, during his sojourn at Walden Pond, Thoreau himself acquired a descriptive wild name: "Hermit."

Thoreau's interest in "tawny grammar" is self-reflexive; he not only holds it up as an abstract ideal, but he also seeks to realize it in his own writing. Thus *Walden* has a deliberately haphazard, meandering, accidental quality to its prose. The language of *Walden* is layered like a geological series, tangled like a willow thicket, darting and shimmering like a school of fish, and excavated from the dark unknown like the burrow of a beast. He built his hut with the bark on (85). In a famous allegorical episode in the "Conclusion" of *Walden,* the Artist of Kouroo epitomizes what Thoreau sought to create in his own work: "He had made a new system in making a staff, a world with full and fair proportions; in which, though the old cities and dynasties had passed away, fairer and more glorious ones had taken their places" (582). Like the intricately carved staff of the Artist of Kouroo, *Walden* is a microcosm of the world in transformation. It seeks to embody the "fair proportions" of the seasonal cycle, the wild, exuberant life of the pond and its denizens, and the contingent, unruly energies of the living Earth as they unfold in temporal process. Nature exists in time, not in some sort of timeless pre-established harmony. "There is more day to dawn. The sun is but a morning star" (587). The task of world-making continues forever.

In his essay "Walking," Thoreau inquires: "Where is the literature which gives expression to Nature?" (676). He calls for a new American poetry and a new kind of language that will embody the wild, unpredictable energies of the natural world:

> He would be a poet who could impress the winds and streams into his service, to speak for him; who nailed words to their primitive senses, as farmers drive down stakes in the spring, which the frost has heaved; who derived his words as often as he used them—transplanted them to his page with earth adhering to their roots; whose words were so true and fresh and natural that they would appear to expand like the buds at the approach of spring, though they lay half smothered between two musty leaves in a library. (676-677)

Although this passage is written in what Emerson would term "the optative mood" ("The Transcendentalist," 199), it nevertheless provides a compelling and memorable expression to a characteristically Romantic conception of natural language. Like Wordsworth and Coleridge, Thoreau is wary of any purely arbitrary relationship between a word and its referent. He wants to "nail words to their primitive senses" in order to nourish the vibrant, image-laden qualities of poetic language. For Thoreau, the historical derivation of a word often provides a clue to its "primitive sense," and for this reason the poet must "derive his words" by showing their origin in the names of concrete material objects. Through careful attention to the various modes of relationship that may exist between words and their natural environment, Thoreau articulates a comprehensive theory of ecolinguistics.

Thoreau develops the concept of natural language most fully in *Walden,* especially in the chapter on "Sounds," which evokes a rich variety of natural noises through the device of onomatopoeia. The lowing of cattle, the song of the whippoorwill, the cry of the screech owl, and the croaking of frogs are represented in phonetic transcription: "*tr-r-r-oonk, tr-r-r-oonk, tr-r-r-oonk!*" (423). Only a false urban sophistication would disregard such natural sounds: "We are in danger of forgetting the language which all things and events speak without metaphor, which alone is copious and standard" (411). Elsewhere in *Walden,* Thoreau often pauses to show the derivation of certain proper names. In "The Ponds," he punningly suggests that Walden Pond "was called, originally, *Walled-in* Pond" (468). He rejects the mercenary proper name attached to Flint's Pond: "Rather let it be named from the fishes that swim in it, the wild fowl or quadrupeds which frequent it, the wild flowers which grow by its shores, or some wild man or child the thread of whose history is interwoven with its own" (479). In "Former Inhabitants," Thoreau evokes the utter solitude and blankness of the snow, a *tabula rasa* as yet unwritten by any creature: "not a rabbit's track, nor even the fine print, the small type, of a meadow mouse was to be seen" (534). But there are occasional human traces to be read in the snow. "Sometimes, notwithstanding the snow, when I returned from my walk at evening I crossed the deep tracks of a woodchopper leading from my door, and found his pile of whittlings on the hearth, and my house filled with the odor of his pipe. Or on a Sunday afternoon, if I chanced to be at home, I heard the cronching of the snow made by the step of a long-headed farmer" (534). The word "cronching" is another instance of onomatopoeia.

Thoreau's visitors often communicated with him through the language of natural objects. "When I return to my house I find that visitors have been there and left their cards, either a bunch of flowers, or a wreath of evergreen, or a name in pencil on a yellow walnut leaf or a chip. . . . One has peeled a willow wand, woven it into a ring, and dropped it on my table" (425). On one memorable occasion, Thoreau met a man whom he regarded as a true Noble Savage, the woodcutter Alec Therien: "Who should come to my lodge this morning but a true Homeric or Paphlagon-ian man,—he had so suitable and poetic a name that I am sorry I cannot print it here,—a Canadian, a wood-chopper and post-maker, who can hole fifty posts in a day, who made his last supper on a woodchuck which his dog caught" (437). Thoreau presumably regarded the name *Therien* as ety-mologically akin to the German word *Thier,* meaning *beast,* and for this rea-son he sees the name as especially "suitable and poetic." Later he remarks, "In him the animal man chiefly was developed" (439). It seems quite fitting to Thoreau that the woodcutter's proper name should mean *beast.*

The chapter "Winter Animals" further examines the noises of nature and the cries of animals. Thoreau hears "the whooping of the ice in the pond, my great bed-fellow in that part of Concord, as if it were restless in its bed and would fain turn over, were troubled with flatulency and bad dreams" (539). The red squirrel, "winding up his clock and chiding all imaginary spectators" (540), "waked me in the dawn, coursing over the roof and up and down the sides of the house, as if sent out of the woods for this purpose" (539-540). The fox "barked a vulpine curse at me" (539). Even the annoying hum of an insect elicits a generous commendation from Thoreau: "I was as much affected by the faint hum of a mosquito making its invisible and unimaginable tour through my apartment at earliest dawn . . . as I could be by any trumpet that ever sang of fame. . . . There was something cosmical about it" (393). In all of these instances, Thoreau expresses his fascination with the incipient language-making abilities of various animals, insects, and even inanimate objects. He is not so much per-sonifying natural objects (and thereby indulging in what Ruskin termed the Pathetic Fallacy) as he is projecting his own human awareness into a very different, utterly inhuman perspective. The hum of the mosquito is "cosmical" because it presents an uncanny aerial perspective upon a famil-iar domestic space. Thoreau imagines himself as a mosquito, humming around the room, which is suddenly opened up (through the eyes of the insect) into a cosmic vastness of scale.

In "Spring" the vibrant, creative energy of the melting sandbank pro-vides an occasion for Thoreau to reflect on a deep analogy between human language and the making of leaves:

The overhanging leaf sees here its prototype. *Internally,* whether in the globe or animal body, it is a moist thick *lobe,* a word especially applicable to the liver and lungs and the *leaves* of fat, (λείβω, *labor, lapsus,* to flow or slip downward, a lapsing; λοβος, *globus,* lobe, globe; also lap, flap, and many other words,) *externally* a dry thin *leaf,* even as the *f* and *v* are a pressed and dried *b.* The radicals of the lobe are *lb,* the soft mass of the *b* (single lobed, or B, double lobed,) with a liquid *l* behind it pressing it forward. In globe, *glb,* the guttural *g* adds to the meaning the capacity of the throat. The feathers and wings of birds are still drier and thinner leaves. Thus, also, you pass from the lumpish grub in the earth to the airy and fluttering butterfly. The very globe continually transcends and translates itself, and becomes winged in its orbit. (566-567)

This passage provides a good example of what Thoreau meant by saying that the poet "should derive his words as often as he used them" ("Walking," 676). He explores the etymology of the words *lobe, globe, leaf,* and *labor,* not merely out of antiquarian curiosity, but in order to demonstrate that human language and natural organisms evolve according to the same underlying principles. In Thoreau's view, these underlying evolutionary principles remain to be discovered; he evidently regards them as mysterious, contingent, and historical in nature, not simply the unfolding of an eternal Idea in the mind of God. Thoreau underlines the analogy between this inscrutable process of leaf-making and the inscrutable hieroglyphics that had only recently been decoded by a French linguist: "What Champollion will decipher this hieroglyphic for us, that we may turn over a new leaf at last?" (568). Thoreau does not claim to know why living forms evolve (and indeed, before the publication of Darwin's *Origin of Species* in 1859, no one could convincingly make such a claim). But he does affirm that the historical evolution of human language bears a close affinity with the "exfoliation" of living forms.

In Thoreau's view, human beings are an integral part of this natural process of exfoliation: "What is man but a mass of thawing clay? The ball of the human finger is but a drop congealed" (567). Boldly anticipating the Gaia Hypothesis, Thoreau beholds the entire globe as "a living earth":

> The earth is not a mere fragment of dead history, stratum upon stratum like the leaves of a book, to be studied by geologists and antiquaries chiefly, but living poetry like the leaves of a tree, which precede flowers and fruit,—not a fossil earth, but *a living earth;* compared with whose great central life all animal and vegetable life is merely parasitic. (568; emphasis added)

Thoreau's view here is often misrepresented as an affirmation of Vitalism, a belief in some occult life-force that drives the universe. But Thoreau is invariably skeptical of any such occult forces, because they imply the exis-

tence of some otherworldly realm. He stubbornly resists such metaphysi-
cal dualism. His is a metaphysic of immanence, and in this passage he is
speaking literally of *a living earth,* a planet that behaves like an organism, as
a single interwoven entity. In modern parlance, he sees the Earth as a single planetary ecosystem.

If the Earth is alive, then possibly it may engage in symbol-making
activity. Thoreau describes the grass as a powerful "symbol" of the Earth's
vibrant energy:

> The grass flames up on the hillsides like a spring fire, . . . as if the earth sent
> forth an inward heat to greet the returning sun; not yellow but green is the
> color of its flame;—the symbol of perpetual youth, the grass-blade, like a
> long green ribbon, streams from the sod into the summer, checked indeed
> by the frost, but anon pushing on again, lifting its spear of last year's hay with
> the fresh life below. (570)

This passage offers a lyrical affirmation of the Earth's inexhaustible fecundity, its ability to produce an endless profusion of complex living forms.
The grass, as it "flames up on the hillsides like a spring fire," is more than
just a parasitical life-form, clinging like a flea to the planet's hide. Rather,
it is a "symbol of perpetual youth," bearing a burden of meaning for those
who know how to read the language of nature. "Not yellow but green is
the color of its flame": the poetry of Earth is written in a green language.

Throughout the text of *Walden,* Thoreau evokes a lived experience of
harmony between the outer and inner worlds. Nature speaks to us, and by
patiently attending to the sights, sounds, textures, and tastes of the world
around us, we can gradually learn to comprehend its latent meanings. The
world of *Walden* is ultimately scrutable, a world that welcomes its human
inhabitants. By dwelling in close proximity to the wild creatures of the forest, Thoreau becomes attuned to the wild, adept in fathoming the elemental meanings of wood, wind, and water. By the end of *Walden,* he has
become a tawny grammarian; he hears books in the babbling brooks, and
sermons in stones. Even the grass speaks to him.

Such an outcome is hardly unexpected, and it is entirely appropriate to
the generic expectations that *Walden* sets up for itself. As pastoral, it evokes
a green world where nature is always peaceful, except where violated by
such bothersome human inventions as the railroad. As georgic, it vindicates
the virtues of agricultural labor and self-reliance. But the natural world did
not always present itself in such a peaceful and accessible form to Thoreau's
imagination. In a dramatic encounter with the vast Maine wilderness, he

was forced to confront the natural world in a harsher, less accommodating mode.

The Unhandselled Globe

While living at Walden Pond in 1846, Thoreau took a long trip by canoe through the Maine woods with his cousin, George Thatcher, and "Uncle George" McCauslin, a local waterman who served as a wilderness guide. He later recounted his adventures in a series of lectures that he presented at the Concord Lyceum, first published as "Ktaadn, and the Maine Woods" in *Union Magazine* (July-November 1848) and also published posthumously as a chapter of *The Maine Woods* (1864). In a vivid narrative climax, Thoreau tells how he climbed to the summit of Katahdin, Maine's highest mountain, where he confronted an utterly inhuman wilderness, startlingly different from the tranquil fields and forests of Concord: "Nature was here something savage and awful, though beautiful" (645). In this elemental encounter with the wild, Thoreau calls into question all that he knows about the relationship between humankind and the natural world. He first realizes the utterly inhuman character of the landscape while passing through the "Burnt Lands," the scene of an old forest fire:

> Perhaps I most fully realized that this was primeval, untamed, and forever untameable *Nature,* or whatever else men call it, while coming down this part of the mountain. We were passing over "Burnt Lands," burnt by lightning, perchance, though they showed no recent marks of fire, hardly so much as a charred stump, but looked rather like a natural pasture for the moose and deer, exceedingly wild and desolate, with occasional strips of timber crossing them, and low poplars springing up, and patches of blueberries here and there. I found myself traversing them familiarly, like some pasture run to waste, or partially reclaimed by man; but when I reflected what man, what brother or sister or kinsman of our race made it and claimed it, I expected the proprietor to rise up and dispute my passage. It is difficult to conceive of a region uninhabited by man. We habitually presume his presence and influence everywhere. And yet we have not seen pure Nature, unless we have seen her thus vast and drear and inhuman, though in the midst of cities. (645)

In this climactic encounter with "pure Nature," Thoreau is forced to confront the limitations of his existing conceptual repertoire. As a creature of civilized human culture, he carries into the wilderness a set of preconceived, largely literary ideas about landscape, which lead him to "read" an open space in the midst of a forest as a "pasture run to waste." But such pastoral conventions only impede the process of his coming to terms with "a region uninhabited by man," a landscape that remains unreadable to an eye trained in the conventional aesthetic appreciation of landscape.

Thoreau struggles to come to terms with the uncanny otherness of this landscape, which he regards as the work of unnamed "Powers." Rejecting the literary conventions of pastoralism, he confronts "the unhandselled globe" in its panoply of "Chaos and Old Night," a phrase that evokes another, more ominous literary archetype: Milton's Satan on his flight through the pathless realm of Chaos (*Paradise Lost,* 2:970). Like his Romantic precursors from Blake through Byron, Thoreau finds in Milton's Satan, and in the underlying archetype of Prometheus, an apt precursor for his own forbidden quest.[20] Yet unlike these English Romantic poets, Thoreau is involved in the exploration of actual space—the Maine wilderness—and in that rugged terrain of raging rivers and dense forests he is confronting the utter solitude of a land completely devoid of human inhabitants. He is thereby engaged in the re-externalization of quest-romance, a characteristic Romantic motif now literally transplanted into the howling American wilderness:

> I looked with awe at the ground I trod on, to see what the Powers had made there, the form and fashion and material of their work. This was that Earth of which we have heard, made out of Chaos and Old Night. Here was no man's garden, but *the unhandselled globe.* It was not lawn, nor pasture, nor mead, nor woodland, nor lea, nor arable, nor waste-land. It was the fresh and natural surface of the planet Earth, as it was made for ever and ever,—to be the dwelling of man, we say,—so Nature made it, and man may use it if he can. Man was not to be associated with it. It was Matter, vast, terrific,—not his Mother Earth that we have heard of, not for him to tread on, or be buried in,—no, it were being too familiar even to let his bones lie there,—the home, this, of Necessity and Fate. (645; emphasis added)

As Thoreau presses onward in his Promethean quest, he brings himself into ever more direct contact with "the unhandselled globe," a vast realm untouched by human cultivation. He contrasts this inhuman wilderness with the more domesticated forest of his native Concord: "Perchance where *our* wild pines stand, and leaves lie on their forest floor, in Concord, there were once reapers, and husbandmen planted grain; but here not even the surface had been scarred by man, but it was a specimen of what God saw fit to make this world" (646).[21] The rough, tangled, disorderly appearance of the Maine wilderness provokes Thoreau to consider a series of ontological questions. *Who* are we? *Where* are we? And what is the role of the human observer in such an inhospitable place?

In addressing these difficult questions, Thoreau starts to feel estranged from his own body, and he ponders the mystery of his physical presence in a material world:

> I stand in awe of my body, this matter to which I am bound has become so strange to me. I fear not spirits, ghosts, of which I am one,—*that* my body might,—but I fear bodies, I tremble to meet them. What is this Titan that has possession of me? Talk of mysteries!—Think of our life in nature,— daily, to be shown matter, to come in contact with it,—rocks, trees, wind on our cheeks! the *solid* earth! the *actual* world! the *common sense! Contact! Contact! Who* are we? *where* are we? (646)

These questions are not merely rhetorical. Thoreau is confronting the utterly inscrutable nature of the wilderness he beholds, and he is coming to realize that the easy answers provided by "common sense," or even by the entire tradition of Western metaphysics, are inadequate to the depth of the mystery presented to the solitary human observer by such irreducibly material phenomena as "rocks, trees, wind on our cheeks." By traveling so far outside the realm of human society, Thoreau has shed his social identity, and he encounters a pre-historical, Paleolithic version of himself wandering free in the forest. Such an irruption of non-social identity is initially terrifying, as if some other being had possession of his body: "What is this Titan that has possession of me?" Yet the terror of this encounter with the wilderness enables Thoreau to recover a deeper, wilder version of himself than he has ever known before. No longer does he regard himself (in unthinking allegiance to the Cartesian tradition) as a ghost in the machine, or as a spirit that resides only temporarily in a physical form. At this crucial moment of identity-formation, he comes to know himself as a Promethean exile from heaven, inhabiting an ineluctably physical body in a vast, inhuman world of matter.

One important consequence of this newly formed sense of identity is that Thoreau no longer feels a strong sense of ontological difference between himself and other living creatures. If personal identity is not constituted socially, but emerges from the physical interaction between person and place, then there no longer exists any firm boundary between humans and other species. Hence Thoreau can refer to the Maine wilderness as "peopled with trout," not merely in a metaphorical sense, but as a strong assertion of the fishes' ontological status as *people:*

It is a country full of evergreen trees, of mossy silver birches and watery maples, the ground dotted with insipid, small, red berries and strewn with damp and moss-grown rocks,—a country diversified with innumerable lakes and rapid streams, *peopled with trout* and various species of *leucisci*. (653; emphasis added)

Thoreau adduces an entire catalog of wild creatures that inhabit the Maine wilderness, leavening the "grim forest" with their presence. The inclusion of "the Indian" in this catalog is not intended to denigrate these indigenous inhabitants, but rather to acknowledge their status as wild denizens of the forest, at home in their ancestral dwelling-place. Indeed, he personifies the forest itself as a "serene infant," with an incipient sentience that is expressed in a few inchoate noises:

Such is the home of the moose, the bear, the caribou, the wolf, the beaver, and the Indian. Who shall describe the inexpressible tenderness and immortal life of the grim forest, where Nature, though it be mid-winter, is ever in her spring, where moss-grown and decaying trees are not old, but seem to enjoy a perpetual youth; and blissful, innocent Nature, like a serene infant, is too happy to make a noise, except by a few tinkling, lisping birds and trickling rills? (653)

The idyllic tone of this passage indicates that Thoreau has come quite a long way from the *Sturm und Drang* of his climactic confrontation with titanic Nature on the slopes of Mount Katahdin. His evocation of the forest as a "serene infant" bespeaks his coming to terms with his own wild identity, as a denizen of the wilderness through which he travels. No longer regarding himself as a Promethean exile from heaven, he has learned to accept his new identity as an inhabitant of the green world.

Another significant consequence of Thoreau's expanded sense of personal identity is his renewed dedication to the preservation of wilderness. Traveling for many weeks in the Maine woods, he has gained a deeper appreciation for all living things that dwell in the wild. Citing the authority of a "higher law," he advocates the protection of the pine trees from the commercial lumbering enterprises that threaten their destruction:

Strange that so few ever come to the woods to see how the pine lives and grows and spires, lifting its evergreen arms to the light,—to see its perfect success; but most are content to behold it in the shape of many broad boards brought to market, and deem *that* its true success! But the pine is no more lumber than man is, and to be made into boards and houses is no more its true and highest use than the truest use of a man is to be cut down and made into manure. There is a higher law affecting our relation to pines as well as to men. A pine cut down, a dead pine, is no more a pine than a dead human carcass is a man. (684-685)

Thoreau affirms a strong sense of identity between humans and pines; both are living things with the potential to thrive, to grow, and to spire toward the light. Just as he did in *Walden*, he appeals to a "higher law" in order to denounce the senseless destruction of living creatures. Thoreau is one of the first American writers to advocate the value of wilderness, and to urge its preservation, not merely on utilitarian or aesthetic grounds, but on the basis of its intrinsic value as a community of living things. Under Thoreau's "higher law," all living things, even pine trees, have a right to existence.

In a subsequent chapter of *The Maine Woods*, Thoreau calls for the establishment of "national preserves" that would provide sanctuary for all indigenous inhabitants of the American wilderness, including the Indians who have hunted there for many generations. Such wilderness preserves will be more authentic, and less disruptive to the existing fabric of civil life, than the forests that formerly provided sporting grounds for English royalty:

> The kings of England formerly had their forests "to hold the king's game," for sport or food, sometimes destroying villages to create or extend them; and I think that they were impelled by a true instinct. Why should not we, who have renounced the king's authority, have *our national preserves*, where no villages need be destroyed, in which the bear and panther, and some even of the hunter race, may still exist, and not be "civilized off the face of the earth,"—our forests, not to hold the king's game merely, but to hold and preserve the king himself also, the lord of creation,—not for idle sport or food, but for inspiration and our own true re-creation? or shall we, like villains, grub them all up, poaching on our own national domains? (712; emphasis added)

As an advocate for wilderness preservation, Thoreau is one of the earliest American writers to conceive the possibility of national parks whose main purpose is "inspiration and our own true re-creation." Such "national preserves" would not exist simply as reservoirs for game or timber; rather, they would exist entirely for the benefit and protection of their indigenous inhabitants: "the bear and panther, and some even of the hunter race." Unlike the creators of the U.S. National Park System, Thoreau envisions these "national preserves" as areas where Indians would be encouraged to continue their traditional ways of life, hunting game and gathering wild plants for subsistence, without outside interference.

Thoreau's most memorable statement of the value of wilderness occurs in the "Spring" chapter of *Walden*. He envisions "the unexplored forests and meadows" as places where modern city-dwellers can become rejuvenated, revitalized, re-created by the presence of the wild:

> Our village life would stagnate if it were not for the unexplored forests and meadows which surround it. We need the tonic of wildness,—to wade sometimes in marshes where the bittern and the meadow-hen lurk, and hear the booming of the snipe; to smell the whispering sedge where only some wilder and more solitary fowl builds her nest, and the mink crawls with its belly close to the ground. At the same time that we are earnest to explore and learn all things, we require that all things be mysterious and unexplorable, that land and sea be infinitely wild, unsurveyed and unfathomed by us because unfathomable. We can never have enough of Nature. We must be refreshed by the sight of inexhaustible vigor, vast and Titanic features, the sea-coast with its wrecks, the wilderness with its living and its decaying trees, the thunder cloud, and the rain which lasts three weeks and produces freshets. We need to witness our own limits transgressed, and some life pasturing freely where we never wander. (575)

Such an eloquent statement of the value of wilderness emerges from Thoreau's own struggle to realize the meanings of his experience in the wild, as he navigated the Concord and Merrimack rivers, sojourned on the shores of Walden Pond, and explored the trackless forests of Maine. He was deeply influenced by the Romantic and Transcendentalist writers in many of his attitudes toward the natural world, and *Walden* might even be read as an extended commentary on Emerson's essay "Self-Reliance." Yet Thoreau learned to question many of the philosophical doctrines of his precursors in the Romantic tradition, especially their unspoken reliance upon an essentially Cartesian conception of the self as an unbounded, autonomous entity, utterly distinct from the world in which it lives and breathes. Such a conception of selfhood, manifested for Coleridge and Emerson in the memorable motif of a transparent eye-ball, became untenable for Thoreau. In his efforts to realize a more authentic relation to the wild, Thoreau eventually developed a new conception of selfhood, largely unprecedented within the Romantic tradition. In a climactic moment of confrontation on the slopes of Mount Katahdin, Thoreau sought to divest himself of his socially constructed identity, and he encountered a pre-historical, Paleolithic version of himself wandering free in the forest. Like a mink crawling with its belly close to the ground, Thoreau learned to immerse himself entirely in a world of matter, with his senses of taste and smell attuned to the most subtle stimuli.

As the intellectual inheritors of Marx and Freud, modern readers tend to be skeptical of any claim that the self is not socially constructed. Such claims are said to be "mystified." Yet Thoreau's endeavor to discover a deeper and more authentic version of himself still offers a viable alternative to the enduring prevalence of the unquestioned values of secular humanism in our society. Like Emerson, Thoreau was engaged in a lifelong effort to discover a ground of ethical value beyond the established, anthropocentric morality of his own time and place. In his strenuous exploration of the trackless wilderness that lay beyond the complacent marketplace of urban American culture, Thoreau found a genuinely external perspective upon the prevailing and largely unexamined values of his own society. Although his tone is sometimes shrill and even puritanical in its condemnation of the complacent acquisitiveness of his contemporaries, he nevertheless managed to articulate an alternative set of moral imperatives that resonate all the more strongly today, in a world where business-as-usual is rapidly destroying the potential of any future life on our planet. *Walden* remains an American classic, not only for the elegance and intensity of its style, but also for the continued salience of its ecological ideas. As an early advocate for the preservation of American wilderness, and as a successful practitioner of a sustainable agrarian lifestyle, Thoreau still provides a useful role model for American readers at the dawn of the twenty-first century.

Chapter 7

John Muir:
A Wind-Storm in the Forests

Among the pantheon of American environmental writers, no single figure looms larger than John Muir (1838-1914). Born in Dunbar, Scotland, John Muir emigrated with his family to the United States at the age of seven, settling on a Wisconsin farm. His father was a strict Calvinist, and Muir grew up in an atmosphere of austerity, strict discipline, and hard work. He attended the University of Wisconsin, becoming an adept student of the natural sciences, particularly chemistry, geology, and botany. In 1864, seeking to avoid military service in the Civil War, Muir vanished into the wilds of northern Michigan and Canada, wandering for several months in utter solitude. He found solace in the sight of a rare white orchid, *Calypso borealis,* blooming far from the presence of any human being. This elusive species formed the subject-matter of Muir's first published writing, "The Calypso Borealis. Botanical Enthusiasm," which appeared in the Boston *Recorder,* December 21, 1866. Muir describes the fervent emotional response evoked by his unexpected discovery of this orchid:

> I did find Calypso—but only once, far in the depths of the very wildest of Canadian dark woods. . . . I never before saw a plant so full of life; so perfectly spiritual, it seemed pure enough for the throne of its Creator. I felt as if I were in the presence of superior beings who welcomed me and beckoned me to come. I sat down beside them and wept for joy.[1]

Muir was deeply impressed by the simple beauty of the orchid, growing by itself in a remote wilderness area, far from any human habitation. He suddenly realized that its existence was entirely distinct from any conceivable human purpose. From this experience Muir gained his first insight into the complete self-sufficiency and intrinsic self-worth of all living things.

Returning to Wisconsin, Muir worked in a rake factory, impressing his employer with his skill in devising new machinery. An industrial accident in 1867 resulted in his almost losing the sight of one eye, and during his recovery from this injury, Muir renounced the "gobble gobble school of economics" and resolved to follow a less materialistic way of life.[2] Inspired by the South American travels of the great naturalists Alexander von Humboldt and Charles Darwin, Muir set forth to explore the Amazon River all the way to its source. After a thousand-mile walk to Florida, camping in swamps and botanizing along the way, Muir fell desperately ill with malaria and abandoned his South American journey. But he still felt the lure of the unexplored wilderness, and in 1868 he traveled by steamship to California. Working as a shepherd, Muir climbed into the Sierra Nevada mountains, where he was astonished by the beauty of the "Range of Light," particularly the awesome crags and pinnacles of Yosemite Valley. For several years he made these mountains his home. Muir's first published book, *The Mountains of California* (1894), established him as a leading advocate for the preservation of wilderness. In his later years, Muir explored wilderness areas throughout the United States, and he became a tireless defender of the National Park system. He published several books, including *My First Summer in the Sierra* (1911), *The Story of My Boyhood and Youth* (1913), *Travels in Alaska* (1915), and *A Thousand-Mile Walk to the Gulf* (1916). In his role as environmental advocate, John Muir was the founder and first president of the Sierra Club, a position that enabled him to bring about the establishment of the National Park system, but which also brought Muir's career to a tragic end with the damming of Hetch Hetchy Valley in Yosemite National Park, an ecological disaster that Muir denounced with prophetic fury, but to no avail. Muir died in 1914, a broken man, defeated in his strenuous efforts to preserve the Hetch Hetchy. Yet through his passionate defense of Yosemite National Park, Muir succeeded in establishing the larger principle of American Wilderness as an inviolable space, exempt from the pressures of economic development.[3]

Aside from his brief stint as an undergraduate at the University of Wisconsin, John Muir was largely self-educated, and his scanty academic credentials would probably not allow him to be employed in any capacity by today's Sierra Club, which has come to be regarded (especially by more radical environmental groups) as a complacent insider organization largely populated by lawyers and lobbyists in tasseled loafers. Muir, by contrast, was always something of an unkempt outsider, a solitary prophet crying in the wilderness. Historians of the American environmental movement have tended to emphasize Muir's rugged individualism, and consequently there has been remarkably little discussion of his highly self-conscious participation in an intellectual tradition of ecological understanding and environmental advocacy that goes back to the English Romantic poets. Muir has sometimes been described as a belated American Transcendentalist, and his connections with Emerson and Thoreau have been thoroughly examined, but his profound awareness and lifetime study of English Romantic poetry, along with Scottish writers of the Romantic period (particularly Robert Burns and Walter Scott), has not been given adequate attention by historians of the environmental movement. Accordingly, this chapter will examine his indebtedness to the British Romantic writers, not only for important ecological concepts, but also for key images and essential rhetorical strategies. As we shall see, in the journal narrative of his first summer in the Sierra Nevada, Muir explicitly acknowledges his Romantic roots, referring at certain key moments to the poetry of Percy Shelley and Robert Burns.

Mountain Manuscript

Muir's journal account of his pastoral wandering in the mountain wilderness of California during the summer of 1869 was later published as *My First Summer in the Sierra* (1911). Although Muir extensively revised his original journal manuscript (mainly for concision and narrative coherence), this book nevertheless retains an exuberant sense of youthful enthusiasm along with an authentic tone of wonder and breathless astonishment at his first encounter with the vast American wilderness. Accompanied by a motley crew of shepherds, his trusty sheepdog Carlo, and some 2,000 sheep, Muir climbed ever higher into the Sierra Nevada, botanizing and geologizing as he went. Although he was employed to protect the sheep from such fierce predators as bears, wolves, and coyotes, Muir nevertheless discovered a growing sense of kinship with all of the Earth's living creatures. In his description of the chaparral, a dense thicket of evergreen shrubs that blankets the Sierra foothills, Muir alludes to the poetry of Robert Burns, observing that "a multitude of birds and 'wee, sleekit, cow'rin, tim'rous beasties' find good homes in its deepest margins."[4] Burns's poem "To a Mouse" provides a handy means for Muir to express his sincere affection for the small creatures that inhabit the chaparral. Unexpectedly bitten by black ants, Muir tolerates the excruciating pain, not as a misfortune, but as an opportunity for self-discovery: "A quick electric flame of pain flashes along the outraged nerves, and you discover for the first time how great is the capacity for sensation you are possessed of" (178). Even the ubiquitous poison oak, "troublesome to most travelers, inflaming the skin and eyes," leads Muir to reflect on its place in the larger scheme of things. It "blends harmoniously with its companion plants, and many a charming flower leans confidingly upon it for protection and shade" (166). The fault is not in the poison oak, but in ourselves, that we are unable to fathom its true purpose for existence: "Like most other things not apparently useful to man, it has few friends, and the blind question, 'Why was it made?' goes on and on with never a guess that first of all it might have been made for itself" (166). Muir is working toward a deep ecological perspective, according to which even apparently noxious species play an important role in the natural world. As he ascends the mountains, they are teaching him how to appreciate the great biological diversity of their flora and fauna.

Muir encountered an astonishing variety of wild creatures during his first extended visit to the Sierra Nevada. In many places his journal reads like an annotated botanical and zoological catalog, as he describes each species and notes its typical associations and habitat. Yet his perspective is far from being that of a detached scientific observer. Muir evokes each living creature as a welcome companion in his travels, often calling them *people* rather than *things*. He is never really alone because he is accompanied by "other people of the so-called solitude—deer in the forest caring for their young; the strong, well-clad, well-fed bears; the lively throng of squirrels; the blessed birds, great and small, stirring and sweetening the groves" (244). He even refers to "plant people" (244) and "such small people as gnats and mosquitoes" (253). Indeed, as he gradually learns to interpret its enigmatic features, the entire wilderness becomes personified: "But most impressive of all is the vast glowing countenance of the wilderness in awful, infinite repose" (244). Like Thoreau, who referred to the Maine wilderness as "peopled with trout," Muir intends such personifications not merely in a metaphorical sense, but as a strong assertion of the fundamental equivalence between wild creatures and human beings. Defying the Cartesian tradition of ontological dualism, Muir stubbornly refuses to accord any special status to humankind. As he pursues his quest deeper into the "Range of Light," he becomes increasingly identified with the landscape that surrounds him, no longer simply a detached observer: "Our flesh-and-bone tabernacle seems transparent as glass to the beauty about us, as if truly an inseparable part of it, thrilling with the air and trees, streams and rocks, in the waves of the sun—a part of all nature" (161). In this way Muir seeks to heal the Cartesian disjuncture between humankind and the natural world. Indeed, he argues that the alienation of Western man from the places he inhabits, and his rapacious use of technology to extract raw materials from deep within the bowels of the Earth, has inexorably led to environmental destruction.

Muir contrasts the destructive industrial technologies of the white man with the more sustainable subsistence practices of the indigenous Indians, with whom Muir became acquainted during his first summer in the Sierra. He notes that the Indians have inhabited this region for many centuries, and yet they have left few traces upon the landscape. "Indians walk softly and hurt the landscape hardly more than the birds and squirrels." Muir recognizes that the Indians often set fires in the surrounding woods "to improve their hunting grounds," but the traces of these fires "vanish in a few centuries" (184). Muir is moved to anger when he contemplates the extensive and irreversible changes in the land that have been wrought in just a few decades by the intrusion of white settlers, especially the rapacious miners who arrived during the California Gold Rush of 1849:

> How different are most of those [marks] of the white man, especially on the lower gold region—roads blasted in the solid rock, wild streams dammed and tamed and turned out of their channels and led along the sides of cañons and valleys to work in mines like slaves . . . imprisoned in iron pipes to strike and wash away hills and miles of the skin of the mountain's face, riddling, stripping every gold gully and flat. These are the white man's marks made in a few feverish years, to say nothing of mills, fields, villages, scattered hundreds of miles along the flank of the Range. (184)

Muir deplores the techniques of hydraulic gold mining, which used powerful jets of water to excavate enormous quantities of soil and gravel. These tailings accumulated in vast piles and caused extensive siltation and flooding downstream in the Sacramento river valley. These destructive mining technologies left marks on the landscape that are still visible today. Yet Muir observes that "Nature is doing what she can" to heal these terrible marks of destruction, "replanting, gardening, sweeping away old dams and flumes, leveling gravel and boulder piles, patiently trying to heal every raw scar" (184). Muir is outraged by the senseless destruction that results from the large-scale extraction of mineral resources from wilderness areas, and he laments the way that wild streams are dammed and made "to work like slaves" in the service of modern industry.[5]

Yet the tone of *My First Summer in the Sierra* is not generally argumentative; it is rather an extended lyrical evocation of the mystery and wonder of the California wilderness and its fascinating denizens. Muir's journal entry for June 29, 1869, records his first observation of the water-ouzel, "a very interesting little bird that flits about the falls and rapids of the main branches of the river" (190). What intrigues Muir about this bird is its resourceful adaptation to a watery environment. "It is not a water-bird in structure, though it gets its living in the water, and never leaves the streams. It is not web-footed, yet it dives fearlessly into deep swirling rapids, evidently to feed at the bottom, using its wings to swim with under water just as ducks and loons do" (190). Muir is more Lamarckian than Darwinian in his understanding of such behavioral adaptations; he does not regard the water-ouzel's unusual way of using its wings as the result of natural selection acting upon random genetic mutations, but rather as the emergence of a distinctive set of character traits within the context of a particular local environment. Muir calls attention to the close functional relationship between the bird and its "genial climate," and he suggests that the ambient noise of the waterfall has affected its song:

> What a romantic life this little bird leads on the most beautiful portions of the streams, in a *genial climate* with shade and cool water and spray to temper the summer heat. No wonder it is a fine singer, considering the stream songs it hears day and night. Every breath the little poet draws is part of a song, for all the air about the rapids and falls is beaten into music, and its first lessons must begin before it is born by the thrilling and quivering of the eggs in unison with the tones of the falls. (190; emphasis added)

Although most modern readers would probably dismiss such Lamarckian speculations as merely fanciful, we should still recognize that Muir intends this passage as a serious attempt at scientific explanation. If all living creatures possess sentience, just as humans do, then cultural evolution must also be possible for them. Thus, in Muir's view, the water-ouzel's behavior is not merely the product of natural selection operating externally upon the species; its inner mental life must play a major role in the way it comes to exist in a given place. As a "little poet" it creates songs in harmony with the sounds of its environment. To borrow a phrase from Wallace Stevens, the songs of the water-ouzel are the poems of its climate.

Not all of the animals in this wilderness are so blithe, cheerful, and harmless as the water-ouzel. Muir's journal achieves a dramatic climax in his encounter with a bear. Working against the grain of traditional American folk-tales about bear-hunting (which typically entail a battle to the death against a supposedly pernicious predator), Muir goes forth into this narrative situation unarmed and without belligerent intent. But he still has a lesson to learn from this encounter, because the bear is not playing by the rules, either:

> I had been told that this sort of bear, the cinnamon, always ran from his bad brother man, never showing fight unless wounded or in defense of young. . . . After examining at leisure, noting the sharp muzzle thrust inquiringly forward, the long shaggy hair on his broad chest, the stiff, erect ears nearly buried in hair, and the slow, heavy way he moved his head, I thought I should like to see his gait in running, so I made a sudden rush at him, shouting and swinging my hat to frighten him, expecting to see him make haste to get away. But to my dismay he did not run or show any sign of running. On the contrary, he stood his ground ready to fight and defend himself, lowered his head, thrust it forward, and looked sharply and fiercely at me. Then I suddenly began to fear that upon me would fall the work of running; but I was afraid to run, and therefore, like the bear, held my ground. (230-231)

After some tense moments, this perilous encounter is resolved through the bear's dignified departure:

> We stood staring at each other in solemn silence within a dozen yards or thereabouts, while I fervently hoped that the power of the human eye over wild beasts would prove to be as great as it is said to be. How long our awfully strenuous interview lasted, I don't know; but at length in the slow fullness of time he pulled his huge paws down off the log, and with magnificent deliberation turned and walked leisurely up the meadow, stopping frequently to look back over his shoulder to see whether I was pursuing him, then moving on again, evidently neither fearing me very much nor trusting me. (231)

Muir is humbled by this experience, yet it also proves educational for him. In his encounter with "a broad, rusty bundle of ungovernable wildness," he comes to realize the utter unpredictability of all living creatures, and he pauses to reflect upon the bear's self-confidence as top predator within its normal habitat: "In the great cañons Bruin reigns supreme. Happy fellow, whom no famine can reach while one of his thousand kinds of food is spared him" (231). Having learned to respect the bear as an omnivorous fellow-inhabitant of the wilderness, Muir also recognizes the dangerous folly of his own prior belief in "the power of the human eye over wild beasts." Humans possess no such magical powers of intimidation, especially in a remote wilderness area where the large predators are rarely hunted.

Merely by refusing to flee from a human intruder, the bear has taught Muir a valuable lesson in humility.

Even the mute rocks provide Muir with valuable scientific information. One of his main objectives in climbing the "Range of Light" (309) was to learn more about its geology, with particular attention to the role of glaciers in the creation of Yosemite Valley. As an avid reader of the glacial theories of Louis Agassiz, Muir was well-prepared to recognize the characteristic traces of glacial activity, and he was delighted to discover that the Sierra Nevada abounded in such traces. He observed glacial erratics, boulders "brought from a distance, as difference in color and composition shows, quarried and carried and laid down here each in its place" (210). Muir goes on to explain how these boulders were carried to their present location:

> And with what tool were they quarried and carried? On the pavement we find its marks. The most resisting unweathered portion of the surface is scored and striated in a rigidly parallel way, indicating that the region has been overswept by a glacier from the northeastward, grinding down the general mass of the mountains, scoring and polishing, producing a strange, raw, wiped appearance, and dropping whatever boulders it chanced to be carrying at the time it was melted at the close of the Glacial Period. A fine discovery this. (210)

The "marks" inscribed upon these pavements were left by ancient glaciers as they overswept the entire Sierra Nevada. Muir was the first geologist to realize the fundamental importance of glaciers in shaping the mountain range, and specifically Yosemite Valley; most professional geologists of the time (including Josiah Whitney, the California State Geologist) believed that Yosemite was formed by a catastrophic subsidence caused by an earthquake.[6] Muir refused to accept that the grand appearances of Yosemite could be the result of such a bizarre, unaccountable catastrophe. He preferred to interpret its impressive geological features as the result of a more subtle and gradual, yet still vast and sublime, process of glacial erosion.

Muir refers to the glaciers as "tools" because he regards them, quite literally, as instruments of Creation in the hands of God. Such a conception is entirely in keeping with his pantheistic sense of the world as an unmediated expression of divine energy. Indeed, in a memorable phrase, Muir describes the entire universe as a single interwoven entity:

> This quick, inevitable interest attaching to everything seems marvelous until the hand of God becomes visible; then it seems reasonable that what inter-

ests Him may well interest us. When we try to pick out anything by itself, we find it hitched to everything in the universe. (245)

In certain respects, such an ecological understanding of world-formation harks back to the physico-theology of John Ray and William Derham, but Muir would have rejected their fundamental belief that the universe was a machine cleverly constructed by a watchmaker God.[7] In Muir's worldview, the divine world-making energies are immanent, not transcendent, and the visible changes in the natural world are not only the way that we come to know God; they are also the way that God comes to know Himself. Particularly in the mountains, the divine workmanship is revealed:

> Nature as a poet, an enthusiastic workingman, becomes more and more visible the farther and higher we go; for the mountains are fountains—beginning places, however related to sources beyond mortal ken. (245)

By describing Nature as "an enthusiastic workingman," Muir offers a homely, artisanal image for the divine process of world-formation. Moreover, if nature is the poetry of God, then the task of the geologist is to interpret the Book of Nature, seeking to discover the meanings hidden in the riddle of the rocks.[8]

Muir frequently uses the traditional metaphor of the Book of Nature to describe his own activity of geological inquiry, although he often finds the meaning of the rocks inscrutable. Yosemite Valley, "with its wonderful cliffs and groves, [is] a grand page of mountain manuscript that I would gladly give my life to be able to read" (211). Yet even if the "mountain manuscript" cannot be fully comprehended, it offers enough hints and glimmers of meaning, like a difficult poem, to keep the human interpreter fully engaged. Muir finds no reason to "bewail our poor inevitable ignorance," since there is always some immediate pleasure to be found in the beauty of the visible creation: "Some of the external beauty is always in sight, enough to keep every fibre of us tingling, and this we are able to gloriously enjoy though the methods of its creation may lie beyond our ken" (211). Rational inquiry and aesthetic appreciation are complementary, not mutually exclusive, in Muir's response to the vast mountain landscape.

Like John Clare, Muir occasionally uses the rhetorical figure of prosopopoeia to convey his intuitive sense that all of nature is animated. Not only animals and birds, but even rocks and trees, are presented as having the power to express themselves in articulate language. Muir evokes the words of all creatures as they awaken in the morning:

> Every morning, arising from the death of sleep, the happy plants and all our fellow animal creatures great and small, and even the rocks, seemed to be shouting, "Awake, awake, rejoice, rejoice, come love us and join in our song. Come! Come!" (191)

At another dramatic moment in *My First Summer in the Sierra*, Muir alludes to Shelley's poem "The Cloud" as an especially memorable instance of prosopopoeia:

> Never in all my travels have I found anything more truly novel and interesting than these midday mountains of the sky, their fine tones of color, majestic visible growth, and ever-changing scenery and general effects, though mostly as well let alone as far as description goes. I oftentimes think of Shelley's cloud poem, "I sift the snow on the mountains below." (239)

Through this allusion to Shelley's poem, Muir explicitly acknowledges the Romantic roots of his pantheistic conception of nature. By attributing sentience to all natural phenomena, even such ephemeral objects as clouds, Muir is relying upon one of Shelley's favorite rhetorical techniques; such personifications occur not only in "The Cloud" but also throughout *Prometheus Unbound,* where characters from Greek mythology rub shoulders with the Earth, Moon, and Ocean. In "Mont Blanc" (a poem that fascinated Muir), Shelley attributes voice to the mountain, and a "mysterious tongue" to the wilderness that surrounds it.[9] Muir's allusion to Shelley's "The Cloud" marks a deep affinity in their means of expressing the sentient dimensions of non-human life, particularly in remote mountain and glacial landscapes.

"How do we know that space is ungrateful?"

After spending his first summer shepherding and exploring in the Sierra, Muir settled in Yosemite Valley, finding part-time work operating a sawmill (where he insisted on cutting only windfallen timber) and occasionally guiding groups of tourists around the valley. The most eminent visitor to Yosemite Valley during Muir's residence there was Ralph Waldo Emerson, who arrived in May 1871. At the age of 68, Emerson was an American author of international renown, and his essays and poems were already familiar to Muir, who read them avidly during his years at the University of Wisconsin. Upon his arrival, Muir wrote a note inviting Emerson to go on an extended camping trip together in the high Sierra, and the following morning Emerson paid a friendly visit to Muir in the little "hang-nest" where he lived, perched on the side of the sawmill. Many years later, Muir recalled this visit from Emerson as one of the two supreme moments of his life (the other being his discovery of the *Calypso borealis* blooming alone in the Canadian wilderness).[10] The two men found great pleasure in each other's company, and Muir agreed to guide Emerson and his companions to a majestic grove of Sequoias, not far from Yosemite Valley. In a chapter of *Our National Parks* (1901) entitled "Forests of Yosemite Park," Muir describes his boisterous high spirits as he led Emerson around the Valley and among the Big Trees:

> He seemed as serene as a sequoia, his head in the empyrean; and forgetting his age, plans, duties, ties of every sort, I proposed an immeasurable camping trip back into the heart of the mountains. He seemed anxious to go, but considerately mentioned his party. I said: "Never mind. The mountains are calling; run away, and let plans and parties and dragging lowland duties all 'gang tapsal-teerie.' We'll go up a cañon singing your own song, 'Good-by, proud world! I'm going home,' in divine earnest. Up there lies a new heaven and a new earth; let us go to the show." (786–787)

With considerable audacity, Muir quotes to Emerson the first line of own poem, "Good-bye," a lyric that evokes the pleasure of escape from the cares of civilization into the wilderness, "Where arches green, the livelong day, / Echo the blackbird's roundelay."[11] As they rode together among the majestic trees, Muir quoted another of Emerson's poems to him, as if he were calling Emerson back to the doctrines of natural wisdom that he had espoused in his younger days:

> Next day we rode through the magnificent forests of the Merced basin, and I kept calling his attention to the sugar pines, quoting his wood-notes, "Come listen to what the pine tree saith," etc., pointing out the noblest as kings and high priests, the most eloquent and commanding preachers of all the mountain forests. (787)

Muir alludes here to one of Emerson's most powerful evocations of the beauty of wilderness, "Woodnotes II," a poem spoken entirely in the voice of a pine tree. It was evidently this feature of Emerson's poem—another instance of prosopopoeia—that attracted Muir's attention, since he describes the surrounding sugar pines as "eloquent and commanding preachers," attributing to them the power of speech. Indeed, Emerson evokes the eloquence of the tree by means of a characteristically Romantic metaphor, the Aeolian harp, in the following passage:

> Song wakes in my pinnacles
> When the wind swells.
> Soundeth the prophetic wind,
> The shadows shake on the rock behind,
> And the countless leaves of the pine are strings
> Tuned to the lay the wood-god sings. ("Woodnotes II," 43)

Like a vast, living Aeolian harp, the pine tree is wakened to prophetic song when the wind blows through its "countless leaves."[12] Muir himself uses a similar figure of the Aeolian harp in *My First Summer in the Sierra,* perhaps thinking of Emerson's "Woodnotes" as he writes of

> trees that are the kings of their race, their ranks nobly marshaled to view, spire above spire, crown above crown, waving their long, leafy arms, tossing their cones like ringing bells—blessed sun-fed mountaineers rejoicing in their strength, every tree tuneful, a harp for the winds and the sun. (201)

Presumably Emerson was treated to this sort of eloquence (and much more) during his tour of the forests with Muir. Although Muir was disappointed that Emerson would not camp out with him under the Big Trees, he nevertheless found great joy in the presence of the older man, who appeared to Muir in the guise of a prophet and poetic precursor in the vocation of Nature. Their brief encounter in Yosemite Valley is one of the most congenial and significant moments in the history of American nature writing.

After Emerson returned to his home in Concord, Massachusetts, Muir sent him several letters of friendship, replete with lyrical description and wilderness exhortation. In February 1872, Emerson replied to Muir in a brief, yet eloquent letter that Muir treasured for the rest of his life. Apologizing for his long silence, Emerson gently encourages Muir to return to the East Coast for an extended visit in his home:

> I have everywhere testified to my friends, who should also be yours, my happiness in finding you—the right man in the right place—in your mountain tabernacle, and have expected when your guardian angel would pronounce that your probation and sequestration in the solitudes and snows had reached their term, and you were to bring your ripe fruits so rare and precious into

waiting society. . . . So I pray you to bring to an early close your absolute contracts with any yet unvisited glaciers or volcanoes, roll up your drawings, herbariums and poems, and come to the Atlantic Coast.[13]

Emerson's affection for his young disciple, sequestrated among the solitudes and snows of the California wilderness, is quite apparent here. Along with this generous letter of invitation, Emerson sent Muir a gift of two volumes of his collected essays. Although Muir never paid Emerson a return visit in Concord, he did read these two volumes with great care, highlighting key passages and making extensive marginal commentary. These marginal comments on Emerson's essays continue their personal colloquy while extending Muir's sense of his own areas of critical departure from Emerson's ideas about nature.

Like most marginalia intended only for private reference, Muir's comments on Emerson's essays may exaggerate the extent of his disagreement with the elder philosopher, if taken out of context. Muir certainly found much to admire, and much to emulate, in Emerson's writings. But on certain points Muir found himself offering sharp rejoinders to Emerson's assertions. In the following excerpts from Emerson's collected essays, Muir's marginal comments are shown in italics:

> Emerson: "The squirrel hoards nuts, and the bee gathers honey, without knowing what they do." Muir: *How do we know this.*
> Nature "takes no thought for the morrow." *Are not buds and seeds thought for the morrow.*
> "It never troubles the sun that some of his rays fall wide and vain into ungrateful space, and only a small part on the reflecting planet." *How do we know that space is ungrateful.*
> "The soul that ascends to worship the great God is plain and true; has no rose-color." *Why not? God's sky has rose color and so has his flower.*
> "The beauty of nature must always seem unreal and mocking, until the landscape has human figures." *God is in it.*
> "The trees are imperfect men, and seem to bemoan their imprisonment, rooted in the ground." *No.*
> "There is in the woods and waters a certain enticement and flattery, together with a failure to yield a present satisfaction. This disappointment is felt in every landscape." *No—always we find more than we expect.*[14]

In each of these instances, Muir is responding to Emerson's assertions from a deep ecological perspective, rejecting any implication that humankind has a special ontological status in the greater scheme of things. He challenges

Emerson's assertion that squirrels and bees lack foresight, and he suggests that even buds and seeds provide evidence of "thought for the morrow." Emerson supposes that the empty void surrounding the earth is "ungrateful" for the sun's warmth, but Muir finds reason to question this premise. Muir poses the unanswerable question, "How do we know that space is ungrateful?" If the entire universe is pervaded with sentient being, then perhaps even interplanetary space may contain glimmers or sparks of affective awareness. Who are we to say otherwise? And who is Emerson to determine the color of souls? By asking such impertinent questions, Muir is cutting to the very core of Emerson's residual anthropocentrism, thereby laying the intellectual groundwork for his own deep ecological worldview.[15]

Muir's critique of Emerson arises mainly from Muir's underlying concern that Emerson has not remained true to his own most seminal insights into the meaning of the American landscape. Like many of his contemporaries, Muir had been inspired by Emerson's famous "transparent eyeball" passage in *Nature,* which articulates a deep sense of kinship between individual human beings and the "currents of the Universal Being" that circulate through them. By invoking the presence of such divine energies within the natural world, Emerson had indicated the possibility of a posthumanistic perspective in American ethics and aesthetics. And Muir was in fundamental accord with Emerson's lifelong quest to redeem the American landscape from a merely utilitarian conception of its possibilities. But Muir detects a latent ethic of anthropocentrism lurking in certain passages of Emerson's essays, particularly in those unguarded moments when Emerson reveals an unexamined belief in the domestication of landscape and a less-than-profound knowledge of natural history. As he emerged from his stimulating encounter with Emerson, Muir was still seeking adequate rhetorical means to express his sense of absolute identity with the non-human beings that surrounded him in the California wilderness—the profusion of plants and animals, the fast-flowing streams of water and air, even the silent stones beneath his feet. He eventually discovered such means of expression in the poetry of the English Romantics.

Aeolian Music

John Muir's first published book, *The Mountains of California* (1894), was assembled from a series of essays that he had previously published in popular magazines: *Harper's, Scribner's, Century,* and the *Overland Monthly,* from 1875 to 1882.[16] More than just a hasty compilation, each chapter was thoroughly revised and expanded from its periodical version, and the book had an enduring impact upon the public recognition of America's wilderness heritage. *The Mountains of California* established Muir's public identity as an eloquent advocate for the preservation of wilderness areas and the conservation of forests and watersheds, while it also advanced his scientific argument for the role of glacial erosion in the formation of the Sierra Nevada. Throughout this work, he combines precise scientific observation with a more exalted conception of nature that harks back to the Romantic poets in its intensity of vision and exuberance of detail. Perhaps the clearest example of Muir's intellectual affinity with the Romantic movement occurs in his use of the Aeolian harp image, which appears in a climactic episode of the chapter entitled "A Wind-Storm in the Forests":

> Toward midday, after a long, tingling scramble through copses of hazel and ceanothus, I gained the summit of the highest ridge in the neighborhood; and then it occurred to me that it would be a fine thing to climb one of the trees to obtain a wider outlook and get my ear close to the Aeolian music of its topmost needles. . . . After cautiously casting about, I made choice of the tallest of a group of Douglas Spruces that were growing close together like a tuft of grass, no one of which seemed likely to fall unless all the rest fell with it. Though comparatively young, they were about 100 feet high, and their lithe, brushy tops were rocking and swirling in wild ecstasy. Being accustomed to climb trees in making botanical studies, I experienced no difficulty in reaching the top of this one, and never before did I enjoy so noble an exhilaration of motion. The slender tops fairly flapped and swished in the passionate torrent, bending and swirling backward and forward, round and round, tracing indescribable combinations of vertical and horizontal curves, while I clung with muscles firm braced, like a bobolink on a reed. (469)

Muir's description of this tree-climbing episode lends a remarkable concreteness and immediacy to the conventional and even somewhat shopworn image of the Aeolian harp. Unwilling to remain aloof as a passive observer of the windstorm, he climbs into the treetops in order to participate in their wild ecstasy of motion. Clinging to the branches "like a bobolink on a reed," Muir casts off his detached scientific persona and becomes an integral part of the scene he beholds. This act of integration partly depends upon Muir's acceptance of physical danger; the thrill of clinging to the branch arises from the thrill of his own mortality, which binds him ever more closely to the natural cycles of death and rebirth.

The Aeolian harp image recurs frequently in Muir's writing, and this image may have enabled him to conceive the relation between nature and the human mind in ways that he could not have done without it. In a letter to Charles Warren Stoddard (a California poet), written in February 1872, during his extended residence in Yosemite Valley, Muir uses this image to evoke the transforming power of nature as it sweeps over the human senses:

> You must not hope that I can teach you, I am only a baby slowly learning my mountain alphabet but I can freely promise that Nature will do great things for you. . . . Come then to the mountains and bathe in fountain Love. Stand upon our Domes and let spirit winds blow through you and you will sing effortless as an Eolian harp.[17]

In writing to a fellow poet about the very nature of poetic vocation, Muir adopts a prophetic tone, evoking the Aeolian metaphor as a means of establishing a bond between poetic "making" and the ongoing process of creation in the natural world.

The image of the Aeolian harp enables Muir to express his vision of the natural world as a place of continuous process, where everything must change in order to make way for something else. In one of his "campfire aphorisms," Muir explores this implication:

> There is always heard, even on the stillest days, a kind of fine aeolian harp music in the air. This is always heard—a sort of world harp, giving out immortal unceasing melody, in unison with all the stars of the sky, for this is still the morning of creation and the sound of work in world-making is eternal.[18]

In this passage the ecological dimension of the Aeolian harp metaphor is made quite explicit. Muir bears witness to the vast dynamic interrelationships that prevail, not only among living things, but among "all the stars in the sky"; his is a cosmic ecology that celebrates the eternal process of world-making on a scale that exceeds any possible human knowledge.[19]

Although (as we have seen) the image of the Aeolian harp does occur in the writings of Emerson and Thoreau, it originally derives from the English Romantic poets, and it finds its fullest thematic development in the poetry of Coleridge and Shelley. In "The Eolian Harp," Coleridge inaugurates a crucial Romantic metaphor that seeks to express the vital interconnection of human beings with other organisms, and he engages in a powerfully evocative speculation about the underlying nature of nature:

> And what if all of animated nature
> Be but organic Harps diversely fram'd
> That tremble into thought, as o'er them sweeps

Plastic and vast, one intellectual breeze,
At once the Soul of each, and God of all? (45-48)

This dangerously pantheistic speculation is quickly quashed by Coleridge's irritable and rather squeamishly orthodox wife ("my pensive Sara"), but the poem's internal dialectic should not blind us to the significance of the Aeolian harp metaphor as a basis for environmental awareness. This image has become something of a cliché in Romantic studies, but I would nevertheless suggest that it deserves a fresh look, since it constitutes one of the earliest and most influential poetic paradigms for an ecological understanding of the natural world.

M. H. Abrams was probably the first literary critic to point out the environmental significance of the Aeolian harp in his famous essay, "The Correspondent Breeze," first published in 1957:

> The wind, as an invisible power known only by its effects, had an even greater part to play than water, light, and clouds in the Romantic revolt against the world-view of the Enlightenment. In addition, the moving air lent itself preeminently to the aim of tying man back into the environment from which, Wordsworth and Coleridge felt, he had been excluded by post-Cartesian dualism and mechanism.[20]

This Abrams essay has been roundly criticized for essentializing a metaphor without due regard to its qualifying context, but we should nevertheless recall the essay's main point, which was that the image of the Aeolian harp made certain thoughts thinkable to the Romantic poets that might otherwise have remained unexpressed. The Aeolian harp was more than just a plaything of idle poets; it facilitated a tectonic shift in the way that Western culture conceived its relation to the natural world.

Percy Shelley made a notable innovation upon the Aeolian harp metaphor in his "Ode to the West Wind." In the final stanza of this poem, Shelley presents himself as an Aeolian harp, a human exponent of the West Wind's profound meaning and message:

> Make me thy lyre, even as the forest is:
> What if my leaves are falling like its own!
> The tumult of thy mighty harmonies
>
> Will take from both a deep, autumnal tone,
> Sweet though in sadness. Be thou, Spirit fierce,
> My spirit! Be thou me, impetuous one!

> Drive my dead thoughts over the universe
> Like withered leaves to quicken a new birth! (57-64)

Shelley offers himself as a "lyre" to bear the full force of the West Wind, represented in this poem as a turbulent, tempestuous wind of autumn that spreads death and destruction across the world. Although the poem presents a scene of universal devastation, its tone is prevailingly optimistic, since the advent of autumn presages the eventual turn of the seasons, when "thine azure sister of the Spring shall blow / Her clarion o'er the dreaming earth" (9-10).

Of all the instances of the Aeolian harp metaphor previously cited, Shelley's "Ode to the West Wind" comes closest in tone and spirit to John Muir's evocation of the wind-harp in "A Wind-Storm in the Forests." Like Shelley, Muir presents himself as a human embodiment of the Aeolian harp, and he anticipates that the passage of the wind over his "leaves" will spread the prophetic message of "my words among mankind" (as Shelley describes the ultimate effect of his verse). Muir may well have had Shelley's poem in mind as he clambered up the Douglas Spruce and clung to its swaying branches "like a bobolink on a reed." Muir literalizes Shelley's metaphorical equivalence between himself and a forest; Muir actually becomes an integral part of the tree as it "flapped and swished in the passionate torrent, bending and swirling backward and forward, round and round, tracing indescribable combinations of vertical and horizontal curves" (469). Even after he descends back to Earth, Muir carries within himself a deeper appreciation for the sentient life of trees; he realizes that trees and men have much in common as they travel the galaxy together:

> We all travel the milky way together, trees and men; but it never occurred to me until this storm-day, while swinging in the wind, that trees are travelers, in the ordinary sense. They make many journeys, not extensive ones, it is true; but our own little journeys, away and back again, are only little more than tree-wavings—many of them not so much. (472-473)

Building upon the Aeolian harp metaphor, Muir uses the occasion of his renewed experience of identification with the forest to explore the meaning of the "travels" that trees make as they swing back and forth in the wind. On a cosmic scale, "our own little journeys" have hardly any greater extent or significance than those of trees; we wander forth from home and back again, often without any noticeable gain in wisdom. Muir's own travels in the Sierra Nevada, far from any settled residence or occupation, present a re-externalized version of the archetypal Romantic quest. Like many other Romantic questers, Muir finds himself most truly when he is farthest from home, where he encounters the utterly inhuman otherness of temporal experience. For Muir, however, the imminent loss of personal identity seems to pose no threat; he is happy enough to merge his being into the larger existence of the forest that surrounds him.

John Muir is more than simply a popularizer of Romantic ideas; he was engaged for most of his adult life in a careful close reading and critical response to the work of the English Romantic poets. Muir's personal library (which is now located in the Huntington Library collection) includes copies of the poetical works of Blake, Wordsworth, Keats, Shelley, and Byron; it also includes five volumes of poetry and prose by Coleridge. Muir's annotations to Coleridge's *Poetical Works, Biographia Literaria, Lectures on Shakespeare, Table Talk,* and *Theory of Life* reveal a remarkable degree of intellectual engagement with Coleridge's holistic conception of the natural world, and they provide clear evidence of Muir's indebtedness to Coleridge's poetic language and imagery.[21] In the following section of this chapter, I will not attempt to summarize the remarkable extent and variety of Muir's annotations to the English Romantic poets, but rather present a single case study of Coleridge's influence on the conception and design of one of Muir's most popular and influential literary works.

Man and Beast

Muir's annotations to Coleridge date from the late 1880s and 1890s, when he was primarily engaged in composing two major works: an extended narrative account of his *Travels in Alaska* (published posthumously in 1915) and a short story entitled *Stickeen* (first published in a periodical of 1897, and in enlarged book form in 1909). Muir's annotations are closely involved with the composition of both of these works, which emerge through a process of dialogue between Muir and Coleridge. I shall focus on the result of this dialogue in Muir's composition of *Stickeen,* which was based on an actual episode that occurred during Muir's exploration of Alaska in 1880. This story describes how Muir became acquainted with a dog named Stickeen, a rather unfriendly little mongrel that nevertheless displayed appealing traits of wildness, independence, and raw courage. Like the ascetic philosopher Diogenes, the dog stands entirely aloof from humankind, remaining utterly wild even in the midst of human society:

> Stickeen seemed a very Diogenes, asking only to be let alone: a true child of
> the wilderness, holding the even tenor of his hidden life with the silence and
> serenity of nature. His strength of character lay in his eyes. They looked as
> old as the hills, and as young, and as wild. (556).

Yet despite the dog's aloofness, Muir comes to feel a sneaking affection for
him, especially when they find themselves confronted with a life-threatening
situation. The climax of the story occurs when the dog follows Muir across
a glacier and they are suddenly trapped in a maze of crevasses. Echoing
Robert Burns's poem "To a Mouse," Muir exclaims, "But poor Stickeen,
the wee, hairy, sleekit beastie, think of him!" (566). At great personal risk,
both Muir and Stickeen manage to extricate themselves from the ice and
find their way back to civilization. The story develops this simple plot in a
dramatic and compelling manner. At the heart of its meaning is Muir's discovery of an intimate bond of companionship that links him with the dog
and, implicitly, with all forms of life.

Muir worked out the details of his *Stickeen* story with painstaking care
in a large notebook and in the flyleaves of several books.[22] Although it is
an uncomplicated tale, it evidently distills a great deal of thought and experience that needed to be worked out in dialogue with other authors, of
whom the most important is Coleridge. Muir's five Coleridge volumes are
laden with annotations that testify to his deep and fruitful engagement with
Coleridge's ideas. Especially interesting is Muir's response to "The Rime of
the Ancient Mariner," in which he takes special note of a passage describing the "sweet jargonings" of the "troop of spirits blest" that inhabit the
dead bodies of the Mariner's comrades. The following passage, cited in the
introduction to Coleridge's *Poetical Works,* was marked by Muir with a vertical stroke in the margin; evidently curious about its context, Muir turned
to the poem itself and marked the same passage with a vertical stroke:

> Sometimes a–dropping from the sky
> I heard the sky-lark sing;
> Sometimes all little birds that are,
> How they seemed to fill the sea and air
> With their sweet jargoning!
>
> And now 'twas like all instruments,
> Now like a lonely flute;
> And now it is an angel's song,
> That makes the heavens be mute.

It ceased; yet still the sails made on
A pleasant noise till noon,
A noise like of a hidden brook
In the leafy month of June,
That to the sleeping woods all night
Singeth a quiet tune.[23]

It is somewhat puzzling to consider why this was the only passage in the entire poem to have been explicitly noted by Muir. We might instead have expected the sublime arctic scenery, or the kaleidoscopic sea-snakes, to have captured his attention. This passage, however, most clearly addresses a theme that was uppermost in Muir's mind as he composed *Stickeen:* the language of the "brute creation." The "sweet jargonings" of the skylarks are metaphorically related by Coleridge to the sounds of human instruments, the songs of angels, and the "singing" of a quiet brook. All created beings, and even inanimate objects, are accorded some form of linguistic expression in this passage. In a related annotation, Muir applies these words to a description of the sound made by streams of water flowing deep within the glacier: "The streams of the Gl[acier] filled all the rent ice & the air above with their 'sweet jargoning.' "[24] Muir extends Coleridge's poetic image to a more radical environmental usage, suggesting that the inanimate creation has its own language, and its own way of responding to the Aeolian influences of the One Life.

Although Muir was an avid admirer of Coleridge's poetry, he was critical of certain aspects of Coleridge's philosophy, particularly Coleridge's stress on the uniqueness of the human faculty of reason. In an annotation to Coleridge's commentary on *The Tempest,* Muir takes a swipe at Coleridge's assertion that animals lack reason and have no "moral sense." Muir asks: "Man & beast. Both moral?"[25] Muir proceeds to describe his own impressions of Stickeen, the "furious ebullition of his fears," the "passionate exuberance of joy," and concludes: "he plainly & reasonably dreaded losing life as if like a philosopher he knew the value of it. He was gifted with the faculties of hope & fear—[we were] fellow-mortals." In Muir's view, the dog displayed "Energy of thought—powers of mind" comparable to what human beings might manifest under similar circumstances.[26]

Muir goes on to question one of Coleridge's speculations about animal language: "Brute animals says Coleridge have the vowel sounds only man the consonants. But Stickine uttered his woe in all the human language— at least so it seemed to me."[27] Here again, Muir seeks to break down the conceptual boundaries that separate humankind from the rest of creation. No single aspect of cognition, language, or "moral sense" can serve as a litmus test to distinguish man from beast. In Muir's view, they differ in degree, not in kind.

While contesting the Christian humanism of the later Coleridge, Muir found himself deeply sympathetic to the more radical views of the youthful Pantisocrat, author of the poem "To a Young Ass" and "The Rime of the Ancient Mariner." Both of these poems express a kinship with all forms of life—even such unlovable beasts as asses and sea-snakes—that Coleridge was later to qualify from a more conservative philosophical perspective. While quarreling with some of Coleridge's philosophical assertions, however, Muir clearly learned a great deal from Coleridge's affirmation of the concept of organic form, and from Coleridge's holistic treatment of the continuum of animal species in his *Theory of Life*. Muir was able to grasp the contribution of Coleridge's thought to his own sense of cosmic ecology, while remaining somewhat critical of Coleridge's retreat from his youthful ideals.

Clearly the most vital and important influence on Muir's short story was Coleridge's poetry; Muir's annotations are closely oriented toward passages of natural description that he could relate to his Alaskan explorations, and the exotic appeal of Coleridge's supernatural poems is especially apparent. Like "The Rime of the Ancient Mariner," *Stickeen* is a parable about the kinship of all life. Both works recount the tale of an unlikely partnership between man and beast. Stickeen, like the Albatross, is a denizen of the remote polar regions, his name referring to his obscure origin within a local Indian tribe whose name was also given to a nearby river. Muir describes Stickeen as aloof, indifferent to humans and their concerns, disobedient, wild, and distinctly unanthropomorphic, mysterious in all of his ways and doings. He embodies the unknowability of the wilderness, the wider world where humans often find themselves off-balance, confused, and disoriented. Muir's plain, parabolic narrative tells how in a moment of crisis, Stickeen's strange soul revealed itself, and how a partnership was created that widened Muir's sense of kinship, making him realize his essential connection and responsibility to other living things. "At first the least promising and least known of my dog-friends, [Stickeen] suddenly became the best known of them all. Our storm-battle for life brought him to light, and through him as through a window I have ever since been looking with deeper sympathy into all my fellow mortals" (571).

Stickeen was one of Muir's most popular works in his own lifetime, although it has fallen into disfavor in an era that resists such edifying narratives. Like "The Rime of the Ancient Mariner," it might be regarded as having *too much* moral.[28] But it does seek to establish, in a way that no abstract philosophical argument possibly could, an ethical basis for Deep Ecology; specifically, the view that intrinsic moral value may be attributed to things outside the human sphere, beyond the merely utilitarian accomplishment of human purposes. The world exists, and deserves to exist, without any special regard to our personal needs and desires. Muir goes beyond the mere aestheticization of nature; he cares for wilderness and wild creatures, not merely because they are visually appealing and offer the intellectual pleasure of discovery to the human observer, but because they deserve to exist in and for themselves. Alligators, rattlesnakes, and mosquitoes have just as much right to exist as we do. It is one thing to assert this view, and it is another to make one's readers feel it compellingly. Yet the fate of the Earth may hinge upon such views becoming accepted and thoughtfully integrated within the core values of our society. Such honest and unsophisticated tales as *Stickeen* may have a vital role to play in the evolution of our post-industrial culture.

Chapter 8

Mary Austin:
The Land of Little Rain

Mary Hunter Austin (1868-1934) was the author of 34 books and more than 250 articles, essays, short stories, and poems on such diverse subjects as anthropology, folklore, politics, metaphysics, and poetics. She was an ardent feminist, championing women's suffrage and birth control, and a staunch environmental advocate, devoted to sustainable development, local control of natural resources, and the preservation of America's wild places.[1]

Born in Carlinville, Illinois, Austin attended Blackburn College and developed an early sense of vocation as a professional writer. Her first published essay, "One Hundred Miles on Horseback" (1887), describes her family's epic journey by covered wagon to a homestead in the remote valley of the Kern River in Southern California.[2] Here she met her future husband, Wallace Stafford Austin, and moved with him to the high desert country of the Owens Valley, east of the Sierra Nevada. Her husband proved feckless and improvident, and their marriage failed after the birth of a daughter who was mentally disabled; but even as her marriage crumbled, Mary Austin fell in love with the stark beauty of the Owens Valley and the wild creatures that inhabited it. Austin's classic evocation of the California desert, *The Land of Little Rain* (1903), is unsurpassed in its treatment of the harsh beauty of that landscape. Austin tempers John Muir's exuberant celebration of American Wilderness by introducing a more austere depiction of the desert creatures that live in a permanent condition of scarcity. She provides a sensitive characterization of the Paiute and Shoshone Indians, based on her intimate acquaintance with their way of life. In "The Basket Maker," one of the later chapters in *The Land of Little Rain,* Austin discovers that she has much in common with Seyavi, a Paiute woman abandoned by her husband who finds that she can live very well without a man.

Mary Austin was actively engaged in the tragic struggle of the people of the Owens Valley to defend their water supply from acquisition by the city of Los Angeles. When this struggle failed, and the valley's agricultural economy was slated for destruction, Austin left the region forever, moving first to San Francisco, then to New York and London, eventually finding a permanent home in Santa Fe, New Mexico, where she wrote *The Land of Journeys' Ending* (1924) and many other works about the American West. Her autobiography, *Earth Horizon* (1932), provides a vivid account of her eventful career as a writer. Austin's struggle for existence in a harsh land, complicated by a troubled relationship with her husband, resulted in an ecofeminist vision of the natural world that still serves as an influential model for contemporary environmental writers.[3]

Nurslings of the Sky

The Land of Little Rain was Austin's first published book, and it still remains her most popular and influential work. It is memorable both as an exquisitely detailed work of natural history and as a lyrical evocation of the desolate, windswept expanses of the Owens Valley and the Mojave Desert. As Roderick Nash has pointed out, the desert landscape was still a largely unknown, godforsaken territory to most American readers at the turn of the twentieth century.[4] It was commonly depicted in popular literature as a dangerous, forbidding place, frequented only by warlike savages, oracular Mormons, foolhardy prospectors, and rugged pioneers who were just passing through on their way to a more arable, healthful, and visually appealing place of settlement. As a domain of mystery and terror, the desert was susceptible to occasional artistic and literary treatment as an instance of the *sublime,* but it was not generally regarded as *beautiful,* and hence it was tacitly dismissed as an unfit subject for aesthetic appreciation. But these traditional attitudes were beginning to change around the turn of the century, as railroads crossed the continent, wild rivers were dammed, Indians were forcibly resettled on reservations, and the American wilderness gradually became more accessible and less threatening. For the wealthier classes, tourism became possible at such scenic destinations as Yellowstone and Yosemite National Parks; and the demand by armchair travelers for descriptive accounts of the American West became insatiable.

New magazines such as *The Overland Monthly* (founded in 1868, the year of Austin's birth) arose to meet this growing demand for Western travel literature, and several of the established Eastern magazines, including *Harper's* and *The Atlantic,* published frequent articles that evoked the splendors of the vast Western landscape. Both John Muir and Mary Austin published much of their early nature writing as articles in various popular journals before it appeared in book form. In particular, Mary Austin published three short stories in *The Overland Monthly* during the 1890s, and *The Land of Little Rain* was serialized in *The Atlantic* in 1902-1903.[5] In this way, Austin found a receptive audience for her work, and she managed to depict an unfamiliar landscape in a way that authentically conveyed its stern reality, yet rendered it appealing to a largely urban readership. By looking at the desert landscape in a new way, Mary Austin discovered an unexpected elegance of adaptation in its flora and fauna, a subtle play of sunlight on sand and rock, and an undiscovered pathos in the life stories of its human inhabitants. *The Land of Little Rain* is one of the first literary works ever to evoke the harsh, elemental beauty of the American desert.

The book's opening paragraphs alert the reader to the stark, forbidding topography of this country. Far from being an inviting pastoral landscape, the desert presents itself as a grim succession of jagged hills, a wasteland apparently devoid of life:

> This is the nature of that country. There are hills, rounded, blunt, burned, squeezed up out of chaos, chrome and vermilion painted, aspiring to the snow-line. Between the hills lie high level-looking plains full of intolerable sun glare, or narrow valleys drowned in a blue haze. The hill surface is streaked with ash drift and black, unweathered lava flows. After rains water accumulates in the hollows of small closed valleys, and, evaporating, leaves hard dry levels of pure desertness that get the local name of dry lakes. Where the mountains are steep and the rains heavy, the pool is never quite dry, but dark and bitter, rimmed about with the efflorescence of alkaline deposits. A thin crust of it lies along the marsh over the vegetating area, which has neither beauty nor freshness.[6]

Austin's lean, austere prose style bespeaks the inhospitable nature of this terrain, which offers "neither beauty nor freshness" to the human observer. Lacking beauty in the conventional sense, the desert seems (at least initially) to be without redeeming qualities. *The Land of Little Rain* begins in the same manner as Milton's *Paradise Lost,* with the protagonist marooned in a bleak, fiery landscape. It presents the desert as a land of scarcity, where even the life-giving rain visits the land with violence:

> Since this is a hill country one expects to find springs, but not to depend upon them; for when found they are often brackish and unwholesome, or maddening, slow dribbles in a thirsty soil. Here you find the hot sink of Death Valley, or high rolling districts where the air has always a tang of frost. Here are the long heavy winds and breathless calms on the tilted mesas where dust devils dance, whirling up into a wide, pale sky. Here you have no rain when all the earth cries for it, or quick downpours called cloud-bursts for violence. (5)

Such a frightful landscape, where springs are "unwholesome" and "dust devils dance," would seem to offer very little to the human observer. Like Milton's fallen angel, Austin's protagonist rouses herself from dejection and embarks upon a journey of exploration through these bleak lands, to see what can be made of her unpromising situation. The subsequent narrative unfolds as a journey of discovery, as she follows hidden pathways to seek the wellsprings of life. As Austin proceeds ever deeper into the labyrinth of hills "squeezed up out of chaos," she finds in Milton's Satan, and in the underlying archetype of Prometheus, an apt precursor for her own symbolic quest. *The Land of Little Rain* bears a strong affinity to the genre of quest-romance, re-externalized upon the vast desert landscape of the American West.[7]

Austin soon discovers that the land around her is not as bleak as it seems. "Void of life it never is, however dry the air and villainous the soil" (3). As she becomes more fully acquainted with the land, she finds that it contains a diverse flora and fauna, each organism cunningly adapted to life under extreme conditions of heat and cold, drought and moisture:

> The desert floras shame us with their cheerful adaptations to the seasonal limitations. Their whole duty is to flower and fruit, and they do it hardly, or with tropical luxuriance, as the rain admits. It is recorded in the report of the Death Valley expedition that after a year of abundant rains, on the Colorado desert was found a specimen of Amaranthus ten feet high. A year later the same species in the same place matured in the drought at four inches. One hopes the land may breed like qualities in her human offspring, not tritely to "try," but to do. (7)

Austin presents the fundamental biological concept of adaptation through the example of an Amaranthus that always manages to bear seeds, despite variable conditions of rainfall. Such a hardy and resilient species "shames" the human observer because it adapts "cheerfully" to the prevailing environmental conditions. Where an American settler might complain about the lack of rainfall, or set about trying to "tame" the desert through massive irrigation projects, the local flora and fauna simply accept the land as it is, and lead their lives accordingly. Austin hopes that the desert, personified here as a female entity, may teach her human inhabitants a like lesson of acceptance and endurance.

Austin observes that each kind of plant grows in a "particular habitat," determined by "the angle of the slope, the frontage of a hill, [and] the structure of the soil" (9). In examining the relation of each species to its habitat, she finds much to admire in the variety of "expedients" that the desert plants have developed to cope with extremely arid conditions:

> Very fertile are the desert plants in expedients to prevent evaporation, turning their foliage edgewise toward the sun, growing silky hairs, exuding viscid gum. The wind, which has a long sweep, harries and helps them. It rolls up dunes about the stocky stems, encompassing and protective, and above the dunes, which may be, as with the mesquite, three times as high as a man, the blossoming twigs flourish and bear fruit. (8)

Here the relationship between living plants and their habitat is not adversarial, but (to a certain extent) cooperative, especially when the surrounding sand is piled around their stems into "encompassing and protective" dunes. The desert is further feminized in this description, since it provides a sheltering, womb-like protection for the hardy plants that grow in its midst.

Although the desert provides a hospitable dwelling-place for its indigenous flora and fauna, it nevertheless remains a hazardous place for human beings to venture. Austin describes the terrible fate of the gold-seekers who perished in Death Valley in 1849:

> It is related that the final breakdown of that hapless party that gave Death Valley its forbidding name occurred in a locality where shallow wells would have saved them. But how were they to know that? Properly equipped it is possible to go safely across that ghastly sink, yet every year it takes its toll of death, and yet men find there sun-dried mummies, of whom no trace or recollection is preserved. To underestimate one's thirst, to pass a given landmark to the right or left, to find a dry spring where one looked for running water—there is no help for any of these things. (8-9)

The desert exacts "its toll of death" from those who encounter it unprepared. But it is not intrinsically a place of death and desolation; Austin emphasizes that the desert provides room for an astonishing diversity of plant and animal species. Because of the scarcity of water in this arid environment, all of these plants are engaged in a Darwinian struggle for existence:

> Other yuccas, cacti, low herbs, a thousand sorts, one finds journeying east from the coastwise hills. There is neither poverty of soil nor species to account for the sparseness of desert growth, but simply that each plant requires more room. So much earth must be preëmpted to extract so much moisture. The real struggle for existence, the real brain of the plant, is underground; above there is room for a rounded perfect growth. In Death Valley, reputed the very core of desolation, are nearly two hundred identified species. (12)

Through the competitive process that Darwin termed natural selection, the arid desert soil engenders a great variety of plant species, each adapted to its own ecological niche. Austin counters the traditional representation of the desert as a place of utter desolation by observing that even in Death Valley there has evolved a diverse flora and fauna, each species elegantly adapted to the prevailing environmental conditions of heat and aridity. Austin is one of the first American nature writers to appreciate the remarkable biodiversity of the desert environment.

Austin's profound understanding of the desert ecosystem is evident in her description of its intricate food chain, involving plants, insects, herbivores, and carnivores:

> There is no special preponderance of self-fertilized or wind-fertilized plants, but everywhere the demand for and evidence of insect life. Now where there are seeds and insects there will be birds and small mammals, and where these are, will come the slinking, sharp-toothed kind that prey on them. Go as far as you dare into the heart of a lonely land, you cannot go so far that life and death are not before you. (13)

Austin does not shrink from observing nature "red in tooth and claw" (as Tennyson once characterized the prevalence of violent death in the natural world).[8] She acknowledges that death is part of life, and (as we shall see) she is fascinated by the roles that predators and scavengers play in the cycle of nature.

One of Austin's great strengths as a nature writer lies in her ability to depict, with concision and coherence, the complex interactions among all the living things that inhabit the desert ecosystem:

> Painted lizards slip in and out of rock crevices, and pant on the hot white sands. Birds, hummingbirds even, nest in the cactus scrub; woodpeckers befriend the demoniac yuccas; out of the stark, treeless waste rings the music

of the night-singing mockingbird. If it be summer and the sun well down, there will be a burrowing owl to call. Strange, furry, tricksy things dart across the open places, or sit motionless in the conning towers of the creosote. The poet may have "named all the birds without a gun," but not the fairy-footed, ground-inhabiting, furtive, small folk of the rainless regions. They are too many and too swift; how many you would not believe without seeing the footprint tracings in the sand. (13-14)

Austin's succinct yet image-laden prose evokes the diverse community of living things that inhabit the "rainless regions," with particular attention given to the complex relationships that have evolved among different species. Some of these relationships are benign or symbiotic, such as the birds that nest in cactus scrub, or the woodpecker that "befriends" the yucca by removing parasites from its leaves. Other creatures exist in predator-prey relationships, such as the owl and the "furtive, small folk" that it hunts by night. This entire complex web of relationships is woven into a diverse, resilient ecosystem that almost defies the ability of human beings to fathom or describe. In the passage just cited, Austin quotes Emerson's poem "Forbearance," in which the poet claims to have "named all the birds without a gun,"[9] but she criticizes Emerson's implicit assumption that nature is entirely knowable, or that a complete taxonomic catalog of species can ever be accomplished. Like John Muir, Austin discerns a latent ethic of anthropocentrism lurking in Emerson's writings, as when Emerson claims that "the whole of nature is a metaphor of the human mind" (*Nature*, 24). Austin is skeptical of any such assertion of perfect congruity between nature and our conception of it. Rather, she suggests that our knowledge of the natural world will always remain incomplete; we will never finish describing the species that inhabit a particular region, and we will never fully comprehend the interactions among species that comprise a complex ecosystem. The natural world will always be an inscrutable palimpsest to the human observer, inscribed with unreadable footprints in the sand.

Austin further develops the theme of nature's inscrutability in the second chapter of *The Land of Little Rain,* entitled "Water Trails of the Carrizo." As she travels deeper into the desert, she notices a vast network of trails that "spread out faint and fanwise toward the homes of gopher and ground rat and squirrel" (25). These trails, which provide access for these small mammals to nearby water-holes, are almost invisible to the human observer:

But however faint to man-sight, they are sufficiently plain to the furred and feathered folk who travel them. Getting down to the eye level of rat and squirrel kind, one perceives what might easily be wide and winding roads to us if they occurred in thick plantations of trees three times the height of a man. It needs but a slender thread of bareness to make a mouse trail in the forest of the sod. To the little people the water trails are as country roads, with scents as sign-boards. (25)

Here again, Austin stresses the inadequacy of human perception to the comprehension of natural phenomena. This inadequacy is partly a problem of perspective, since "it seems that man-height is the least fortunate of all heights from which to study trails" (26). Only by "getting down to the eye level" of small mammals can we begin to understand their world. Like Thoreau and Muir, Austin refers to the animals as "little people," not merely in a metaphorical sense, but as a strong affirmation of the fundamental equivalence between wild creatures and human beings. Throughout *The Land of Little Rain,* she suggests that the desert animals have much to teach us about survival in that harsh environment. In particular, the animal trails of the Carrizo provide an unerring guide to local water-holes for those who know how to read and interpret them. Austin claims that these animal trails are more reliable than any printed map or guidebook: "No matter what the maps say, or your memory, trust them; they *know*" (29). Austin italicizes the word *know* in order to emphasize a significant epistemological assertion. As a naturalist, Austin seeks to overcome the perennial subject-object dichotomy of Western science by becoming a dweller in the world that she describes. She is not only learning *about* the small creatures that inhabit the desert, but also *from* them.

In the following chapter, entitled "The Scavengers," Austin describes the life-cycle of the birds and mammals that survive in the desert by eating carrion. These scavenger species are not commonly encountered in the literary tradition of nature writing, presumably because they are generally regarded as dirty, ugly, frightful beasts that contribute nothing to the beauty of nature. But for Austin they are an integral part of "the economy of nature," a phrase that occurs twice in this chapter, and she does not shrink from describing how they feed upon dead cattle, and even dead humans, that succumb from heat and thirst in the desert. Austin evinces strong curiosity, and even a sneaking affection, for these frightful creatures, and she zestfully describes their grotesque noises:

There are three kinds of noises buzzards make,—it is impossible to call them notes,—raucous and elemental. There is a short croak of alarm, and the same syllable in a modified tone to serve all the purposes of ordinary conversation. The old birds have a kind of throaty chuckling to their young, but if they have any love song I have not heard it. The young yawp in the nest a little, with more breath than noise. (51)

Austin finds that she can learn a great deal from these hideous creatures. In particular, she is fascinated by the way that scavengers of different species exchange information concerning the whereabouts of various food sources. The coyote, for example, "never comes out of his lair for killing, in the country of the carrion crows, but looks up first to see where they may be gathering" (54). Austin observes that coyotes, buzzards, hawks, and eagles carefully monitor each other's behavior to find out where a kill has been made, or is in progress:

> Probably we never fully credit the interdependence of wild creatures, and their cognizance of the affairs of their own kind. When the five coyotes that range the Tejon from Pasteria to Tunawai planned a relay race to bring down an antelope strayed from the band, beside myself to watch, an eagle swung down from Mt. Pinos, buzzards materialized out of invisible ether, and hawks came trooping like small boys to a street fight. Rabbits sat up in the chaparral and cocked their ears, feeling themselves quite safe for the once as the hawk swung near them. Nothing happens in the deep wood that the blue jays are not all agog to tell. The hawk follows the badger, the coyote the carrion crow, and from their aerial stations the buzzards watch each other. (55-56)

By describing such an intricate array of interactions between various species of birds and mammals, Austin seeks to substantiate her claim that wild creatures are interdependent in complex ways that human beings will never fully comprehend. Such interdependence of species cannot be adequately described as a series of binary predator-prey relationships, but encompasses a rich network of symbolic exchanges among animals of different species, at all levels of the food chain. Moreover, Austin recognizes that such information-sharing behaviors involve both instinctual and learned elements, some of which are passed along by parents to their offspring. "What would be worth knowing is how much of their neighbor's affairs the new generations learn for themselves, and how much they are taught of their elders" (56). Many of Austin's questions about the communicative behavior of wild animals have been addressed in recent decades by the scientific discipline of ethology, but Austin remains correct in her assertion that there is much we do not know about "the interdependence of wild creatures."

Austin is painfully aware that the "economy of nature" may be irrevocably damaged by the intrusion of human beings and their destructive technologies. Although she admires and respects the Paiute and Shoshone peoples who have lived in harmony with the desert for many generations, she deplores the blundering presence and the disfiguring traces left by modern American travelers:

> Man is a great blunderer going about the woods, and there is no other except the bear makes so much noise. Being so well warned beforehand, it is a very stupid animal, or a very bold one, that cannot keep safely hid. The cunningest hunter is hunted in turn, and what he leaves of his kill is meat for some other. That is the economy of nature, but with it all there is not sufficient account taken of the works of man. There is no other scavenger that eats tin cans, and no wild thing leaves a like disfigurement on the forest floor. (60)

The disfigurement of the forest floor by tin cans poses a severe threat to the economy of nature because such human junk is not recyclable; it simply accumulates, clogging and eventually disrupting a wide range of natural cycles. Although Austin may appear to be making a petty complaint about litterbugs in the forest, she is actually broaching a much more serious topic: namely, the threat posed by non-recyclable waste to the continuing survival of life anywhere on the Earth. Not only wilderness areas are threatened by the indiscriminate disposal of solid waste; the entire economy of nature, including the water we drink and the air we breathe, is threatened by the disruption of the natural cycles that sustain and nourish life on the entire planet. From a twenty-first-century perspective, Austin's concerns about the deleterious long-term effects of human waste upon natural systems are quite serious, credible, and well-founded.

But Austin does not dwell upon the negative effects of humans on the natural world; she is far more interested in describing the effects that nature may have on humankind. Although she initially presents the desert landscape as bleak and forbidding, subsequent chapters of *The Land of Little Rain* engage the reader in her own gradual process of learning to see this terrain in a new way, and to appreciate its austere beauty. The book's penultimate chapter, "Nurslings of the Sky," offers a lyrical summation of all that she has discovered about the desert's hidden power to rouse and awaken the human spirit. The chapter title is taken from Percy Shelley's poem "The Cloud," and throughout this chapter Austin evinces a Shelleyan perspective upon storms as enigmatic exponents of hidden purposes and powers in the natural world. Like Shelley, she personifies the clouds, which "come walking," "lock hands," and "dance" across the sky:

Days when the hollows are steeped in a warm, winey flood the clouds come walking on the floor of heaven, flat and pearly gray beneath, rounded and pearly white above. They gather flock-wise, moving on the level currents that roll about the peaks, lock hands and settle with the cooler air, drawing a veil about those places where they do their work. If their meeting or parting takes place at sunrise or sunset, as it often does, one gets the splendor of the apocalypse. There will be cloud pillars miles high, snow-capped, glorified, and preserving an orderly perspective before the unbarred door of the sun, or perhaps mere ghosts of clouds that dance to some pied piper of an unfelt wind. (248)

By personifying the clouds, Austin suggests that they are something more than merely empirical phenomena. As she approaches the end of her quest-narrative, Austin is learning to "read" the appearances of earth and sky in ways that reveal her intellectual roots in the English Romantic poets, as she seeks to elucidate the hidden sources of meaning in the desert landscape.

Elsewhere in this chapter, Austin attributes "presence and intention" to storms, in terms that echo both the ebullient pantheism of John Muir and the Transcendental idealism of Emerson:

The first effect of cloud study is a sense of presence and intention in storm processes. Weather does not happen. It is the visible manifestation of the Spirit moving itself in the void. It gathers itself together under the heavens; rains, snows, yearns mightily in wind, smiles; and the Weather Bureau, situated advantageously for that very business, taps the record on his instruments and going out into the street denies his God, not having gathered the sense of what he has seen. Hardly anybody takes account of the fact that John Muir, who knows more of mountain storms than any other, is a devout man. (247)

In Austin's view, "weather does not happen"; it is not just a random occurrence. Drawing upon the Transcendentalist terminology of Emerson's *Nature,* and the vatic rhythms of the first verse of Genesis, she declares weather to be "a visible manifestation of the Spirit moving itself in the Void." The narrow-minded empiricists who work for the Weather Bureau cannot see the larger meanings of weather because they are too wrapped up in their "instruments"; only those of broader and more comprehensive vision are able to fathom what is before their eyes. Austin invokes John Muir as one such seer; she is presumably thinking of the climactic chapter of *The Mountains of California,* "A Wind-Storm in the Forests," as an instance of his prophetic insight into the hidden significance of such phenomena. Steeped in such skyey influences, Muir has become "a devout man."

But Austin does more than merely echo the words and ideas of her precursors in the Romantic tradition of nature writing. By choosing the chapter title "Nurslings of the Sky," Austin emphasizes the feminine, nurturing aspect of storms, and she continues the implicit feminization of nature through another literary allusion, from Tennyson's "Lotos-Eaters":

> [The storm] rays out and draws to it some floating films from secret cañons. Rain begins, "slow dropping veil of thinnest lawn;" a wind comes up and drives the formless thing across a meadow, or a dull lake pitted by the glancing drops, dissolving as it drives. Such rains relieve like tears. (251)

Austin personifies the rain as a female being, clad in "veil of thinnest lawn," who offers welcome relief to the dry landscape and its thirsty human inhabitants. Such emotional catharsis goes beyond the literal satisfaction of thirst; the rain offers succor, seduction, and the satisfaction of spiritual hunger at the end of a long quest. Like the enchanted sailors in Tennyson's "Lotos-Eaters," but without their tone of melancholy defeatism, the inhabitants of the desert draw comfort, sustenance, and hope from the simple presence of water.[10] In the heart of a barren land, Austin has finally arrived at the wellsprings of life, where the nature of nature is revealed as a nurturing female presence.

The Iliad of the Pines

Although Austin makes few overt allusions to previous writers in *The Land of Little Rain,* this work is clearly indebted, both in form and content, to the English and American literary traditions.[11] She describes the formation of her literary tastes in her third-person autobiography, *Earth Horizon,* where she mentions that her father had bought "first American editions of Keats and Shelley, Mrs. Browning and Ruskin" and strove "to keep pace with the writers of genuine distinction in the United States: with Herman Melville, Hawthorne, Poe, and Longfellow, particularly with Emerson."[12] Austin describes how Emerson came to affect her style during her college years:

> Oddly, the only writer out of those days who affected her style was Emerson. I don't know why. The predilection showed itself early in her college

life. Possibly his death in '82 had revived public attention in his work, and that in turn had recalled associations with her father, among whose books she had found an early edition of the "Poems," and "Representative Men." (*Earth Horizon,* 165)

Emerson was one of several writers who had a profound early impact on Austin's formation as a writer. As a child, she read Milton's *Paradise Lost* with great fascination, and she memorized Tennyson's "Lady of Shalott" and portions of Byron's *Childe Harold's Pilgrimage* (*Earth Horizon,* 105, 63, 165). She was an avid reader of popular magazines, where she encountered the short stories of Bret Harte, a chronicler of Western frontier life. Although she admired Harte's efforts to forge a new kind of regional writing, she deplored his tendency to rehash stock characters and situations, and in *The Land of Little Rain* she suggests that when Harte found "his particular local color fading from the West, he did what he considered the only safe thing, and carried his youthful impression away to be worked out untroubled by any newer fact" (105). In Austin's view, a true regional writing must emerge from places actually lived in, not merely remembered.

Among contemporary American women writers, Austin admired the fiction of Harriet Beecher Stowe, Sarah Orne Jewett, and Willa Cather, specifically for the authentic regional voices that they brought to the task of writing fiction, and she learned from them how to develop her craft and follow her vocation as a woman writer. Jewett provided an especially compelling female role model for Austin's writing about the natural world. Jewett's modernity of voice in such works as *A White Heron* (1886) and *The Country of the Pointed Firs* (1896)—specifically, her impressionistic mode of description and her elliptical presentation of theme—provided Austin with an effective way to convey her impressions of wild and scenic places from a limited individual perspective, without resorting to the standard Victorian device of an omniscient narrator. Among the most prominent British writers of the late nineteenth century, Austin mentions Rudyard Kipling as a formative influence during the years that she was working on *The Land of Little Rain.* Kipling's short story collection *Plain Tales from the Hills* (1888) provided a compelling literary model for Austin's plain-spoken, hard-boiled, proto-Modernist prose description of exotic climes and cultures. Austin recalls her fascination with Kipling's short fiction:

The Kipling tales, with their slightly mocking detachment, their air of completely disengaging the author from any responsibility for the moral implications of the scene and the people of whom he wrote, had at least pointed

the way for a use of the sort of material of which I found myself possessed. . . . Mr. Kipling had, happily, made his tales so completely strange and
far away that comparison failed. (*Earth Horizon,* 230)

Kipling provides an intriguing model for Austin's prose style because the
Oriental exoticism of his landscapes (set mostly in India) was in many ways
analogous to the Western exoticism of the land she sought to describe in
The Land of Little Rain. Both in her depiction of Native American cultures
and in her description of the land itself, Austin draws upon Kipling's direct,
non-judgmental manner of presentation and his sympathetic affinity for
wanderers, beggars, urchins, and outcasts.

Despite her thoughtful and imaginative response to all of these literary
models, Austin found herself having to invent the most essential features of
her own prose style. Of all American writers, only John Muir came close
to the kind of writing that she needed to depict a land that was truly
beyond the ken of most American readers. Austin profoundly admired
Muir's work, and she refers approvingly to *The Mountains of California* in
The Land of Little Rain. Three decades later, Austin wrote of herself and
Muir as united in their common appreciation for "natural America, the
land, its pattern of seasons and prospects, its beauty and drama and revelation."[13] In a popular magazine article entitled "Beyond the Hudson" (1930),
Austin complains about the narrow-minded literary world of New York,
which has failed to recognize the merits of any American regional writer
outside of New England and the Hudson River Valley. The literary establishment admires Thoreau, but ignores such writers as Austin and Muir:

> I know very well that it is not out of the *knowledge* of writers for *The Sat-
> urday Review,* that John Muir and I myself—to mention no others—have
> written lovingly and knowledgeably of their California and New Mex-
> ico. . . . The Glaciers of Alaska and the Cactus Country have been treated
> as tenderly, as informedly, as scientifically, and as interpretatively by the two
> authors mentioned, as ever was Walden by its Hermit. (432)

In this remarkable manifesto, Austin goes on to describe and defend her
own writing practice, and to indicate in what respects it differs from that
of Thoreau and his precursors in the English and American traditions of
nature writing:

> Before the editor of *The Saturday Review* advises anyone to begin writing
> lovingly of the American scene, I suggest that he discover in advance what

it will cost. Everyone knows how many years Thoreau spent over *Walden,* but Thoreau wrote in a country which had already been lived in for a couple of hundred years by English speaking people, and he had behind him the literary tradition of Izaak Walton, [Gilbert] White of Selborne, Richard Jeffries, and those other writers of English country life whom Mr. Canby so admires. He wrote of a country so little different from England, that practically all the natural science and the plant and animal lore of England served him. But when John Muir and I undertook to establish a tradition of literary description of our own beloved lands, it was quite another matter. The units of that land were of the size of European empires, the topography was that of a continental axis. The plants, the birds, and the animals had few of them any common names, so that, if the writers wished to speak of what they saw, they had to master the natural sciences of botany, zoölogy, geology, and topography, at least so far as their land was concerned. The land was but imperfectly mapped. The very names which were available for description, such as barrancas, cumbres, and sierras, were un-English and had no English equivalents. Every now and then to this day, when I try to write of the land I love, some peevish critic, in West 23rd Street, frets at me because I dare to describe it in words he does not know. And yet in spite of the fact that the editor of *The Saturday Review* seems not to know what they have done, I insist that John Muir and I have established a literary tradition for dealing with the American scene on the Western scale which will not soon be discarded.

Austin's vehemence in this essay emerges from her deep frustration with the narrowness, intolerance, and provinciality of the literary taste that prevails among New York publishers and reviewers. Such a dominant urban intelligentsia will inevitably gravitate toward the known and familiar, at the expense of literary works that use unfamiliar words to present unfamiliar landscapes. Austin declares common cause with John Muir in defending their shared ways of writing about the wild Western landscape, whose indigenous culture and vast topography far exceed the comprehension of contemporary American readers. Austin takes evident pride in proclaiming that she and Muir have established "a tradition of literary description of our own beloved lands."

Austin was personally acquainted with Muir, whom she encountered shortly after the publication of *The Land of Little Rain* in 1903. She describes her first meeting with him "at the center of an intimate circle of writers and painters of San Francisco":

I recall John Muir most distinctly, a tall lean man with the habit of talking much, the habit of soliloquizing. He told stories of his life in the wild, and of angels; angels that saved him; that lifted and carried him; that showed him where to put his feet; he believed them. I told him one of mine; except that I didn't see mine. I had been lifted and carried; I had been carried out of the way of danger; and he believed me. I remember them still. (*Earth Horizon,* 298)

Austin remembers Muir as a *raconteur,* a teller of "stories of his life in the wild," and as a visionary, who spoke of the angels that saved him on the sheer granite cliffs of the Sierra. Austin's own encounters with the wild had presented her with similar visionary experiences, although her own guardian angels had remained invisible (yet just as real to her). Elsewhere in *Earth Horizon,* Austin reflects more deeply upon the spiritual dimension of her response to the natural world:

> This is the way a Naturist is taken with the land, with the spirit trying to be evoked out of it. . . . It is time somebody gave a true report. All the public expects of the experience of practicing Naturists is the appearance, the habits, the incidents of the wild; when the Naturist reports upon himself, it is mistaken for poetizing. I know something of what went on in Muir . . . for him, quite simply, the spirits of the wild were angels, who bore him on their wings through perilous places. But for Mary, the pietistic identifications of the angels she had heard of prevented such identification. (*Earth Horizon,* 188)

Austin clearly shares Muir's profound belief in "the spirits of the wild," but she resists his "pietistic" identification of these spirits as angels.

The essential distinction between Austin and Muir lies in their subtly different attitudes toward Christianity. Both Muir and Austin grew up within the strictures of fairly repressive Protestant churches, and both eventually rebelled against the religion of their fathers, seeking a less dogmatic, more intuitive way of relating to the spiritual dimension of their experiences in the natural world. Whereas Muir remained something of a Christian pantheist throughout his career as a writer, Austin breaks definitively with the entire traditional framework of Christian belief, choosing instead to identify herself as a "Naturist." Rather than espousing a fixed and coherent set of religious doctrines, she presents her belief system mainly as a quest for meaning in a world endowed with spiritual presences. In *Earth Horizon,* Austin describes how she was haunted from an early age by an "experiential pang":

> There was something else there besides what you find in the books; a lurking, evasive Something, wistful, cruel, ardent; something that rustled and ran, that hung half-remotely, insistent upon being noticed, fled from pursuit, and when

you turned from it, leaped suddenly and fastened on your vitals. . . . Then, and ever afterward, in the wide, dry washes and along the edge of the chaparral, Mary was beset with the need of being alone with this insistent experiential pang for which the wise Greeks had the clearest name concepts . . . fauns, satyrs, the ultimate Pan. (*Earth Horizon,* 187)

For Austin, the ultimate repository of meaning and value resides just beyond the borders of perception, "in the wide, dry washes and along the edge of the chaparral." Her vocation as a writer is to seek for that hidden significance; and *The Land of Little Rain* is narratively structured as a quest along these border zones for the elusive spiritual dimension of experience.

Austin explores her vocation as a writer most explicitly in two consecutive chapters of *The Land of Little Rain.* In "The Basket Maker," she discovers that she has much in common with Seyavi, a Paiute woman abandoned by her husband who discovers that she can live very well without a man. In many respects, the Basket Maker's life story resembles that of Austin herself, who likewise had to fend for herself when her husband proved feckless, unreliable, and ultimately unable to support her and her infant daughter. Austin learns a great deal from Seyavi about the conflicting demands of marriage, motherhood, and career. Even more important, Austin learns the true meaning of artistic vocation for a woman writer:

Seyavi made baskets for love and sold them for money, in a generation that preferred iron pots for utility. Every Indian woman is an artist,—sees, feels, creates, but does not philosophize about her processes. Seyavi's bowls are wonders of technical precision, inside and out, the palm finds no fault with them, but the subtlest appeal is in the sense that warns us of humanness in the way the design spreads into the flare of the bowl. (168-169)

The traditional craft of weaving provides an apt metaphor for Austin's own craft of writing. Like Seyavi, she makes books for love and sells them for money, in an era that prefers iron pots for utility. *The Land of Little Rain* is pervaded by the personality of its maker, not obtrusively, but in the subtle appeal of its design.

The following chapter, "The Streets of the Mountains," offers some further reflection upon the craft of writing. It describes how Austin climbed into the high Sierra, where she encountered the landscape that John Muir had so lovingly described. Her chapter title pays subtle homage to Muir, who wrote in *The Mountains of California* that "these cañons make . . . a kind of mountain streets full of charming life and light" (*Nature Writings,*

317). Surrounded by high mountain peaks and a vast forest of pines, Austin ponders the possibility of a more expressive kind of lyric utterance, "the Iliad of the pines":

> It is a pity we have let the gift of lyric improvisation die out. Sitting islanded on some gray peak above the encompassing wood, the soul is lifted up to sing the Iliad of the pines. They have no voice but the wind, and no sound of them rises up to the high places. But the waters, the evidences of their power, that go down the steep and stony ways, the outlets of ice-bordered pools, the young rivers swaying with the force of their running, they sing and shout and trumpet at the falls, and the noise of it far outreaches the forest spires. (192)

Austin wonders what song would be adequate to the expression of the pine forest, and the wilderness that it represents. The pines themselves have no voice, but the waters that arise under their branches "sing and shout and trumpet at the falls." By analogy, if the land itself is silent, the task of the poet is to speak *for* it, not simply *about* it. Austin envisages a craft of writing that would express the very being of a particular place, flowing forth from the land as water from hidden springs.

Throughout *The Land of Little Rain,* Austin presents the desert landscape in a voice that is remarkably innovative for its time, and that still offers a suggestive model for contemporary nature writers. Her style is marked by its relative impersonality, especially when compared with that of her American precursors, such as Thoreau and Muir, whose frequent use of the first-person pronoun "I" tends to foreground the "eye" of the observer, rather than the thing observed. Austin, in contrast, uses the first-person pronoun rarely, in most cases to narrate an anecdote of some particular encounter in the wild; otherwise she generally employs a third-person descriptive voice and, most innovatively, a second-person form of address. Thus, for example, she warns the reader, "Go as far as *you* dare in the heart of a lonely land, *you* cannot go so far that life and death are not before *you*" (13; emphasis added). The pronoun "you" is rarely encountered in nature writing, with the exception of promotional pamphlets and guidebooks that purport to instruct the reader on how to navigate in unfamiliar terrain. Austin's book could hardly be considered a guidebook—indeed, she takes pains to conceal the actual location of many of the places that she writes about—but it does draw upon the unspoken generic conventions of promotional literature. In *Earth Horizon* she describes the literary marketplace in which she published *The Land of Little Rain:*

At that time almost the whole expressive energy of California went into what was beginning to be called "publicity" literature; highly objective and extravagantly descriptive articles about the region which Charles Dudley Warner had just named "Our Italy," and other more particular matter designed to increase the number of real estate investors, prospective orange-growers and vineyarders. (*Earth Horizon,* 229)

In her own work, Austin frequently draws upon certain generic features of "publicity" literature while adapting them to her own, very different pur-poses. Specifically, Austin adopts a "highly objective" mode of presentation, an intensely descriptive style, and a second-person pronoun that engages the reader in a shared task of exploring the unknown landscape. Austin often uses imperative verb forms to warn, cajole, instruct, or encourage the reader: "*Venture* to look for some seldom-touched water-hole. . . . *Watch* a coyote come out of his lair. . . . *Wait* long enough at the Lone Tree Spring and sooner or later they will all come in" (28, 30, 34; emphasis added). Austin engages the reader in an active, dialogical process of coming to know the land. Through the innovative deployment of these stylistic ele-ments, she endeavors to create a new kind of writing that would express the very being of a particular place: the Iliad of the pines.

Androcentric Culture

Even as Mary Austin was writing *The Land of Little Rain,* discovering her vocation as a writer, and finding her voice amid the austere beauty of the Owens Valley, the seeds of that region's destruction were already being sown. Her husband, Stafford Wallace Austin, was employed in 1905 as Reg-istrar of the federal Land Office in Independence, California, and by virtue of this position he was among the first to become aware of the surrepti-tious efforts being made by Frederick Eaton, employed as an agent for the City of Los Angeles, to purchase water rights throughout the Owens Val-ley. Eaton was working secretly in concert with the civil engineer William Mulholland, and the U.S. Reclamation Service administrator J. B. Lippin-cott, to acquire a new water supply for the City of Los Angeles. Under their audacious plan, the entire watershed of the Owens River would be diverted through a massive, 223-mile aqueduct to supply the rapidly grow-ing urban population of Los Angeles. Such a vast diversion of water resources had never before been attempted in American history, and the sheer audacity of the scheme was a key to its success: to the ordinary layperson, it seemed utterly incredible. The long-term environmental cost of this scheme would be the total desolation of the Owens Valley, whose agrarian way of life depended upon the life-giving streams that flowed down from the annual snowfall of the High Sierra into its wells, cisterns, and irrigation channels. Stafford and Mary Austin were among the first to foresee the severity of the environmental impact of the Los Angeles Aqueduct upon the Owens Valley, and they both took immediate action to defend the local way of life. In August 1905, Stafford wrote directly to President Theodore Roosevelt, charging that Lippincott had conspired with Eaton "to betray the Government."[14] Meanwhile, in September 1905, Mary Austin published an editorial in the *San Francisco Chronicle* denouncing the federal Reclamation Service for its covert assistance to Los Angeles:

> Every considerable city in the State is or is about to be confronted by a water problem. But what is to be gained by the commonwealth if it robs Peter to pay Paul? Is all this worthwhile in order that Los Angeles should be just so big? . . . It is worthwhile for other cities to consider that as this case proceeds their water problems are likely to be shaped by it more or less. Shall the question of domestic water in California be determined by craft and graft and bitterness and long-drawn wasteful struggles, or conducted with rightness and dignity to an equal conclusion?[15]

In this editorial, Austin appeals to her readers' democratic sense of decency and fair play, and with truly prophetic insight she predicts that the future of the Western American landscape will depend upon the outcome of this unequal struggle for water rights.

Despite the Austins' eloquent advocacy and their concerted efforts to organize the local inhabitants to resist the appropriation of their water rights, it was already too late to save the fragile landscape from destruction. Mary Austin was among the few who understood that the Owens Valley was already doomed when it sold its first water right to Los Angeles, since the city would inexorably devour the entire river and all its adjoining lands. She left the valley forever in 1906, foreseeing with tragic insight that its fate was sealed. Subsequent events have only served to vindicate her prophetic vision. In 1907 work began on the construction of the Los Angeles aqueduct, which took six years to build, opening in 1913. Relentlessly the city encroached upon the water resources of the Owens Valley, despite the guerrilla action of farmers who attempted in 1924 to blow up the aqueduct with dynamite, until the valley became a place of utter desolation. By the 1970s the Owens Valley had lost virtually all of its agriculture and most of its population. In *Cadillac Desert: The American West and Its Disappearing Water,* Marc Reisner describes how the Owens Valley "went beyond desert and took on the appearance of the Bonneville Salt Flats. When the winds of convection blow, huge clouds of alkaline dust boil off the valley floor; people now live in the Owens Valley at some risk to their health."[16] In 1987, when a film version of *The Land of Little Rain* was being made for public television, the producers found they could not shoot it in the Owens Valley, due to its environmental devastation, and ultimately they had to settle for a film location in the San Luis Valley of Colorado.[17]

Mary Austin wrote about the Owens Valley struggle and its aftermath in *The Ford,* a novel published in 1917.[18] This novel transposes the story to a fictive setting, "Tierra Longa," where the simple agrarian lifestyle of the farmers and ranchers is threatened by the subterfuge of a nefarious, alcoholic agent, Elwood, who seeks to purchase their water rights for an undisclosed purpose. *The Ford* is a *roman à clef* whose fictional characters may readily be identified with real historical figures: Elwood is evidently a fictional version of Eaton, while his fictional partner, Jevens, an ominous figure dressed all in black, may be identified with Mulholland, who accompanied Eaton on a secret, preliminary survey of the valley's water resources in September 1904. The fictional character Lattimore, a federal surveyor who resigns to join the water district of a great city, may be identified with Lippincott, who was employed by the U.S. Reclamation Service before he resigned in May 1905 to work for the Los Angeles Aqueduct project. However, throughout *The Ford,* Austin is less concerned with the historical details of the irrigation battle than she is with the underlying motives of its main adversaries: the agents of the booming industrial city and the ragtag band of settlers who oppose their nefarious scheme to divert the water away from the land. Austin does not present this narrative simply as a struggle of good versus evil; both sides have complex, largely selfish motives, and the fatal flaw of the farmers is their failure to organize in their own common interest.

Lacking a deep, intuitive connection to the land, the settlers fail to foresee the scope of the machinations being waged against them. Over the course of the novel, Austin's authorial persona (embodied by a wise, self-reliant woman named Anne Brent) comes to realize that both sides in this struggle share a common cultural failing, endemic to the entire project of "taming" the Western landscape. Anne declares:

Society is a sort of mirage, a false appearance due to refraction. . . . I mean most of the things we do and think important only seem so because of all sorts of hang-overs,—political, religious, all sorts of ignorances . . . that's because we have Androcentric culture. (*The Ford,* 233)

Anne's interlocutors are puzzled by the unfamiliar word "androcentric," which she proceeds to explain:

"I mean,"—she went more slowly,—"because everything has been accepted from the point of view of men only, and that's the obvious. Women have a much keener sense of real values. . . . Look at the land; I'm learning a lot about the land, and the first thing to learn is that you can absolutely find out what land is good for, and in time you'll find out that, no matter what you feel about it, it only belongs to the people who can do those things." (*The Ford,* 233-234)

In this critique of "Androcentric culture," and in her articulation of an alternative relationship to the land, Austin embarks upon a project of ecofeminist revision. She rejects a merely instrumental relationship to the land, which is practiced both by the settlers who grow market crops and the agents who seek to extract water resources for a distant urban population. Such "Androcentric culture" is invisible, yet ineluctable, because it permeates everything: politics, religion, and all human knowledge. Man-centered culture is unavoidably exploitive in its approach to the land, plundering its natural resources and leaving behind a wake of destruction. Both sides in this novel fail to realize the land's true potential, what it is "truly good for." "Women have a much keener sense of real values" because they have a deeper and more intuitive feel for the real potential of the Western landscape, drawn from their long cultural memory of working with the land in a sustainable manner and seeking to dwell in harmony with its rhythms instead of struggling to "tame" it. Since Austin generally personifies the desert as an elusive female presence, she regards women as having a special affinity for its sounds and silences, its harsh textures and hidden potentialities. Against all odds, *The Ford* has a happy ending, as its shallow young lovers get married off, the plotters repent of their wicked deeds, and the wise woman of the hills retreats to a rural enclave to live out her pastoral idyll. Unfortunately, in real life, the Owens Valley had no such happy ending, and Austin found no such Arcadia. She went forth from the ruined land, and from the ruins of her marriage, into a wandering life of exile. Like the protagonist in her short story "The Walking Woman," Austin found herself wandering homeless in a world of desolation, without friends or family, on an endless, questing journey outward from her lost paradise.[19]

Sacred Mountains

After her departure from the Owens Valley in 1906, Austin spent several years in New York City, where she became involved with the women's movement and developed her career as a professional writer. But even during this period of urban existence, her work continued to be deeply affected by the lands and peoples of the American West. Austin published several books that dealt with the remembered landscapes of California: *Lost Borders* (1909), a collection of short stories; *The Arrow Maker* (1911), a play about a Paiute medicine woman; and *California: Land of the Sun* (1914), a lyrical evocation of the state's varied landscapes. In 1918 Austin visited Santa Fe to study Indian poetry, and from that point onward she began to feel at home in the arid lands of the American Southwest. During 1922 and 1923 she made several trips by automobile through remote wilderness areas of New Mexico and Arizona, and in 1925 she settled permanently in Santa Fe, building her *Casa Querida* (Beloved House) in the traditional Spanish adobe style, which she admired as an elegant, sustainable form of ecological design.[20] Austin's later work articulates a profound sense of dwelling-in-place as she explores the arid mountains and deserts of the American Southwest.

In *The American Rhythm* (1923), Austin examines the historical relationship between place and poetry, describing how the deep rhythms of agricultural work and wilderness travel have inflected the cadences of lyric poetry and oratorical prose throughout American history. She devotes careful attention to the Native American traditions of poetry, arguing "that all verse forms which are found worthy the use of great poets are aboriginal, in the sense that they are developed from the soil native to the culture that perfected them."[21] Like Emerson and Thoreau, Austin boldly declares literary independence from the decadent, militaristic culture of the Old World, and she claims that the American landscape has had a deep generational impact upon the making of poetry:

> Streams of rhythmic sights and sounds flowed in upon the becoming race of Americans from every natural feature. The great hegira from northern and central Europe had been largely motivated by the desire to escape from the over-humanized aspects of those lands. There was hunger in man for free flung mountain ridges, untrimmed forests, evidence of structure and growth. Life set itself to new processions of seed time and harvest, the skin newly tuned to seasonal variations, the very blood humming to new altitudes. The rhythm of walking always a recognizable background for our thoughts,

altered from the militaristic stride to the jog of the wide, unrutted earth. Explorer, fur-trader, King's agent, whoever for three centuries followed it, must have carried a record of its foot work in his walk, a wider swing and recovery to his mind. (14)

Austin embraces the rhythms of the American land as a basis for poetry, and she celebrates the resonant prose of Lincoln's Gettysburg Address and the incantatory free verse of Walt Whitman as exemplary of the expressive possibilities of the New World.[22] Austin advocates a thorough study of Native American poetry as a basis for a New World poetics, since (in her view) the meters and symbolic repertoire of this indigenous American tradition offer a means of expression that most fully expresses the potentiality of the land itself. Through its thoughtful attention to the relationship between poetry and place, *The American Rhythm* articulates an authentic ecopoetics.

Although Austin is generally hostile to the literary influences of the Old World, she carves out a special exception for the English Romantic poets. She argues that the poetry of Keats and Shelley draws upon the rhythmic tradition of ancient Greek poetry, which expressed a deep, intuitive sense of relationship to its native place. Lurking beneath the luxuriant metrical forms of their poetry she discovers a latent strain of primitivism: "Under the pure lilt of Keats and Shelley it is still possible to follow the patter of naked feet in dances that may no longer be described with propriety, or in rituals in which living beasts were torn apart" (45). Austin contends that the fundamental rhythmic basis of English Romantic poetry is "aboriginal" because it harks back to the primitive, ritualistic character of ancient Greek poetry. According to an eyewitness report, Austin conveyed her enthusiasm for the wild, exuberant, primitivistic aspects of poetry in a lecture that she presented to the Woman's Club in Fort Worth, Texas, on a rainy afternoon in 1928:

> She expounded her theories of the origin of rhythms while someone, in lieu of a drum, thumped the heart-beat of the universe on middle C of the grand piano. Mary chanted Indian poetry, eyes half shut. No one tittered when this tall, gaunt woman lifted her blue velvet skirt and twirled and kicked a Greek dance in her flat heeled shoes, while she chanted Shelley's "To a Skylark." She was illustrating her belief in the Greek origin of English meters. She strode up and down and wielded an axe, orating the *Gettysburg Address*. Here as in Indian chants were native American rhythms. We were fascinated.[23]

According to Austin's primitivistic conception of the origin of metrical forms, the fundamental rhythms of the land itself are expressed in poetry and prose that echoes "the heart-beat of the universe." Her ecstatic performance of these "native American rhythms" was conveyed to her listeners through dance, gesture, and rhythmic recitation, in a way that must have proven profoundly unsettling to her demure audience members at the Fort Worth Woman's Club. Although Austin's broadly syncretic approach to the history of culture would probably be dismissed as "unscientific" by most contemporary anthropologists, her thoughtful investigation of the environmental determinants of metrical form is nevertheless worthy of earnest attention from a strictly literary point of view, since it offers a coherent theory of ecopoetics within the geographical framework of the American landscape.

Austin's intensely emotional engagement with American history and geography is most fully articulated in *The Land of Journeys' Ending* (1924), a nonfictional prose work that represents the culmination of her lyrical response to the arid landscapes of the American West.[24] Once again, the English Romantic poets provide a profoundly resonant set of images for the unfamiliar phenomena that Austin encounters in the desert. Invoking Shelley's "To a Skylark," Austin observes a horned lark, "which, like the lark that Shelley heard, rises as it sings" (305). She reflects more generally upon the literary significance of birds: "For the most part it is the literary interest which is served by birds, man making them to stand for his thought in upper airy reaches of his mind, long before he had any other use for those he could not use for food" (305). Such symbolic significance is accorded to birds both in Western literary tradition and in the poetry of "our Ancients," a term by which Austin refers to Native American culture:

> Thus I might name a hundred species from the broad-tailed hummingbirds, droning like bees about the holy peaks of San Francisco Mountains, to the hermit thrush singing at evening on steep, dark-forested slopes the sacrament of desire, only to find that for you, as for our Ancients, and Keats and Shelley, birds serve best when they serve as symbols for free roving, skyey thought. (307)

Austin invokes the concept of "symbol" in the constitutive, Coleridgean sense. The skylark does not merely serve as an arbitrary sign, but actually participates in the concept (in this case, "freedom") that it renders apparent. Indeed, according to Austin's evolutionary conception of human culture, birds may well have enabled primitive humans to conceive the very possibility of "free roving, skyey thought" before such an abstract idea was part of the human conceptual repertoire. Not only poetic rhythms, but also the abstract concepts that make human cognition possible, are originally derived from primitive human experience of the landscape and its indigenous creatures. Like Emerson, Austin regards the natural world as the birthplace of all human culture. New concepts are born in the struggle of human language to encompass new images, new contingencies of perception in the phenomenal world.

In her discussion of the indigenous origins of New World agriculture, Austin suggests that there exists an underlying affinity between human consciousness and "the soul of the corn." She invokes one of the most perennial Romantic archetypes, the correspondent breeze,[25] as a means of expressing the deep, intuitive relationship between humankind and the natural world:

> There is something inexpressibly stirring thus to happen, where all around is silence and the sun, on plants that have come down this long way with man, as though they gave off something of man's personality, absorbed through centuries of aspiration with him, up from the grass. The soul of the corn passes into the soul of the observer; the insistent beat of consciousness soothes to a murmur, faint as the wind in the corn, of godhead in man, to which the Small-house People, giving ear, were moved like the corn in the wind. It is only in such passages that one realizes that the charm of Amerind life, for the modern American, is the absence of those strains and resistances that stiffen us against the wind forever blowing from some quarter of the universe across our souls. (*Land of Journeys' Ending*, 72-73)

The imagery in this passage is strongly reminiscent of Coleridge's poem "The Eolian Harp," which speculates that "all of animated nature" is wakened into thought by "one intellectual breeze, / At once the Soul of each, and God of all" (lines 44-48). According to Austin, however, only the indigenous peoples of the American Southwest are still capable of attending to the subtle sounds of "the wind in the corn." Large-scale mechanized agriculture has alienated most people from any awareness of the symbiotic affinities that once existed between human beings and the crops that we cultivate for food. Elsewhere in *Land of Journeys' Ending*, Austin deplores the way that modern Americans "go about with a vast impedimenta of Things, clanking entrails of our Frankenstein culture" (345). Like Mary Shelley, Austin was profoundly skeptical of the supposed benefits conferred upon humankind by advanced technology.

Austin's extended meditation on the human significance of the South-western landscape reaches a climactic resolution in her chapter "Sacred Mountains." In a passage that foreshadows the ecological awareness of Aldo Leopold's seminal essay, "Thinking Like a Mountain" (1949), Austin describes her encounter with a barren mountain in the midst of a vast, uninhabited desert landscape:

> I knew a mountain once, over toward Lost Borders, which could both glow and pale, pale after the burning, like a lovely neglected woman who burned to no purpose, a dark mountain, whose bareness was like a pain. After some thousand years nothing grew there but sparse tufted grass, round-branched, rusted cacti, and the knee-high creosote. Occasionally, in hollows where the seldom rains would catch, astralagus ripened a few papery pods, and slim spears of painted-cup. So dry it was, not even lizards darted, nor lichens grew upon the rocks. (386-388)

Austin personifies the mountain as "a lovely neglected woman," a phrase that evokes the pathos of her own lonely life. Having suffered the personal trauma of divorce in 1914, and having lost her daughter to the influenza epidemic of 1918, Austin felt herself very much alone in the world. In her lifelong feelings of solitude and abandonment, Austin identifies deeply with the lonely mountain, and she takes great joy when the mountain finds an animal companion:

> Then after several seasons of less frequent rains, a solitary rabbit found its way there. If by chance I saw it in my visits, I turned quickly and went another way; not for worlds would I have scared it from the mountain. And the second season after, I went there with a man of my acquaintance, and in my excitement to discover that the rabbit had found a mate, I cried out. Unhappily, the man was the sort in whom a mountain wakes only the love of killing, and after he showed me the rabbits dangling bloody from his hand, I felt I could never go there again. But sometimes I have dreamed of it, and in my dream the mountain has a face, and on that face a look of hurt, intolerably familiar. (388)

This seemingly simple anecdote of discovery and loss conveys a deep personal significance. As a green parable, it expresses Austin's intuitive sense of connection with the landscape and its non-human inhabitants. Like "The Rime of the Ancient Mariner," this narrative offers a symbolic meditation upon the environmental consequences of the thoughtless destruction of wild creatures.[26] Although Austin does not oppose hunting in the context of an indigenous subsistence lifestyle, she does deplore the senseless violence that typically accompanied the exploration and development of the Western frontier. She lays particular emphasis upon the gender differences that condition the possibility of human response to this desolate yet vulnerable landscape. To Austin, as a wandering woman, the lonely mountain evokes profound feelings of empathy, but to her male companion it "wakes only the love of killing." Such gender differences have pervaded the entire historical experience of discovery and conquest on the American continent, and they contribute to the ecofeminist ethic that Austin brings to her presentation of the Western landscape.

Austin concludes her chapter on "Sacred Mountains" with some further reflections on the importance of preserving the wild character of such remote, inhospitable landscapes. Like Thoreau and Muir, she argues that the existence of wild places is important because of their intrinsic value, as distinct from any economic utility or aesthetic appreciation that we may derive from them. These "vast, stony undulations" confront the meek denizens of civilized places with the ineluctable truth of their own wild origins:

> For he who does not understand that the wildness of mountains serves us far more than their tameness, understands very little. Slopes given to the plow may serve us less than the vast, stony undulations that are patterned gray and green in the spring, and gray and gold in October, with the quaking aspens. All up the Sangre de Cristo, the pine and aspen patterns make a hieroglyph still undeciphered, except as you find the key to it in the script of pagan thinking at the back of the mind of man. (393-394)

For Austin the wilderness is a hieroglyph whose meaning can never be fully deciphered. The arid environment of the desert, and the resourceful adaptations of its wild flora and fauna, present the human mind with an unspoken, enigmatic significance. Austin suggests that the interpretive key to such places may be found in the "script of pagan thinking" that still resides at the instinctual core of human cognition.

In her yearning for revelation in the natural world, her sympathetic identification with wild creatures, and her nostalgia for the exuberant paganism of ancient Greece, Austin evokes several characteristic themes of English Romantic poetry. But her profound appreciation for the harsh beauty of desert places is unprecedented in the English and American tradition of nature writing. No previous writer in this tradition has conveyed the austere patterns of desert life in such compelling and luminous prose. Austin's ecofeminist ethic, her powerful advocacy for the preservation of the Southwestern landscape, and her provocative efforts to develop an ecological poetics, will remain an important legacy for future environmental writers.

Conclusion: Roads Not Taken

A s suburbs and strip malls continue to devour large tracts of the American heartland, it seems strange that the conceptual under-pinnings of contemporary material culture are not more widely questioned. Yet even among the most sympathetic historians of ecological ideas, the validity of an utterly materialistic worldview remains unchallenged. Karl Kroeber, to take a recent example, suggests that "the Romantic era is especially interesting because in it are discernible beginnings of ideas developed by modern scientists."[1] But Kroeber regards the Romantic writers as merely "proto-ecological," not fully ecological in their thinking, because they lacked an adequate Darwinian concept of evolution. According to Kroeber, Darwinian evolution "regards all life forms in themselves (along with their progenitors and descendants) as evanescent and as shaped by ever-changing environmental processes operating materialistically to no definable end (either naturalistic or transcendental)" (167). Kroeber's account of the prevailing contemporary understanding of biological evolution is quite accurate, and he is certainly correct that the English Romantics and their American progeny did not see the world in such a reductively materialistic way. But that does not mean that the modern view of "environmental processes operating materialistically" is the only possible view, or that it provides a completely adequate framework for understanding how the world works.

Is there a "definable end" to the history of life on Earth? At the level of the individual organism, Charles Darwin's *On the Origin of Species* (1859) provides a compelling and persuasive narrative account of the "survival of the fittest" through a continuous process of natural selection. By this means, every species becomes progressively more adapted to its local environment. Darwin's evolutionary theory, combined with the modern understanding of genetics pioneered by Gregor Mendel, does provide an answer to the question of whether life has an "end" or purpose: every living creature is engaged in a struggle to survive and reproduce, in order to pass along its genes to the next generation. In its most extreme form, this materialistic worldview results in Richard Dawkins's theory of the Selfish Gene: organisms are just mechanisms created by their genes for the purpose of replication. According to Dawkins, "we are survival machines— robot vehicles blindly programmed to preserve the selfish molecules known as genes."[2] This absurdly reductionist theory of the Selfish Gene harks back to the Cartesian view of animals as mindless machines.

Even if Darwin's theory of evolution is correct—and it certainly ranks among the best-established and most durable theories in the entire history of science—it is not a "theory of everything," even within the domain of the environmental sciences. Theories that operate at the local level of an individual organism's struggle for survival need to be complemented by theories that operate at the global level of system dynamics. Charles Darwin himself struggled to reconcile these two points of view, and his famous evocation of the "entangled bank" represents an intuitive effort to comprehend the place of the individual organism within the global ecosystem.[3] But even today, the science of ecology has not fully integrated these two perspectives. Contemporary ecologists operate either from the bottom up (as with local population studies) or from the top down (as with global computer modeling), but they have yet to meet in the middle.[4] The Gaia Hypothesis offers a provisional attempt at synthesis, but it remains controversial and unproven.

Darwin's theory of evolution offers a well-established model for describing the anatomy, behavior, and population dynamics of organisms within a specific environment. But an excessively dogmatic adherence to Darwinism may prevent contemporary scientists from seeing things that the "survival of the fittest" does not adequately explain. Many of the writers discussed in this book—including Coleridge, Thoreau, Muir, and Austin—observed the living world through the lens of an evolutionary theory that was more Lamarckian than Darwinian, because they understood the gradual evolution of terrestrial life to be goal-oriented, driven by an underlying intention. Lamarck's theory of evolution has been generally dismissed, and widely ridiculed, by biologists ever since the advent of Darwinism, but the fact that a theory is unpopular does not make it untrue.[5] Stephen Jay Gould, in an essay entitled "Shades of Lamarck," argues that

Lamarck's theory of evolution as a goal-oriented process does hold true in one very significant area: human cultural evolution. According to Gould,

> We have transformed the entire surface of our planet through the influence of one unaltered biological invention—self-consciousness. . . . This crux in the earth's history has been reached because Lamarckian processes have been unleashed upon it. Human cultural evolution, in strong opposition to our biological history, is Lamarckian in character. What we learn in one generation, we transmit directly by teaching and writing.[6]

Although (as Gould points out) the long-term impact of human material culture upon the global ecosystem has generally been disastrous, the fact that human culture is driven by consciously directed intentional processes offers one small reason for hope. If it is within our power to destroy the planet, then it may also be within our power to change the prevailing course of human history and save the planet. The choice lies within ourselves, and the simple tools of teaching and writing may be used to accomplish such worthy ends. All of the writers examined in this study were engaged, by different means, toward the same goal of changing the historical trajectory of human culture. All of them were critical of modern technological hubris and regarded the Earth as a dwelling-place for an interdependent community of living things.

If the writers of the Romantic era were proto-ecological thinkers because they lacked an adequate basis in scientific theory, then today's most advanced environmental scientists are also proto-ecological because the contemporary science of ecology still lacks a comprehensive theory that can link the local and global perspectives. Ecology is not a mature science in the way that chemistry, physics, and biology are. It is more like neuroscience: it is still seeking answers to many of its most fundamental questions, and still seeking a quantitative model that can "account for the appearances." Among these unanswered questions remains this one above all: Is there a definable end to the history of life on Earth?

Sometimes it is impossible to answer a question because it is phrased in the wrong way, or because we are looking for the answer in the wrong place. The English Romantics and the American Transcendentalists were engaged in lifelong scrutiny of the same fundamental questions as today's most advanced ecologists, but they posed these questions in different terms, and they looked elsewhere for the answers. Their Green Writing is a legacy to our own troubled moment in the history of the Earth. Rather than dismiss or forget about their work, contemporary ecologists would be well advised to reconsider the various conceptual frameworks afforded by the authors examined in the present study. Their diverse individual approaches to the literary representation of the natural world offer many suggestive ideas and seminal thoughts that have been obscured by the continuing cultural dominance of secular humanism. From "The Rime of the Ancient Mariner" to *The Land of Little Rain,* their works offer roads not taken by contemporary material culture. By envisioning alternatives to the unsustainable industrial exploitation of natural resources, these writers provide hints, clues, and intimations of different ways of dwelling on Earth. They offer pathways to a better future than we might otherwise be able to imagine.

Notes

Introduction

1. *The Works of Thoreau,* ed. Henry S. Canby (Boston: Houghton Mifflin, 1937), 668. Subsequent citations of Thoreau's essay "Nature" refer to this edition by page number.

2. Wordsworth's poem "Stepping Westward" was well known to Thoreau, who cites it approvingly in his *Journals.* James McIntosh notes that "Thoreau refers admiringly to several poems of Wordsworth that contain submerged apocalyptic impulses: the Intimations Ode, 'Stepping Westward,' and 'Peter Bell.'" *Thoreau as Romantic Naturalist: His Shifting Stance Toward Nature* (Ithaca, NY: Cornell University Press, 1974), 66.

3. "Stepping Westward," lines 1–8. *The Poetical Works of William Wordsworth,* ed. Ernest de Selincourt and Helen Darbishire, 5 vols. (Oxford: Clarendon Press, 1940–49). Subsequent citations of Wordsworth's poetry refer to this edition by line number.

4. Harold Bloom, *The Anxiety of Influence: A Theory of Poetry* (London: Oxford University Press, 1973).

5. William Cronon, "The Trouble with Wilderness; or, Getting Back to the Wrong Nature," *Uncommon Ground: Toward Reinventing Nature,* ed. William Cronon (New York: Norton, 1995), 69–90.

6. *The Complete Poetical Works of Samuel Taylor Coleridge,* ed. Ernest Hartley Coleridge (Oxford: Clarendon Press, 1912), 1:178–181. Subsequent citations of Coleridge's poetry refer to this edition by line number.

7. Geoffrey Hartman, *The Unremarkable Wordsworth* (Minneapolis: University of Minnesota Press, 1987). Although this book could hardly be characterized as a work of ecocriticism, it does usefully examine "the infinite variety of natural appearances" in Wordsworth's poetry, emphasizing "the way that the

simplest event can enrich the mind" (4). Hartman argues that "Wordsworth's real danger was always the 'sublime'—the public and preacherly dimension" (15).

8. Wordsworth, "Ode: Intimations of Immortality from Recollections of Early Childhood," line 58.

9. William Rueckert, "Literature and Ecology: An Experiment in Ecocriticism," *Iowa Review* 9 (1978): 71–86; reprinted in *The Ecocriticism Reader: Landmarks in Literary Ecology*, ed. Cheryll Glotfelty and Harold Fromm (Athens and London: University of Georgia Press, 1996), 105–123. The history of the term "ecocriticism" is more fully described in *Ecocriticism Reader*, xviii-xx.

10. Roland Barthes, "The Death of the Author," in *Image, Music, Text*, essays selected and translated by Stephen Heath (London: Fontana, 1977). The French terms *langue* and *parole* derive from Ferdinand de Saussure, *Cours de Linguistique Générale* (1916; English translation 1958).

11. Alan Liu, *Wordsworth: The Sense of History* (Stanford, CA: Stanford University Press, 1989), 104.

12. Karl Kroeber, *Ecological Literary Criticism: Romantic Imagining and the Biology of Mind* (New York: Columbia University Press, 1994), 2.

13. David Abram, *The Spell of the Sensuous: Perception and Language in a More-Than-Human World* (New York: Vintage Books, 1996).

14. Abram develops these ideas in "Animism and the Alphabet," *Spell of the Sensuous*, 93–135.

15. M. H. Abrams, *The Correspondent Breeze: Essays on English Romanticism* (New York: Norton, 1984), 216–222.

16. For further discussion of semiotic exchange in predator-prey relationships, see John Coletta, " 'Writing Larks': John Clare's Semiosis of Nature," *The Wordsworth Circle* 28 (Summer 1997): 192–200.

17. The copyright situation that prevailed in Britain and the United States during the nineteenth century actually worked to enhance the free exchange of ideas, since a book published on one side of the Atlantic could generally be distributed on the other side without payment of royalties. Thus British books were often widely available in cheap American editions, and leading American writers such as Washington Irving and Ralph Waldo Emerson found a substantial readership in Britain.

18. On this topic see Lore Metzger, *One Foot in Eden: Modes of Pastoral in Romantic Poetry* (Chapel Hill: University of North Carolina Press, 1986).

19. Kroeber, *Ecological Literary Criticism*, pages 5 and 156, note 9.

20. The history of environmental ideas in Western science and culture is examined in magisterial detail by Clarence J. Glacken, *Traces on the Rhodian Shore: Nature and Culture in Western Thought from Ancient Times to the End of the Eighteenth Century* (Berkeley: University of California Press, 1967). Another excellent historical overview is provided by Peter Marshall,

Nature's Web: An Exploration of Ecological Thinking (London: Simon and Schuster, 1992).

21. On the disastrous consequences of ancient Mediterranean deforestation, see Clive Pointing, *A Green History of the World: The Environment and the Collapse of Great Civilizations* (New York: St. Martin's Press, 1991), 68–78. A more detailed historical narrative is provided by John Robert McNeill, *The Mountains of the Mediterranean World: An Environmental History* (Cambridge: Cambridge University Press, 1992).

22. Raymond Williams rigorously demystifies the pastoral ideal in *The Country and the City* (London: Chatto & Windus, 1973). The ideological determinants of the pastoral mode are further examined by Annabel Patterson, *Pastoral and Ideology: Virgil to Valéry* (Berkeley: University of California Press, 1987).

23. On the figuration of Nature as female (in Renaissance and post-industrial cultures), see Carolyn Merchant, *The Death of Nature: Women, Ecology, and the Scientific Revolution: A Feminist Reappraisal of the Scientific Revolution* (San Francisco: Harper & Row, 1980), 1–41. See also Robert Graves's classic study, *The White Goddess,* and Riane Eisler, "The Gaia Tradition and the Partnership Future: An Ecofeminist Manifesto," in *Reweaving The Word: The Emergence of Ecofeminism,* ed. Irene Diamond and Gloria Feman Orenstein (San Francisco: Sierra Club Books, 1990), 23–34.

24. "Canticle of Brother Sun," translated by Lawrence S. Cunningham, *St. Francis of Assisi* (Boston: Twayne, 1976), 59. The Italian original reads: ". . . matre terra / la quale ne sustenta et governa / et produce diversi fructi con coloriti fiori et herba."

25. St. Francis of Assisi was recognized in 1979 by Pope John Paul II as the patron saint of ecology (according to the *Encyclopedia of Religion*). Nikos Kazantzakis's novel *St. Francis* (1953; English translation, 1962), presents the major events of his life in a lively and provocative form. On St. Francis as a progenitor of modern ecological thought, see Lynn White, "The Historical Roots of Our Ecological Crisis," *Science* 155 (1967): 1203–1207.

26. Richard Mabey, *Gilbert White: A Biography of the Author of The Natural History of Selborne* (London: Century Hutchinson, 1986), 11–12.

27. The early development of nature writing out of a more purely "scientific" approach to natural phenomena is discussed by Thomas J. Lyon, *This Incomperable Lande: A Book of American Nature Writing* (Boston: Houghton Mifflin, 1989). Lyon elucidates the convergence in ecological thought of Romantic transcendentalism (with its holism and organicism) and the scientific concepts of taxonomy, evolution, and symbiosis (20).

28. For further discussion of the voyages of Captain Cook and the professionalization of natural history during the eighteenth century, see Richard H. Grove, *Green Imperialism: Colonial Expansion, Tropical Island Edens, and the Origins of Environmentalism, 1600–1860* (Cambridge: Cambridge University Press, 1994), 311–325.

29. William Cowper, *The Task,* Book 6, in *Cowper: Poetry and Prose,* ed. Brian Spiller (London: Rupert Hart-Davis, 1968), 530. For further information on the history of animal rights, see Roderick Frazier Nash, *The Rights of Nature: A History of Environmental Ethics* (Madison: University of Wisconsin Press, 1989).

30. Cowper, *The Task,* Book 6 (530). "The economy of nature" was an expression commonly used in the later eighteenth century to denote the interdependence of all living things. On the early development of this concept, see Donald Worster, *Nature's Economy: The Roots of Ecology* (San Francisco: Sierra Club Books, 1977) and Robert P. McIntosh, *The Background of Ecology: Concept and Theory* (Cambridge: Cambridge University Press, 1985).

31. *The Letters of John Clare,* ed. Mark Storey (Oxford: Clarendon Press, 1985), 137–138. Hereafter cited as *Letters.*

32. Despite his best efforts to protect the Lake District from the encroachments of modern industrial society, Wordsworth probably did more than anyone to popularize it as a tourist destination through the publication of his poetry and *A Description of the Scenery of the Lakes in the North of England* (first published anonymously in 1810 and often reprinted).

33. Keats mentions the "wordsworthian or egotistical sublime" in a letter to Richard Woodhouse, October 27, 1818. Jonathan Bate sympathetically examines Wordsworth's ecological awareness in *Romantic Ecology: Wordsworth and the Environmental Tradition* (London: Routledge, 1991).

34. Dorothy Wordsworth records this episode in her *Grasmere Journal* entry of April 15, 1802. William Wordsworth's poem "I wandered lonely as a cloud" (composed 1804) was based on Dorothy's account.

35. Gilbert White, *The Natural History of Selborne,* ed. Paul Foster (Oxford: Oxford University Press, 1993), 182.

36. Gilbert White's contribution to the development of natural history writing is examined by William J. Keith, *The Rural Tradition: A Study of the Non-Fiction Prose Writers of the English Countryside* (Toronto: University of Toronto Press, 1974), 39–59.

37. Mabey, *Gilbert White,* 213–214.

38. Clare possessed two different editions of White's *Natural History of Selborne;* cited in *The Natural History Prose Writings of John Clare,* ed. Margaret Grainger (Oxford: Clarendon Press, 1983), 360, 362, 363.

39. Karl Kroeber, *Ecological Literary Criticism: Romantic Imagining and the Biology of Mind* (New York: Columbia University Press, 1994), 75 and 8.

40. The word *ecology* is attested in OED (second edition, 1989) from 1873, while the word *Ökologie* first appeared in German circa 1866. The Greek word οὖκος is defined in Liddell and Scott's *Greek-English Lexicon* as "house . . . [or] any dwelling-place."

Chapter 1

1. *The Notebooks of Samuel Taylor Coleridge,* ed. Kathleen Coburn (Princeton, NJ: Princeton University Press, 1957–), 1:579. Hereafter cited as *Notebooks.*

2. See, for example, the list of local place-names in *Notebooks,* 1:1207.

3. For further discussion of Coleridge's acquaintance with Erasmus Darwin, see Desmond King-Hele, *Erasmus Darwin and the Romantic Poets* (New York: St. Martin's Press, 1986).

4. William Harvey, *An Anatomical Disquisition on the Motion of the Heart and Blood in Animals* (London, 1628).

5. Edmund Halley (1656?-1743), the English astronomer, contributed a scientific description of the hydrological cycle in three brief papers published in the *Philosophical Transactions* in the early 1690s. Halley established that the rate of evaporation from the surface of the Mediterranean was more than sufficient to account for the return of water to the sea by its major rivers. For further information on Halley, see *Dictionary of Scientific Biography,* 6:67.

6. Isaac J. Biberg, "Specimen academicum de Oeconomia Naturae," *Amoenitates Academicae* 2 (1751): 1–58. English translation: "The Oeconomy of Nature," trans. Benjamin Stillingfleet, in *Miscellaneous Tracts Relating to Natural History, Husbandry, and Physick* (London, 1759). Cited from the second London edition (1762), 39.

7. Joseph Priestley, "Observations on Different Kinds of Air," *Philosophical Transactions of the Royal Society* 62 (1772): 147–264.

8. John Pringle, *A Discourse on the Different Kinds of Air, delivered at the anniversary of the Royal Society* (London, 1774).

9. Gilbert White, *The Natural History and Antiquities of Selborne, in the County of Southampton* (London: T. Bensley, 1789; reprinted Menston, England: Scolar Press, 1970).

10. Coleridge was a great admirer of Gilbert White; he annotated *The Natural History of Selborne,* and he shared White's preference for the local vernacular names over the "learned names" for plant species (*Notebooks,* 1:1610). He also shared White's interest in the larger, holistic view of the natural world implicit in the phrase "economy of nature."

11. See John Livingston Lowes, *The Road to Xanadu: A Study in the Ways of the Imagination,* second edition (Boston: Houghton Mifflin, 1930), 69–72, 83–84, and 174. Lowes's meticulous analysis of Coleridge's intellectual development might well have been subtitled "a study in the ecology of mind." For a more detailed discussion of the influence of Darwin's "The Economy of Vegetation" on Coleridge's intended Hymns, see Ian Wylie, *Young Coleridge and the Philosophers of Nature* (Oxford: Clarendon Press, 1989), 73.

12. Robert Southey, letter of September 1794, *Life and Correspondence of Robert Southey,* 1:221. Cited by Lowes, 573, n. 8. Coleridge first uses the words "Pantocracy" [*sic*] and "aspheterized" in a letter to Southey, July 6, 1794, in

Collected Letters of Samuel Taylor Coleridge, ed. E. L. Griggs (Oxford: Clarendon Press, 1956–71), 1:84.

13. Coleridge, *Notebooks,* 1:863. The most significant of Sara Hutchinson's interpolations to this list is the name "Forget me not" (which she substituted for Withering's "Mouse-ear"). As Kathleen Coburn's note to this passage points out, Coleridge later used the term "forget-me-not" in his poem "The Keepsake," which is cited by OED as the first recorded English usage of this word (except for one sixteenth-century citation). Presumably, however, this plant name was current in popular speech. In Coburn's view, "it is not unpleasant to reflect that Coleridge and Sara between them may have been responsible for re-introducing it into English letters."

14. For a list of 700 Coleridgean coinages, see James C. McKusick, " 'Living Words': Samuel Taylor Coleridge and the Genesis of the OED," *Modern Philology* 90 (1992): 1–45. The coinages discussed in the present study represent additional discoveries, not included in the previously published list.

15. The following words from Coleridge's early *Notebooks* are unrecorded in OED: *breezelet* (1:1449), *hillage* (1:1433), *interslope* (1:1449), *kittenract* (1:412), *offrunning* (1:798), *treeage* (1:789), *twisture* (1:1495), and *lacustral* (1:1495; note that the word *lacustral* is recorded in OED with a first citation of 1843). Coleridge's use of certain other words significantly antedates the citations in OED: *bulgy* (1:798) is first recorded in 1848, *rockery* (1:495, 1:855) is first recorded in 1843, *waterslide* (1:804) is first recorded in 1869, and *wavelet* (1:1489) is first recorded with a Coleridge citation of 1810. The word *cloudage* (1:1635) is first recorded in OED with a Coleridge citation of 1818; Coleridge's earlier use of *cloudage* in the *Notebooks* was cited by Fred Shapiro, "Neologisms in Coleridge's *Notebooks,*" *N&Q* 32 (1985): 346–347. The word *greenery* is first recorded in OED with a citation from "Kubla Khan" (1797); this word appears three more times in Coleridge's *Notebooks* of May 1799 (1:410, 411, 417). The words *scabby, scarified,* and *scorious* (1:798) are not coinages, but these three medical terms are used by Coleridge in a new, figurative sense (to describe landforms).

16. *Notebooks,* 1:174. The word *tremendity* is unrecorded in OED; it was cited as a Coleridgean coinage by Joshua Neumann, "Coleridge on the English Language," *PMLA* 63 (1948): 642–661.

17. The term "ecolect" was invented by Hugh Sykes Davies, *Wordsworth and the Worth of Words* (Cambridge: Cambridge University Press, 1986), 274–275. Davies derives "*ecolect,* from the word οἶκος (a household), to describe a variation peculiar to a particular household, or kin group" (319, note 8). In the present study, the term "ecolect" is used in a more comprehensive sense, to denote a language that arises from extended human habitation in a particular place.

18. "The Rime of the Ancyent Marinere," *Argument,* and lines 55–56. All citations of this poem will refer to the 1798 version by line number; this version is reprinted in Coleridge's *Poetical Works,* vol. 2.

19. Coleridge makes a similar point about the eerie "creeking" noise of the rook in "This Lime-Tree Bower My Prison": "No sound is dissonant which tells of Life." *Poetical Works,* 1:181.

20. For much fuller discussion of this historical analogue, see Bernard Smith, "Coleridge's *Ancient Mariner* and Cook's Second Voyage," *Journal of the Warburg and Courtauld Institutes* 19 (1956): 117–154.

21. "Rime of the Ancyent Marinere," *Argument.*

22. Erasmus Darwin, "The Economy of Vegetation," in *The Botanic Garden: A Poem, in Two Parts* (2 vols., London: Joseph Johnson, 1791), vol. 1, additional note 9. Cited by Wylie, *Young Coleridge and the Philosophers of Nature,* 154.

23. Romand Coles, "Ecotones and Environmental Ethics: Adorno and Lopez," in *In the Nature of Things: Language, Politics, and the Environment,* ed. Jane Bennett and William Chaloupka (Minneapolis: University of Minnesota Press, 1993), 243. Citing Barry Lopez, *Arctic Dreams: Imagination and Desire in a Northern Landscape* (New York: Bantam, 1986).

24. Samuel T. Coleridge, *Logic,* ed. J. R. de J. Jackson (Princeton, NJ: Princeton University Press, 1981), 126, and *Biographia Literaria,* ed. James Engell and W. Jackson Bate (Princeton, NJ: Princeton University Press, 1983), 1:86n. The word "offlet" is a Coleridge coinage; its usage in the Logic (circa 1819–1828) antedates the 1838 citation in OED.

25. Lowes, *Road to Xanadu,* 306, citing *The Romaunt of the Rose,* lines 661–662, 671–672, and 715–716, as published in Anderson's *Poets of Great Britain* (1795). Emphasis added.

26. Wilhelm von Humboldt, *Über die Verschiedenheit des menschlichen Sprachbaues und ihren Einfluss auf die geistige Entwicklung des Menschengeschlechts* (Berlin, 1836); translated by Peter Heath as *On Language: The Diversity of Human Language-Structure and its Influence on the Mental Development of Mankind* (Cambridge: Cambridge University Press, 1988), 49. Coleridge describes his 1806 encounter with Humboldt in *The Friend,* ed. Barbara E. Rooke, 2 vols. (Princeton, NJ: Princeton University Press, 1969), 1:510. On the emerging discipline of ecolinguistics, see Einar Haugen, *The Ecology of Language* (Stanford, CA: Stanford University Press, 1972) and Adam Makkai, *Ecolinguistics: Toward a New **Paradigm** for the Science of Language* (London: Pinter Publishers, 1993).

Chapter 2

1. For a more detailed study of these local affiliations, see David McCracken, *Wordsworth and the Lake District: A Guide to the Poems and their Places* (Oxford: Oxford University Press, 1985).

2. William Wordsworth, *The Prelude,* ed. Ernest de Selincourt (London: Oxford University Press, 1928). Subsequent citations of *The Prelude* refer to the 1850 edition of this poem by book and line number.

3. On this topic see Geoffrey H. Hartman, *The Unmediated Vision: An Interpretation of Wordsworth, Hopkins, Rilke, and Valéry* (New Haven, CT: Yale University Press, 1954). The phenomenological approach developed in Hartman's earlier work has strong affinities with the methodology of ecocriticism, especially in its concern for the epistemology of perception.

4. All citations from *Lyrical Ballads* refer to the text of the first edition (London, 1798) by title and line number.

5. The Preface to Coleridge's *Sheet of Sonnets* (1796) advocates a poetic style in harmony with nature: "those Sonnets appear to me the most exquisite, in which moral Sentiments, Affections, or Feelings, are deduced from, and associated with, the scenery of Nature. . . . They create a sweet and indissoluble union between the intellectual and the material world" (Coleridge, *Poetical Works,* vol. 2, 1139). Such a style might well be termed "Green Writing."

6. For a thoughtful discussion of Wordsworth's poetry in the context of contemporary agricultural practices, see Kenneth MacLean, *Agrarian Age: A Background for Wordsworth* (New Haven, CT: Yale University Press, 1950). MacLean provides useful information on Wordsworth's opposition to the enclosure of common lands in Grasmere, citing a local informant: "It was all along of him [Wordsworth] that Grasmere folks have their Common open. Ye may ga now reet up to sky over Grisedale, wi'out laying leg to fence, and all through him" (21).

7. A similar act of usurpation occurs in "Goody Blake, and Harry Gill," another poem from *Lyrical Ballads* (1798). In this narrative poem, which Wordsworth based on an actual incident, the wealthy landowner Harry Gill catches Goody Blake gathering sticks from his hedge for firewood. Although such stick-gathering was customarily permitted on common lands, Harry seizes the poor old woman and threatens her with "vengeance" for her crime. Just as in "The Female Vagrant," the traditional common rights of local inhabitants have been criminalized as acts of "trespass" as a consequence of the enclosure of common lands. (Harry's hedge marks the boundary of his private enclosure.)

8. William Wordsworth, *Guide to the Lakes,* fifth edition (1835), ed. Ernest de Selincourt (Oxford: Oxford University Press, 1906), 52. Hereafter cited as *Guide.* Wordsworth also memorably evokes the extinct Leigh deer in *The River Duddon* (1820), sonnet 2.

9. Karl Kroeber, "'Home at Grasmere': Ecological Holiness," *PMLA* 89 (1974): 134.

10. "Home at Grasmere" is cited by line number from *The Poetical Works of William Wordsworth,* vol. 5, pages 313–338.

11. Paul H. Fry, "Green to the Very Door? The Natural Wordsworth," *Studies in Romanticism* 35 (1996): 535–551.

12. Mary Moorman, *William Wordsworth: A Biography* (Oxford: Clarendon Press, 1965), vol. 2, 563n.

Chapter 3

1. The social and economic impact of enclosure is examined by E. P. Thompson, *The Making of the English Working Class* (New York: Pantheon Books, 1963). Thompson asserts that "enclosure (when all the sophistications are allowed for) was a plain enough case of class robbery, played according to fair rules of property and law laid down by a Parliament of property-owners and lawyers" (218). For a contemporary view, see Arthur Young, *General Report on Enclosures* (London: McMillan, 1808; reprinted New York: Augustus M. Kelley, 1971). Young, a staunch advocate of parliamentary enclosure, nevertheless recognizes that in many cases the poor lose their customary rights to common pasturage and fuel (12–20), and he deplores the widespread "inattention to the property or the customs of the poor" (154).

2. Clare's first published volume was entitled *Poems Descriptive of Rural Life and Scenery* (London: John Taylor and James Hessey, 1820). Clare's response to enclosure is more fully discussed by John Barrell, *The Idea of Landscape and the Sense of Place 1730–1840: An Approach to the Poetry of John Clare* (London: Cambridge University Press, 1972), 98–120, and Johanne Clare, *John Clare and the Bounds of Circumstance* (Kingston and Montreal: McGill-Queen's University Press, 1987), 36–55. See also Robert Waller, "Enclosures: The Ecological Significance of a Poem by John Clare," *Mother Earth, Journal of the Soil Association* 13 (1964): 231–237.

3. *John Clare: Selected Poetry and Prose,* ed. Merryn and Raymond Williams (London: Methuen, 1986), 1–20. Critical studies by John Barrell and Johanne Clare are cited above, note 2.

4. Geoffrey Summerfield, editor, *John Clare: Selected Poetry* (London: Penguin, 1990), 22.

5. *The Early Poems of John Clare 1804–1822,* ed. Eric Robinson & David Powell (Oxford: Clarendon Press, 1989), 1:159. Hereafter cited as *Early Poems* by volume and page number.

6. *John Clare By Himself,* ed. Eric Robinson and David Powell (Manchester: Carcanet Press, 1996), 113–114.

7. John Clare, *The Shepherd's Calendar,* ed. Eric Robinson and Geoffrey Summerfield (London: Oxford University Press, 1964), viii; cited by Merryn and Raymond Williams, *John Clare: Selected Poetry and Prose* (London and New York: Methuen, 1986), 209, 213.

8. History has vindicated Clare's repudiation of the Linnaean taxonomy, since naturalists of the 1820s and 1830s largely abandoned the Linnaean or Sexual System of classification in favor of the more "natural" system pioneered by John Ray, retaining however the established Latin nomenclature. On Clare's preference for Ray over Linnaeus, see his *Natural History Prose Writings,* xliii; the editor notes that Clare's interest in natural history was encouraged by Joseph Henderson, a local amateur naturalist well-versed in the

Linnaean nomenclature. Clare's rejection of the Linnaean scheme was evidently a matter of choice and not the result of sheer ignorance.

9. Clare's complex response to the tradition of "picturesque" writing is examined by Timothy Brownlow, *John Clare and Picturesque Landscape* (Oxford: Clarendon Press, 1983). Especially relevant to the present context is his discussion of natural history writing, 41–66.

10. The rigid monthly framework of *A Shepherd's Calendar* was suggested to Clare by John Taylor in a letter of August 1, 1823 (*Letters*, 278n). Elsewhere in his poetry, Clare rarely conforms to such an explicit chronological scheme.

11. *John Clare: Poems of the Middle Period*, ed. Eric Robinson, David Powell, and P. M. S. Dawson (Oxford: Clarendon Press, 1996–98), 3:173. Hereafter cited as *Middle Period* by volume and page number.

12. "February—A Thaw," *Middle Period*, 1:30.

13. *Natural History Prose Writings*, 70–71.

14. "The Vixen," *John Clare*, ed. Eric Robinson and David Powell (Oxford: Oxford University Press, 1984), 249. Hereafter cited as *John Clare*.

15. "A Sunday with Shepherds and Herdboys," *Middle Period*, 2:18.

16. "Remembrances," *Middle Period*, 4:133.

17. "Summer Evening," *Middle Period*, 4:147.

18. Clare denounces "accursed wealth" in "Helpstone" (*Early Poems*, 1:161); "No Trespassing" signs appear in "The Mores" (*Middle Period*, 2:349); he witnesses the local incursion of railways in *Natural History Writings*, 245.

19. "The Robin's Nest," *Middle Period*, 3:534.

20. Clare depicts an unspoiled, idyllic landscape in the sonnet "Swordy Well" (*Middle Period*, 4:145).

21. This pattern of double meanings (encoded in Clare's nonstandard spelling of such words as "enarmoured," "swarthy/swathy," and "main/mane") is more fully examined by Barbara Strang, "John Clare's Language," in John Clare, *The Rural Muse* (London, 1835; reprinted Northumberland: Mid Northumberland Arts Group, 1982), 162.

22. On the ideological basis of Clare's "green language," see Raymond Williams, *The Country and the City*, 133–141. Williams further examines Clare's use of Northamptonshire dialect in *John Clare: Selected Poetry and Prose*, 205–213.

23. Cultural assimilation is especially apparent in the case of Robert Bloomfield, a contemporary "peasant poet" whose brief popularity around 1800 was due in part to his ability to cultivate a standard poetic diction.

24. *The Midsummer Cushion*, ed. Anne Tibble & R. K. R. Thornton (Northumberland: Mid Northumberland Arts Group, 1979). A small selection of poems from *The Midsummer Cushion*, heavily "corrected" and bowdlerized by an anonymous editor, was published as *The Rural Muse* (London, 1835). The full text of *The Midsummer Cushion* has been definitively re-edited as volumes 3–4 of Clare's *Poems of the Middle Period*.

25. John Clare, Preface to *The Midsummer Cushion, Middle Period,* 3:6.

26. "Sighing for Retirement," *The Later Poems of John Clare 1837–1864,* ed. Eric Robinson and David Powell (Oxford: Clarendon Press, 1984), 1:19.

27. The formal and thematic structure of *The Midsummer Cushion* is more fully analyzed by the editors of the 1979 edition, xii-xiv, although without reference to Clare's implicit ecological paradigm.

28. "The Pewit's Nest" describes a habitat threatened by agricultural "progress." Marginal grass strips were normally eliminated in the process of enclosure, while fallow fields were a feature of medieval crop rotation that gradually became obsolete under modern intensive agriculture.

29. OED defines "plashy" (a.2, sense 2) as "marked as if splashed with colour," noting that this sense is "rare" and citing only Keats, *Hyperion,* 2:45. Clare may be creating this usage independently (as a metaphoric extension of the primary adjectival sense, "that splashes with water"), or he may be echoing Keats's usage here.

30. William Empson, *Some Versions of Pastoral* (London: Chatto & Windus, 1935; reprinted New Directions, n.d.), 23.

31. Clare's Northborough cottage is described in "The Flitting," *Middle Period,* 3:479.

Chapter 4

1. Kroeber, *Ecological Literary Criticism,* 3.

2. Harold Bloom, *Blake's Apocalypse: A Study in Poetic Argument* (Garden City, NY: Doubleday, 1963); Joseph A. Wittreich, *Angel of Apocalypse: Blake's Idea of Milton* (Madison: University of Wisconsin Press, 1975); Morton D. Paley, *The Apocalyptic Sublime* (New Haven, CT: Yale University Press, 1986); see also Steven Goldsmith, *Unbuilding Jerusalem: Apocalypse and Romantic Representation* (Ithaca, NY: Cornell University Press, 1993).

3. "And was Jerusalem builded here, / Among these dark Satanic Mills?" (*Milton,* plate 1). *Blake's Poetry and Designs,* selected and edited by Mary Lynn Johnson and John E. Grant (New York: Norton, 1979). Subsequent citations of Blake's poetry refer to this Norton Critical Edition by title and plate number, except where noted otherwise.

4. The estimated population of Greater London was 1,117,000 in 1801; it increased to 1,327,000 in 1811, 1,600,000 in 1821, and 1,907,000 in 1831. The transient and homeless population is almost certainly undercounted in these figures. These population estimates are derived from B. R. Mitchell, *British Historical Statistics* (Cambridge: Cambridge University Press, 1988), 25 and 27.

5. The first edition of *The Botanic Garden* (London: Joseph Johnson, 1791) includes several engravings by Blake, most notably "Fertilization of Egypt" (after Henry Fuseli), facing page 127, and four views of the Portland Vase.

Blake also engraved "Tornado" after Fuseli, which appeared only in the third edition of *The Botanic Garden.*

6. *Botanic Garden,* vol. 1, Appendix, page 22, additional note 11.

7. Peter Ackroyd, *Blake* (London: Sinclair-Stevenson, 1995), 130.

8. Blake's probable awareness of the Albion Mill was first suggested by Jacob Bronowski, *William Blake: A Man Without a Mask* (London: Secker & Warburg, 1944), 64; revised as *William Blake and the Age of Revolution* (New York: Harper & Row, 1965), 96.

9. *Atlas of Industrializing Britain 1780–1914,* ed. John Langton and R. J. Morris (London: Methuen, 1986), 77 and 79. The chart on page 79 indicates that London in 1800 had 1,000 total horsepower of Boulton and Watt steam engines installed, a figure comparable to any of England's northern industrial cities. Manchester and Birmingham would later greatly surpass London in the growth of their manufacturing base, but in Blake's time London was a major center of industrial production.

10. Blake explicitly refers to these new military devices in *The Four Zoas,* night 8; see David V. Erdman, *Blake: Prophet Against Empire* (first edition 1954; revised edition: Princeton, NJ: Princeton University Press, 1969), 398.

11. *The Poems of William Blake,* ed. W. H. Stevenson, text by David V. Erdman (London: Longman, 1971). This edition is cited only for passages unavailable in the Norton Critical Edition.

12. For more extensive discussion of Blake's mill imagery in the context of Enlightenment epistemology, see Harry White, "Blake and the Mills of Induction," *Blake Newsletter* 10 (1977): 109–112. See also Stuart Peterfreund, *William Blake in a Newtonian World: Essays on Literature as Art and Science* (Norman, OK: University of Oklahoma Press, 1998).

13. For further information on Blake's innovative printmaking techniques, see Robert N. Essick, *William Blake, Printmaker* (Princeton, NJ: Princeton University Press, 1980) and Joseph Viscomi, *Blake and the Idea of the Book* (Princeton, NJ: Princeton University Press, 1993).

14. E. F. Schumacher, *Small is Beautiful: Economics as if People Mattered* (New York: Harper & Row, 1973).

15. Cited from the Longman edition. Capitalization variants from the Longman edition reflect Blake's actual usage, as recorded in *The Complete Poetry and Prose of William Blake,* New Revised Edition, ed. David V. Erdman, with commentary by Harold Bloom (Berkeley: University of California Press, 1982).

16. Samuel Taylor Coleridge, *Notebooks,* 1:1098, recording Humphrey Davy's January-February 1802 lectures on chemistry.

17. The "clouded hills that belch forth storms & fire" may refer specifically to underground fires in coal mines, a common sight in deep-pit coal-mining regions. Such fires often burn out of control for many years. During the early 1960s, for example, there was an enormous underground coal-mine

fire in the vicinity of Carbondale, Pennsylvania, resulting in plumes of sulphurous smoke and steam that emanated from small crevices in the earth. Entire houses would disappear when the ground suddenly collapsed beneath them, and the surrounding region was blanketed in a dark, smoky haze. (Personal observation by James McKusick.)

18. Blake's first volume, *Poetical Sketches,* was privately printed in 1783; it follows the conventional arrangement of poems according to the four seasons, established by Alexander Pope's *Pastorals* (1709) and James Thomson's *The Seasons* (1726–30).

19. The term "Ecotopia" was coined by Ernest Callenbach, *Ecotopia: A Novel about Ecology, People and Politics in 1999* (Berkeley: Banyan Tree Books, 1975).

20. For more complete discussion of the "Wild Thyme" (and its possible pun on "Time"), see William Blake, *Milton a Poem and the Final Illuminated Works,* ed. Robert N. Essick and Joseph Viscomi (Princeton, NJ: Princeton University Press, 1993), 194. Blake's "Wild Thyme" echoes one of Shakespeare's best-known passages, "I know a bank where the wild thyme grows" (*Midsummer Night's Dream* II.i.249), where this fragrant herb decks the magical bower of Titania.

21. The building of the city of Golgonooza is further elaborated in *Jerusalem,* 12:21 to 14:34. For an excellent discussion of Blake's vision of an ideal cityscape, see Kenneth Johnston, "Blake's Cities: Romantic Forms of Urban Renewal," *Blake's Visionary Forms Dramatic,* ed. David V. Erdman and John E. Grant (Princeton, NJ: Princeton University Press, 1970), 413–442.

22. Personal communication, Donna Meadows, Dartmouth College, September 1975.

23. Mary Shelley, *The Last Man,* ed. Anne McWhir (Peterborough, Ontario, Canada: Broadview Press, 1996). Subsequent citations refer to this edition by page number.

24. See Audrey A. Fisch, "Plaguing Politics: AIDS, Deconstruction, and *The Last Man,*" in *The Other Mary Shelley,* ed. Audrey A. Fisch, Anne K. Mellor, and Esther Schor (New York: Oxford University Press, 1993), 267–286. In "The Last Man: Apocalypse without Millennium" (Fisch 107–123), Morton Paley argues that Mary Shelley depicts apocalypse without its redemptive aftermath, unlike Blake's *Jerusalem* or Percy Shelley's *Prometheus Unbound.* On the topic of influenza, see William Ian Beveridge, *Influenza: The Last Great Plague,* revised edition (New York: Prodist, 1978) and Alfred W. Crosby, *America's Forgotten Pandemic: The Influenza of 1918* (Cambridge: Cambridge University Press, 1989). According to Beveridge, "the total deaths [in 1918 from influenza] throughout the world were estimated at 15–25 million—the greatest visitation ever experienced by the human race" (32).

25. The *miasma* theory of disease was prevalent among medical experts in Europe from the fourteenth century until the late nineteenth century.

According to this theory, epidemic diseases such as bubonic plague were spread by contaminated air. See Sheldon Watts, *Epidemics and History: Disease, Power, and Imperialism* (New Haven, CT: Yale University Press, 1997), 8–15.

26. Bill McKibben, *The End of Nature* (New York: Viking Penguin, 1990).

27. George Rippey Stewart, *Earth Abides* (New York: Random House, 1949); Rachel Carson, *Silent Spring* (Boston, 1962).

28. Kroeber, *Ecological Literary Criticism,* 5 and 156, note 9.

Chapter 5

1. Ralph Waldo Emerson, *Essays & Lectures,* ed. Joel Porte (New York: Library of America, 1983), 1299. Subsequent citations of Emerson's essays and lectures refer to this edition by page number.

2. For biographical information on Emerson, I am indebted to Robert D. Richardson, *Emerson: The Mind on Fire: A Biography* (Berkeley: University of California Press, 1995).

3. F. O. Matthiessen, *American Renaissance: Art and Expression in the Age of Emerson and Whitman* (London and New York: Oxford University Press, 1941).

4. Stanley Cavell, *In Quest of the Ordinary: Lines of Skepticism and Romanticism* (Chicago: University of Chicago Press, 1988), 27.

5. Kenneth Walter Cameron, *Ralph Waldo Emerson's Reading* (1941; reprinted New York: Haskell House Publishers, 1973), 46.

6. Coleridge, *Biographia Literaria,* ed. James Engell and Walter Jackson Bate, 1:304.

7. *Biographia Literaria,* 1:304.

8. *Biographia Literaria,* 1:80–81.

9. Wordsworth, "Ode: Intimations of Immortality," line 112. In the essay "Spiritual Laws," Emerson alludes to Wordsworth's Intimations Ode: "'Earth fills her lap with splendors' *not her own*" (313). Wordsworth actually wrote, "Earth fills her lap with pleasures of her own" (line 78). Emerson is evidently "correcting" Wordsworth's poem from the standpoint of his own transcendental idealism.

10. *The Journals and Miscellaneous Notebooks of Ralph Waldo Emerson,* ed. W. H. Gilman and A. R. Ferguson (Cambridge, MA, 1964), 6:38. The phrase is copied from Coleridge, *Aids to Reflection,* ed. John Beer (Princeton, NJ: Princeton University Press, 1993), 118.

11. The American reception of *Aids to Reflection,* particularly among the emerging community of Transcendentalists, is more fully described in John Beer's preface to the edition cited above (cxvi-cxxviii). For an excellent discussion of the convoluted intellectual relationship between Coleridge and Emerson, see Anthony Harding, "Coleridge and Transcendentalism," *The*

Coleridge Connection: Essays for Thomas McFarland, ed. Richard Gravil and Molly Lefebure (New York: St. Martin's Press, 1990), 233–253.

12. *The Letters of Ralph Waldo Emerson,* ed. R. L. Rusk (New York, 1939), 1:291.

13. Cameron, *Ralph Waldo Emerson's Reading,* 17, 21.

14. Walter Harding, *Emerson's Library* (Charlottesville: University Press of Virginia, 1967), 64. Emerson's personal library contained volumes of poetry by all six of the major Romantic poets: Blake, Wordsworth, Coleridge, Byron, Shelley, and Keats.

15. *Journals and Miscellaneous Notebooks of Ralph Waldo Emerson,* 4:401–410.

16. In his *Life of John Sterling* (1851), Thomas Carlyle recorded his personal impression of Coleridge in the late 1820s: "Coleridge sat on the brow of Highgate Hill, in those years, looking down on London and its smoke-tumult, like a sage escaped from the inanity of life's battle. . . . He had, especially among young enquiring men, a higher than literary, a kind of prophetic or magician character" (Part 1, Chapter 8).

17. Emerson, *Journals,* June 1871.

18. In fact, no American writer seriously addressed the possibility that global environmental change might result from human economic activity until the publication of *Man and Nature* in 1864 by George Perkins Marsh.

19. Emerson, "Ode, Inscribed to W. H. Channing," *Poems* (1847). William Henry Channing (1810–1884) was a prominent clergyman and social reformer (not to be confused with Emerson's close friend, William Ellery Channing).

20. Immanuel Kant, *Critique of Pure Reason* (1781), part 2, section 3, Table of Categories. Kant posits three Categories of Relation: (1) Inherence and Subsistence; (2) Causality and Dependence; (3) Community.

21. Lovelock, J. E. [James Ephraim], *Gaia: A New Look at Life on Earth* (Oxford: Oxford University Press, 1995). Lovelock traces the intellectual history of the Gaia Hypothesis back to the Scottish geologist James Hutton, who argued at a meeting of the Royal Society of Edinburgh in 1785 that the Earth's crust is not a rigid, crystalline structure, but a slow-moving fluid dynamic. According to Hutton, the Earth as a whole may be considered "as a planetary body, or as a globe sustaining plants and animals, which may be termed *a living world." Transactions of the Royal Society of Edinburgh,* vol. 1, part 2 (1788): 209–304.

22. Throughout the history of the English language, the words *thought* and *think* have always referred to an abstract process of cognition. According to *The American Heritage Dictionary,* third edition (1992), the word *thought* derives from the Old English *(ge)thōht,* which derives from the Indo-European root *tong-,* meaning "to think, feel."

23. According to John Horne Tooke: "Remember, where we now say, *I Think,* the antient expression was—*Me thinketh,* i.e. *Me Thingeth, It Thingeth me."*

ΕΠΕΑ ΠΤΕΡΟΕΝΤΑ, *or, The Diversions of Purley* (London, 1786–1805), 2:406. Coleridge mentions Horne Tooke's book in his preface to *Aids to Reflection* (7), and Emerson may have consulted this book himself. For further discussion of Coleridge and Horne Tooke, see James C. McKusick, *Coleridge's Philosophy of Language* (New Haven, CT: Yale University Press, 1986), 33–52.

24. Coleridge's concept of the symbol is most fully developed in *The Statesman's Manual,* where he argues that "a Symbol is characterized by . . . the translucence of the Eternal through and in the Temporal." *Lay Sermons,* ed. R. J. White (Princeton, NJ: Princeton University Press, 1972), 30. This volume comprises *The Statesman's Manual* (1816) and *A Lay Sermon* (1817); hereafter cited as *Lay Sermons.*

25. Emerson copied into his *Journals* (6:173) another trenchant description of the symbol from Coleridge's poem "The Destiny of Nations": "For all that meets the bodily sense I deem / Symbolical, one mighty alphabet / For infant minds" (lines 18–20). In this passage, a symbolic correspondence is established between the objects of perception and the repertoire of Platonic ideas.

26. Coleridge, *Biographia Literaria,* 1:85; Emerson copied the phrase "truth becomes power through domestication" from this source into his *Journals,* 6:35, 6:191. Emerson's apothegm, "every object rightly seen, unlocks a new faculty of the soul," first appears in his *Journals* 5:189; compare 3:283. This apothegm is not a direct quotation from Coleridge, but it does embody an idea expressed by Coleridge in *Aids to Reflection:* "The Mistakes of scientific men have never injured Christianity, while every new truth discovered by them has either added to its evidence, or prepared the mind for its reception" (245).

27. The quality of *translucence* is also frequently attributed by Coleridge to the human faculty of Reason. "A Symbol is characterized by a translucence of . . . the Eternal through and in the Temporal" (*Lay Sermons,* 30).

28. Samuel Gilman, "Ralph Waldo Emerson," *Southern Rose* 7 (November 24, 1838): 100–106; reprinted in *Emerson and Thoreau: The Contemporary Reviews,* ed. Joel Myerson (New York: Cambridge University Press, 1992), 58.

29. In the introduction to *Nature,* Emerson lists "sex" among the natural phenomena he finds inexplicable (7). This passage is cited as an example of Emerson's "defects" by Francis Bowen, "Transcendentalism," *Christian Examiner* 21 (January 1837): 371–385; reprinted in *Emerson and Thoreau: The Contemporary Reviews,* 5.

30. Samuel Taylor Coleridge, *Logic,* ed. J. R. de J. Jackson (Princeton, NJ: Princeton University Press, 1981), 170–1. For further discussion of Coleridge's linguistic turn, see McKusick, *Coleridge's Philosophy of Language,* 143.

31. Coleridge's "true and original realism" (*Biographia Literaria,* 1:262) appeals to the concept of natural language in order to refute Kant's skeptical objections to the possibility of our knowing the *Ding an sich* (thing-in-itself).
32. "Farming" (1858), Emerson, *Works,* 7:143.

Chapter 6

1. Henry David Thoreau, "The Commercial Spirit of Modern Times," cited by Walter Harding, *The Days of Henry Thoreau: A Biography* (New York: Knopf, 1962; reprinted Princeton, NJ: Princeton University Press, 1992), 50.
2. Thoreau, *Journal,* comprising volumes 7–20 of *The Writings of Henry David Thoreau* (Boston: Houghton Mifflin, 1906). These journal volumes are independently numbered 1–14, and they are cited in the text as *Journal* by independent volume number.
3. Ralph Waldo Emerson, "Thoreau," *Atlantic Monthly* 10 (August 1862): 239–249; reprinted in *Emerson and Thoreau: The Contemporary Reviews,* ed. Joel Myerson, 428.
4. Thoreau's "canonization" as an environmental writer is thoughtfully examined by Lawrence Buell, *The Environmental Imagination: Thoreau, Nature Writing, and the Formation of American Culture* (Cambridge, MA: Harvard University Press, 1995), 339–369.
5. For more complete information on Thoreau's personal library, see *Thoreau's Reading: A Study in Intellectual History, with Bibliographical Catalogue,* ed. Robert Sattelmeyer (Princeton, NJ: Princeton University Press, 1988). Emerson's review of *The Poetical Works of Coleridge, Shelley, and Keats* appears in "Thoughts on Modern Literature," *The Dial* (October 1840); reprinted in Emerson, *Essays and Lectures* (New York: Library of America, 1983), 1159.
6. This chronology of Thoreau's reading of Coleridge is derived from *Thoreau's Reading,* 155–156.
7. Thoreau, *Journal,* ed. E. H. Witherell et. al. (Princeton, NJ: Princeton University Press, 1981), 1:222. This phrase appears in *Aids to Reflection,* ed. John Beer (1993), 72.
8. On this topic see Harold Bloom, "The Internalization of Quest-Romance," *The Yale Review* 58 (Summer 1969); reprinted in *Romanticism and Consciousness: Essays in Criticism,* ed. Harold Bloom (New York: Norton, 1970), 3–24.
9. *Henry David Thoreau: A Week on the Concord and Merrimack Rivers; Walden; or, Life in the Woods; The Maine Woods; Cape Cod,* ed. Robert F. Sayre (New York: Library of America, 1985), 14. Subsequent citations of Thoreau's book publications refer to this edition by page number.
10. The hardest part of Lewis and Clark's expedition came in 1805, when they reached the Great Falls of the Missouri and realized that they would have to portage their boats for several miles over rugged terrain. They improvised wheels for their boats and continued overland. Thoreau was quite familiar

with the exploits of these famous explorers; he mentions "Lewis and Clarke" [sic] in *Walden,* 578. In *A Week* he claims that an explorer of Cranberry Island (on the Concord River) may "get as good a freezing there as anywhere on the Northwest Coast" (9), referring to the place where Lewis and Clark spent a miserably cold winter.

11. In *A Week,* Thoreau refers to Columbus (50, 214, 265, 310, 317), Cook (54), Ledyard (96), and Ross (297).

12. Another contemporary instance of quest-romance, with an inward or psychological dimension, is Tennyson's "Lady of Shalott," cited by Thoreau as a chapter epigraph to "Tuesday" in *A Week,* 146.

13. According to the *Liddell-Scott-Jones Lexicon of Classical Greek,* Greek word ὕλη is defined as (I) forest, woodland; (II) wood cut down, firewood, fuel, brushwood, timber, twigs; (III.1) the stuff of which a thing is made, material; (III.2) in Philosophy, matter, first in Aristotle; (III.3) matter for a poem or treatise; (IV) sediment.

14. In affirming the ineluctable materiality of human cognition, Thoreau parts company with Emerson, whose version of transcendental idealism (following in the footsteps of Kant) allowed pure categories of the Understanding to exist independent of any material embodiment.

15. Thoreau mentions John Evelyn's *Sylva, or a Discourse of Forest-Trees* (1664) in *A Week on the Concord and Merrimack Rivers* (45) and he quotes from this work in *Walden,* 330. *Sylva* presents a philosophical and aesthetic justification for the reforestation of England. Evelyn delves deeply into the ancient traditions of sacred groves, and he advocates a new way of seeing forests: not merely as game-hunting preserves, or as sources of raw material, but as having intangible aesthetic value, and an intrinsic sacred character, worthy of nurturance and preservation.

16. Emerson, *Journals,* November 10, 1838.

17. Lamarck's theory of evolution was first propounded in his *Système des animaux sans vertèbres* (1801), which asserts that all life forms have arisen from a continuous process of gradual modification throughout the history of the Earth. Lamarck believed that the acquired characteristics of individual organisms are passed on to the next generation; in a famous example, he argued that giraffes acquire longer necks by stretching them to reach higher in the trees. Lamarck's theory emphasizes the creative response of organisms to their environments.

18. Stanley Cavell, *The Senses of Walden,* expanded edition (San Francisco: North Point Press, 1981), 22.

19. On Romantic vegetarianism, see Timothy Morton, *Shelley and the Revolution in Taste: The Body and the Natural World* (Cambridge: Cambridge University Press, 1994).

20. Harold Bloom, "The Internalization of Quest-Romance," points out that "the Romantics tended to take Milton's Satan as the archetype of the hero-

ically defeated Promethean quester" (9). Bloom adds that "the special puzzle of Romanticism is the dialectical role that nature had to take in the revival of romance" (9)

21. Later in *The Maine Woods,* Thoreau reflects more deeply on "the difference between that wild forest which once occupied our oldest townships, and the tame one which I find there to-day" (708), concluding that "the Maine wilderness differs essentially from ours" (709).

Chapter 7

1. John Muir, "The Calypso Borealis," in William F. Kimes and Mamie B. Kimes, *John Muir: A Reading Bibliography,* second edition (Fresno, CA: Panorama West Books, 1986), 1.

2. Autobiographical fragments, cited in Linnie Marsh Wolfe, *Son of the Wilderness: The Life of John Muir* (New York: Knopf, 1945), 102.

3. For biographical information on Muir, I am indebted to Frederick Turner, *Rediscovering America: John Muir in His Time and Ours* (New York: Viking, 1985). The development of Muir's sense of vocation, from a serene extoller of the beauties of nature to a passionate defender of wilderness, is cogently described in an essay by Paul Sheats, "After Yosemite: John Muir and the Southern Sierra," *John Muir: Life and Work* (Albuquerque: University of New Mexico Press, 1993), 244–264.

4. *My First Summer in the Sierra,* in *John Muir: Nature Writings,* ed. William Cronon (New York: Library of America, 1997), 163. Subsequent citations of Muir's nature writings refer to this edition by page number.

5. Muir's metaphorical description of the streams being made "to work like slaves" is remarkably similar to that of John Clare, whose "Lament of Swordy Well" deplored the way that "vile enclosure came and made / A parish slave of me" (183–184). This resemblance is evidently an analogy rather than an example of "influence," since Muir was not familiar with Clare's poetry.

6. Josiah Whitney's *Yosemite Guide-Book* (1869) argued that Yosemite Valley was formed by catastrophic subsidence, a view that Muir ridicules as "a violent hypothesis, which furnishes a kind of Tophet for the reception of bad mountains." John Muir, *Studies in the Sierra,* ed. William E. Colby (San Francisco: Sierra Club, 1950), 18.

7. The doctrine of physico-theology was first expounded by John Ray, *The Wisdom of God Manifested in the Works of the Creation* (1691) and further developed by William Derham, *Physico-Theology, or, A Demonstration of the Being and Attributes of God from His Works of Creation* (1713). For further discussion, see introduction above, page 21.

8. The concept of the Book of Nature has a long history, and is perhaps ultimately traceable to Romans 1:20, which says that God's "invisible nature,

namely his eternal power and deity, has been clearly understood in the things that have been made." English theologians frequently describe God's manifestation in nature by means of this metaphor; Sir Thomas Browne, for example, says that "there are *two Books* from whence I collect my divinity; besides that written one of God, another of His servant Nature, that universal and publick Manuscript, that lies expans'd unto the Eyes of all" (*Religio Medici* [1643], part I, chapter 15); cited by Ernst R. Curtius, *European Literature and the Latin Middle Ages* (Princeton, NJ: Princeton University Press, 1953), 323. Curtius surveys the history of the Book of Nature topos on 319–26. See also Geoffrey Hartman, *Beyond Formalism* (New Haven, CT: Yale University Press, 1970), 53–56. John Muir presents an elaborated version of this concept in "Yellowstone National Park," where he invites the reader to "take a look at a few tertiary volumes of the grand geological library of the park, and see how God writes history" (757).

9. Muir made extensive annotations in the endpapers of *The Poetical Works of Percy Bysshe Shelley,* edited by Mrs. Shelley, 4 vols. in 2 (Boston: Houghton, Osgood & Co., 1880); he noted with special interest the "beaming ice" described in "Mont Blanc." This volume is now in the John Muir Collection, Huntington Library.

10. Wolfe, *Son of the Wilderness,* 147.

11. Ralph Waldo Emerson, *Collected Poems and Translations,* ed. Harold Bloom and Paul Kane (New York: Library of America, 1994), 30. Subsequent citations of Emerson's poems refer to this edition by page number.

12. The image of the Aeolian harp occurs frequently in Emerson's writing, most memorably in the essay "Nature" from *Essays: Second Series:* "the musical streaming odorous south wind, which converts all trees to windharps" (542). See also Emerson's poems "The Harp" and "Maiden Speech of the Aeolian Harp," both published in *Selected Poems* (1876). Thoreau uses Aeolian harp imagery on several occasions in *Walden,* using it to express a vital emotional link between man and nature: "There can be no black melancholy to him who lives in the midst of Nature and has his senses still. There never was such a storm but it was Aeolian music to a healthy and innocent ear" (426). Elsewhere in this work, Thoreau refers to "a vibration of the universal lyre" (420) and "the music of the harp which trembles round the world" (497).

13. William Frederic Badè, *The Life and Letters of John Muir* (Boston and New York: Houghton Mifflin, 1924), 1:259–60. The original autograph letter from Emerson is in the Bancroft Collection at the University of California, Berkeley.

14. Stephen Fox, *The American Conservation Movement: John Muir and His Legacy* (Madison: University of Wisconsin Press, 1981), 6. John Muir's annotated copy of *The Prose Works of Ralph Waldo Emerson* now resides in the Yale Beinecke Library.

15. For further analysis of the formation of Muir's deep ecological worldview, see James D. Heffernan, "Why Wilderness? John Muir's 'Deep Ecology,'" *John Muir: Life and Work,* ed. Sally M. Miller (Albuquerque: University of New Mexico Press, 1993), 102–117.

16. For a complete list of Muir's periodical publications, see Kimes, *John Muir: A Reading Bibliography.*

17. Typescript copy of letter from Muir to Charles Warren Stoddard, c. February 20, 1872. In "John Muir. Collection of letters & papers" (C-H 101, pt. 1), Bancroft Library, University of California, Berkeley.

18. John Muir Papers, John Muir Center for Regional Studies, University of the Pacific, Stockton, California. Cited by Richard F. Fleck, "John Muir's Transcendental Imagery," in *John Muir: Life and Work,* 139.

19. M. H. Abrams uses the term "cosmic ecology" to describe a key contribution of Coleridge's *Statesman's Manual* to our modern worldview. *The Correspondent Breeze,* 216–222.

20. Abrams, *The Correspondent Breeze,* 42.

21. Muir's personal library includes the following works: *Poetical Works of Samuel Taylor Coleridge* (London: George Bell, 1885), vol. 1 only; *Biographia Literaria . . . and Two Lay Sermons* (London: George Bell, 1889); *Lectures and Notes on Shakspere and Other English Poets* (London: George Bell, 1888); *The Table Talk and Omniana* (London: George Bell, 1888); *Miscellanies, Aesthetic and Literary: to Which Is Added The Theory of Life* (London: George Bell, 1885). All of these books are inscribed "Wm. Keith," which indicates that Muir obtained them from William Keith, a close personal friend who first met Muir during an artistic excursion in Yosemite in the fall of 1872.

22. For a more detailed examination of Muir's compositional process, see Ronald H. Limbaugh, *John Muir's "Stickeen" and the Lessons of Nature* (Fairbanks: University of Alaska Press, 1996). Limbaugh attentively describes the various manuscript drafts and sources for the book, and provides a bibliography of works annotated by Muir.

23. John Muir Collection, Huntington Library, Coleridge's *Poetical Works* (1885), vol. 1, pages cxxxiii and 173. The cited passage is marked with a vertical stroke on both of these pages.

24. John Muir Collection, Huntington Library, pencil annotations to Coleridge's *Poetical Works,* endpapers.

25. John Muir Collection, Huntington Library, pencil annotations to Coleridge's *Lectures and Notes on Shakspere,* endpapers.

26. John Muir Collection, Huntington Library, pencil annotations to Coleridge's *Lectures and Notes on Shakspere,* endpapers.

27. John Muir Collection, Huntington Library, pencil annotations to Coleridge's *Table Talk and Omniana,* endpapers.

28. Responding to the criticism that "The Rime of the Ancient Mariner" was improbable and had no moral, Coleridge replied "that in my judgment the

chief fault of the poem was that it had too much moral, and that too openly obtruded upon the reader." *Table Talk,* ed. Carl Woodring (Princeton, NJ: Princeton University Press, 1990), 1:272–273.

Chapter 8

1. The most complete available bibliography of Mary Austin's published work was compiled by Dudley Taylor Wynn, *A Critical Study of the Writings of Mary Hunter Austin* (Ph.D. Thesis, New York University, 1939). A copy of this thesis is available in the Huntington Library, which also houses the Mary (Hunter) Austin Collection of papers and documents. Despite its thoroughness, Wynn's bibliography is incomplete. Note to graduate students: a full descriptive bibliography of Austin's publications remains a desideratum!

2. Mary Austin, "One Hundred Miles on Horseback," *The Blackburnian* (May 1887); reprinted in *A Mary Austin Reader,* ed. Esther F. Lanigan (Tucson: University of Arizona Press, 1996), 23–28.

3. For biographical information I am indebted to Esther Lanigan Stineman, *Mary Austin: Song of a Maverick* (New Haven, CT: Yale University Press, 1989).

4. Roderick Frazier Nash, "Wilderness Values and the Colorado River," *New Courses for the Colorado River,* ed. Gary D. Weatherford and F. Lee Brown (Albuquerque: University of New Mexico Press, 1986), 201–224. Nash writes: "Hardly a Walden Pond, the wilderness along the Colorado did not initially support the transcendental assumption of the divinity inherent in nature" (207). Nash goes on to describe the gradual development of appreciation for this rugged desert landscape through the contributions of the explorer John Wesley Powell, the artist Thomas Moran, the photographer Timothy O'Sullivan, the painters John Marin and Georgia O'Keefe, and the writers Mary Austin, Willa Cather, Joseph Wood Krutch, Wallace Stegner, and Edward Abbey.

5. Austin published three short stories in *The Overland Monthly:* "The Mother of Felipe" (November 1892), "The Wooing of the Señorita" (1897), and "The Conversion of Ah Lew Sing" (October 1897). Separate chapters of *The Land of Little Rain* were serialized in *The Atlantic:* "Jimville: A Bret Harte Town," *Atlantic* 90 (November 1902): 690–694; "The Land of Little Rain," *Atlantic* 91 (January 1903): 96–99; "The Basket Maker," *Atlantic* 91 (February 1903): 235–238; "The Little Town of the Grape Vines," *Atlantic* 91 (June 1903): 822–825. *The Overland Monthly,* based in San Francisco, also published work by John Muir, Bret Harte, Ambrose Bierce, and Charles Warren Stoddard; for further historical detail on this periodical see Francis Walker, *San Francisco's Literary Frontier* (New York: Knopf, 1937).

6. Mary Austin, *The Land of Little Rain* (Boston and New York: Houghton Mifflin, 1903), 4. Subsequent citations of this work refer to the first edition

by page number. No other edition of this work provides a reliable text or a facsimile reproduction of its elegant graphic design, which is replete with marginal embellishments and full-page illustrations.

7. The ubiquitous Romantic genre of quest-romance, and its re-externalized American version, is more fully discussed in chapter 6, pages 145 and 164.

8. Tennyson, *In Memoriam,* section 56, line 15.

9. Emerson, "Forbearance," line 1, first published in *Poems* (1847). Austin's personal library contained a copy of Emerson's *Poems* (Boston, 1857) and *Representative Men* (Boston, 1857), as well as books of poetry by Coleridge, Shelley, and Keats. Information on Austin's personal library is derived from the Huntington Library's Austin Collection, which contains a "List of books in the library of Mary Austin" (Ephemera Boxes 132 and 133).

10. Austin alludes to Alfred, Lord Tennyson, "The Lotos-Eaters," line 11. In the first chapter of *The Land of Little Rain,* she invokes the Lotus archetype more explicitly: "the rainbow hills, the tender bluish mists, the luminous radiance of the spring, have the lotus charm" (16).

11. In "How I Learned to Read and Write" (composed 1921), Austin denies that she intentionally deployed a literary "style" in *The Land of Little Rain,* claiming that she wrote in "the way that I supposed highly cultivated people talked to one another" (*Mary Austin Reader,* 151). Such a claim is not inconsistent with the observation that her style is inflected by numerous British and American precursors, since many stylistic influences are often entirely unconscious.

12. Mary Austin, *Earth Horizon: Autobiography* (Boston: Houghton Mifflin, 1932), 34.

13. Mary Austin, "Beyond the Hudson," *Saturday Review of Literature* 7 (December 6, 1930): 432 and 444. This impassioned manifesto deserves to be much better known; it is Austin's most incisive discussion of her place in the American tradition of nature writing. Bylined "Santa Fe, New Mexico," it was written in protest against an article in a preceding issue by H. S. Canby, who complained that no current American writer had "given evidence of special love for the land that produced him." H. S. Canby, "The Promise of American Life," *Saturday Review of Literature* 7 (1930): 301–303.

14. Stafford W. Austin to President Theodore Roosevelt, August 4, 1905, NA BUREC RG 115 63–B; cited by William L. Kahrl, *Water and Power: The Conflict over Los Angeles' Water Supply in the Owens Valley* (Berkeley: University of California Press, 1982), 107.

15. *San Francisco Chronicle,* September 3, 1905; cited by Kahrl, 107.

16. Marc Reisner, *Cadillac Desert: The American West and Its Disappearing Water* (New York: Viking, 1986), 105. In chapter 2, "The Red Queen" (54–107), Reisner describes how the city of Los Angeles captured the water of the Owens Valley by means of "chicanery, subterfuge, spies, bribery, a campaign of divide-and-conquer, and a strategy of lies to get the water it needed. In

the end it milked the valley bone-dry, impoverishing it, while the water made a number of prominent Los Angeleans very, very rich" (65). In a curious historical irony, one of the Los Angeles businessmen who profited magnificently from the Aqueduct project was Henry E. Huntington, in whose library the papers of Mary Austin now reside.

17. David Mazel, "American Literary Environmentalism as Domestic Orientalism," *The Ecocriticism Reader*, 137–138.

18. Mary Austin, *The Ford* (Boston and New York: Houghton Mifflin, 1917; reprinted with a foreword by John Walton, Berkeley: University of California Press, 1997).

19. "The Walking Woman," *Lost Borders* (New York and London: Harper, 1909; reprinted with *The Land of Little Rain* in *The Country of Lost Borders,* edited by Marjorie Pryse, New Brunswick, NJ: Rutgers University Press, 1987), 255–263. The autobiographical dimension of this story is insightfully examined by David Wyatt, *The Fall into Eden: Landscape and Imagination in California* (Cambridge: Cambridge University Press, 1986), 76–80.

20. The Mary Austin House (*La Casa Querida*) is located at 439 Camino del Monte Sol in Santa Fe, New Mexico. Now occupied by a commercial art gallery, the house and its enclosed patio have been kept as close as possible to their historic form.

21. Mary Austin, *The American Rhythm: Studies and Reëxpressions of Amerindian Songs* (Boston: Houghton Mifflin, 1923; revised edition, 1930), 44. Subsequent citations of this work refer to the 1930 edition by page number.

22. Austin's enthusiasm for Whitman is tempered by her disapproval of his swaggering self-confidence: "His whole personality swaggered with what more or less dominated the movement of the American procession, the consciousness of being entirely adequate to the environment. America was a woman, and the poet, though slightly befuddled by her effect upon him, had proved his manhood upon her" (*The American Rhythm,* 17).

23. Mabel Major, "Mary Austin in Ft. Worth," *The New Mexico Quarterly* 4:4 (November 1934): 307–310.

24. Mary Austin, *The Land of Journeys' Ending* (New York & London: Century, 1924; facsimile reprint with an introduction by Larry Evers, Tucson: University of Arizona Press, 1983). Subsequent citations of this work refer to the facsimile reprint edition by page number.

25. On this recurrent image in Romantic poetry, see Abrams, *The Correspondent Breeze,* discussed in chapter 7, pages 185–188.

26. Austin alludes to Coleridge's "Rime of the Ancient Mariner" in *The American Rhythm:* "Sitting on the sunny side of the wickiup, considering with the elders of Sagharewite how it came to be called the Place-where-they-gave-him-mush-that-was-afraid, I thought of doctors disputing in the temple, of academicians loitering amid olive groves, and occasionally I thought of the Ancient Mariner. For when you have invited a strange people to

unfold their mysteries you must by no means show yourself bored by the unfoldment" (39). Austin evidently imagines herself in the role of the impatient Wedding Guest.

Conclusion

1. Karl Kroeber, "Proto-Evolutionary Bards and Post-Ecological Critics," *Keats-Shelley Journal* 48 (1999): 167.
2. Richard Dawkins, *The Selfish Gene* (New York: Oxford University Press, 1976).
3. The "entangled bank" is a recurrent image in Darwin's *On the Origin of Species* (London, 1859), 74–75, 489–490. For further analysis of this image, see Joel B. Hagen, *An Entangled Bank: The Origins of Ecosystem Ecology* (New Brunswick, NJ: Rutgers University Press, 1992). This book perceptively examines the Darwinian roots of the modern ecosystem concept.
4. For further discussion of the "fundamental gulf" between the conceptual models of population ecology and systems ecology, see Peter J. Bowler, *The Norton History of the Environmental Sciences* (New York: Norton, 1992), 537–546.
5. Indeed, the molecular biologist Edward J. Steele claims to have evidence that a Lamarckian hereditary mechanism is at work within the mammalian immune system. See Steele et. al., *Lamarck's Signature: How Retrogenes Are Changing Darwin's Natural Selection Paradigm* (Cambridge, MA: Perseus Books, 1998).
6. Stephen Jay Gould, "Shades of Lamarck," *The Panda's Thumb: More Reflections in Natural History* (New York: Norton, 1980), 83–84.

Index